THE ADULT JOKE BOOK

A Hilarious Collection of
Bawdy, Ridiculous and
Politically Incorrect Jokes

By Johnny Sharpe

INDEX

Published by
Arcturus Publishing Limited
For Index Books
Henson Way
Kettering
Northamptonshire
NN16 8PX

ISBN 1-900032-38-4

This edition published 1999

Printed and bound in Finland

Text layout by Blue Design
Cover design by Paul Ashby

© Arcturus Publishing Limited
1-7 Shand Street, London SE1 2ES

CONTENTS

IN YOUR ANIMAL KINGDOM

THIS man loved his pet ferret so much he never went anywhere without it. One night he went to the cinema but was told that ferrets were not allowed in. Unperturbed, he went round the corner and stuffed the ferret down his trousers, then bought his ticket and sat down to enjoy the film. However after half an hour the ferret became very restless, so the man opened his flies to give the animal some air. Two girls were sitting next to him and suddenly one turned to the other and whispered urgently, "Tracy, that man next to me has got his willy out."

"Never mind, just ignore him," replied the friend.

"I can't," she gasped, "it's nibbling my knee."

★   ★   ★

WHAT'S the difference between a sheep and a Lada?
You don't feel quite so embarrassed being seen getting out of the back of a sheep.

★   ★   ★

AN elephant and a monkey were strolling through the jungle when suddenly the elephant fell down a large hole.

Quickly the monkey ran for help and waved down a Rolls Royce on a nearby road. Hearing of his friend's plight, they hurried back to the hole, dropped a rope down and pulled the elephant out.

Some months later the monkey fell down a steep hole but was rescued quite easily when the elephant dropped his donger down for the monkey to climb up.

So it just goes to show that you don't need a Rolls Royce if you've got a big dick.

A RABBIT and a mouse found themselves squatting down side by side in the woods. The rabbit turned to the mouse and asked, "Do you have trouble with crap sticking to your fur?"
"No" said the mouse.
"Oh good." And with that the rabbit picked up the mouse and wiped his arse with him.

★ ★ ★

IT was the monthly meeting of the Paranormal Society and the subject of the evening's discussion was ghosts. The speaker got up and asked the audience whether any of them had had an intimate relationship with a ghost and a man at the back put his hand up but said he didn't really want to talk about it.
"Oh come now, don't be shy," said the organiser and after much coaxing the man approached the platform.
"Now Ladies and Gentlemen, I'm delighted to say we have some-one with us tonight who has had an intimate relationship with a ghost."
"What?" gasped the man, stopping dead in his tracks. "I thought you said goats."

★ ★ ★

"NOW listen, sons" said daddy hedgehog. "You're old enough to leave home and there are many dangers out there, the worst one being that busy road. If you ever need to cross it, but a car comes along before you get to the other side, just make sure you're standing in the middle of the lane and it will go over you without causing harm. Look, I'll show you."
The hedgehog went out to the middle of the lane and waited for an on-coming car.
"Here comes one!" he shouted. "Now watch how its ..." but that's all he had time to say before there was a sickening

crunchy sound and poor dad was flattened.

"Oh dear," said one of the sons, "I meant to ask him about three wheelers."

★ ★ ★

TWO visiting athletes took time off to go on safari but they got separated from the rest of the party and soon found themselves face to face with a very angry lion. One of them immediately bent down to put his running shoes on and the other said, puzzled, "It's no good doing that, you'll never outrun the beast."

"I know," replied the first, "but if I can outrun you, that's all I have to do."

★ ★ ★

A MOTORIST was having trouble with his car and stopped to see what the problem was. He'd been peering under the bonnet for a few minutes when a voice behind him said, "It'll be the carburettor."

Startled, the motorist looked around but all he could see was an old cow in the nearby field. He felt spooked out by the whole episode so jumped quickly back in the car and headed for the nearest garage. Later, as the mechanic was inspecting the car, the motorist recounted his experience.

"Was it a black and white cow with a crooked horn?"

"Yes, it was," he replied.

"Oh don't listen to her, she'll never make a good mechanic."

★ ★ ★

HOW do you know when you've passed a rhinoceros?
You can't close the toilet lid.

★ ★ ★

A DEADLY germ is chasing an arsehole through the park when the arsehole bumps into a wandering genie.

"Oh please help me get away from this deadly germ," he pleads.

"OK" says the genie, "I've got nothing on this afternoon. I'll disguise you as a cat, just sit quietly in that tree over there."

A moment later the deadly germ appears and goes up to the cat.

"Have you seen an arsehole around here?"

The cat shakes his head and the germ is about to leave when he notices the cat is hanging on for grim death.

"You're an odd cat, why are you shaking so much? I thought cats were at home up trees."

The cat doesn't answer.

"Come on," says the germ," have you got nothing to say for yourself?"

By this time the cat is so terrified he opens his mouth to speak and out comes a particularly noxious fart.

★ ★ ★

TWO parrots are sitting on a perch and one says to the other, "Can you smell fish?"

★ ★ ★

WHAT do you call a flock of sheep tied to a lamp post?
A Leisure Centre.

★ ★ ★

WHAT have you got there, Bob?" asks his mate.
"It's an elephant that fucks cats."
"Get away, that's got to be impossible!"

"Listen, I'll show you. See that cat over there?" And as he looks the elephant goes over and squashes it with his foot. "See, I told you.".

★ ★ ★

WHAT can cows do that women can't?
Stand up to their tits in water without getting their fannies wet.

★ ★ ★

A MAN went to the pet shop to buy a parrot but the only one on offer cost £500.
"Why is it so expensive?" he asked.
"Ah well, it's a very special parrot, it lays square eggs," said the pet shop owner.
"How very odd. OK, I'll take it, but just one thing - does it talk?"
"Well, it's got the ability to talk but up to now all I've heard is 'Aagh, oooh, buugerr....'."

★ ★ ★

A MAN walked into a club with a pet snake under his arms.
"Hey, you can't bring that snake in here, he might bite one of our members," said the Manager.
"Oh that's no problem, you just get a friend to suck the poison out."
"But what if he bites someone up the backside?"
"Well, then you really find out who your friends are."

★ ★ ★

IT'S Christmas Eve and there's a knock on the door, but when Jack opens it he can't see anyone until he looks down and notices a snail.

"Go on, piss off!" he says and kicks it away.

Easter comes round and there's a knock at the door and when Jack opens it, he sees the same snail on the doorstep.

"What's wrong with you then? Got the hump or something?"

★ ★ ★

A MAN goes into the vet's.

"Say aaah...." says the vet.

"Why?" asks the man.

"Because your dog died half an hour ago."

★ ★ ★

A MAN, a parrot and a budgie were standing on the edge of Beachy Head. Suddenly the man jumped off and hit the rocks below with a mighty thud, dying instantly.

"Fuck that," said the parrot, "I don't think much of this parrot-glid-ing."

"And I'm not into budgie jumping, either," said his companion.

★ ★ ★

PAUSE for thought:

Should mountain goats be illegal?

★ ★ ★

A RANDY old gorilla was walking through the wildlife park when he saw a lion bending over, drinking from the water hole. Unable to restrain himself, he came up quietly behind the animal, grabbed him by the front paws and gave him a good rogering. Once free, the lion went berserk, determined to take revenge on his attacker. Meanwhile, the gorilla had raced back into the undergrowth where he came across a lone hunter. He got rid of the man, took off his clothes and put them on himself, covering up his fur with a long coat and pulling a hat low down on his forehead. In the man's belongings there was also a newspaper which he held up in front of his face and started to read. A moment later, the lion came along, saw the 'would be' hunter and asked him if he'd seen a gorilla.

"You mean the gorilla that molested a lion down by the watering hole?" he said.

"Bloody hell!" said the astonished lion. "Don't tell me it's in the papers already."

★ ★ ★

A WOMAN was given a parrot for her birthday but the bird had grown up with a 'bad attitude' and some of the foulest language she had ever heard. Try as hard as she could - teaching it new words, soothing it with music - she could not get the parrot to change. One day, he was even worse than usual. She got so angry that she put him in the freezer and closed the door. The bird could be heard squawking, kicking and screaming, and then all went quiet. Frightened that she may have harmed him, she quickly opened the door and the parrot calmly stepped out.

"I am very sorry that I might have offended you with my bad language and beg for your forgiveness. I will try as hard as I can to change my ways" he said.

Astonished at the change in the bird's attitude, she was just about to ask him why, when he said, "By the way, may I ask what the chicken did?"

★ ★ ★

WHAT do you call a man with 14 rabbits up his arse?
Warren.

ONCE there was a small private zoo that was dependent on public contributions to pay for its upkeep. However, times were tough and the zoo was losing money hand over fist. Somehow the owner had to raise some cash. He came up with a brilliant idea. The next day, notices went up that anyone who could make the most ferocious lion jump straight up in the air would win £1,000. The entry fee would be £50. Many people tried, but no-one succeeded and much to the owner's delight, a lot of money was raised. Then, two days later, a small rather insipid man arrived at the zoo and offered his £50 to take up the bet. Feeling quite safe, the owner took him over to the lion's cage and called for witnesses. When a crowd had gathered, the man produced a wooden truncheon from within his coat, swung it around in the air and hit the lion's balls as hard as possible. With an almighty growl, the lion jumped three foot into the air. Very dispirited, the man handed over the £1,000 prize. A couple of months passed and the owner was forced to think up another bet. This time he decided to challenge people to make the lion shake his head from side to side within 15 seconds of meeting it. It was a roaring success and the financial situation started to improve. Alas, to his horror, the small insipid man appeared one week later and handed over his entry fee. He went over to the lion and whispered, "Do you remember me?"

The lion nodded apprehensively.

"Do you want me to do the same as I did last time?"

And the lion shook his head vigorously.

★　★　★

TWO men on safari were cooling down by dangling their feet in the river. Suddenly, one of them screams. "Aoh, an alligator has just bitten off my foot."

"Which one?"

"I don't bloody know, when you've seen one, you've seen them all."

★　★　★

A MAN buys two dogs from the pet shop and no matter what he does he can't stop them from shagging each other. He tries throwing cold water over them, putting pepper on their backsides, and then changing their diet - but nothing works. In desperation he rings the vet in the middle of the night to tell him the problem.

"Here's a good idea," says the vet. "Why don't you take the telephone over to the dogs and give each of them a ring."

"Will that really work?" replies the astonished man.

"Well it damn well worked for me," says the vet as he slams down the phone.

★　★　★

OUT in the middle of the jungle a hunter spots a gorilla standing in a clearing. He takes aim and fires but when he goes to collect his prize, there's no sign of the animal.

Suddenly there's a voice behind him.

"I'm fed up being target practice for you lot. Now get down on your knees and give me a blow job."

The hunter has no choice but to comply, thankful he has got off with his life. However, the next day he returns with a bigger and better gun, spies the gorilla and fires. Again he misses and again he is forced to see to the big brute.

Determined to succeed, the man returns on a third day, this time with telescopic sight, and tries again.

Once more he fails and as he gets down on his knees to give the gorilla another blow job the animal says to him, "You know, I'm beginning to think it's more than the hunting you're after."

A MAN goes hunting with his two dogs and a monkey and his fellow hunters ask him what the monkey is for.

He replies "When the dogs have cornered the animal up a tree the monkey goes in and shoots it at close range."

Later in the day they hear the dogs barking so a gun is handed to the monkey and he shins up the tree only to return a few seconds later. He jumps to the ground and immediately shoots the dog dead.

"Bloody hell" exclaims one of the hunters. "Why did he do that?"

The man replied, "If there's one thing he can't stand, it's liars."

★ ★ ★

TWO old ladies visiting the zoo land up at the giraffe enclosure and are amazed to find the giraffe's testicles just inches from their faces. One of the old ladies can't help herself and leans through the fence squeezing one of the testicles in her hand. All at once the animal jumps into the air, clears the fencing and gallops off into the distance. The zookeeper rushes out to find out what has happened and when he hears the two old ladies explain, he immediately drops his pants.

"Here, you'd better do the same to me, I've got to catch that son of a bitch!"

★ ★ ★

A MAN goes to buy some rat poison. The shopkeeper gives him a bottle of powder and tells him to sprinkle it round his hole. Exasperated, the man replies, "If I could get that close I'd step on him!"

★ ★ ★

A RATHER shy girl is visiting the zoo when suddenly as she passes the monkey house, a huge ape grabs her, pulls her over the moat and gives her a good seeing to. Afterwards she is taken to hospital in a state of shock and it is almost a week before she is allowed any visitors. When she does eventually have friends to see her and they ask how she is, she replies, "Terrible, he hasn't phoned, sent a letter..."

⋆ ⋆ ⋆

A WOMAN is left a pair of parrots in her aunt's will and immediately rings the vet to ask him how she can tell which was the male and which the female.
The vet tells her to creep down first thing in the morning and if she catches them mating, then the one on top was the male and she should mark him with some tape. This the woman does and on catching them in the act she puts a white tape around the male bird's neck. A couple of days later the vicar comes to tea and on seeing him the male parrot says, "Ah ha, I see you've been caught mounting a woman as well."

⋆ ⋆ ⋆

A MAN and a parrot find themselves sitting next to each other on a plane. As the stewardess comes along the man asks for a coffee, at which point the parrot shouts, "Get me a brandy and be quick about it!"
A little upset by his attitude, the stewardess goes off and returns with the brandy but not the coffee.
"Excuse me miss, you've forgotten my coffee" he tells her.
"Oh sorry" she replies and is just about to go when the parrot shouts even louder, "And get me another brandy you incompetent cow!"
This time she's very upset but returns quickly with the brandy hav-

ing forgotten once again to get the man's coffee. Maybe if I take the same attitude as this parrot I might get results, he thinks to himself.

"Hey, get me my coffee quick or you'll be sorry, you silly bitch."

In no time at all the stewardess returns with two male colleagues who drag both the man and the parrot from their seats and throw them out of the emergency hatch. As the man passes the parrot on the way down, the bird turns to him and says, "For someone who can't fly, you've sure got a foul mouth on you."

★ ★ ★

IN another part of the parish a woman has a parrot who uses such foul language she has to keep him covered up when visitors call round. One day the vicar comes to tea and on hearing about her problem suggests he take the parrot back to his house where he has a female parrot who is forever on her knees praying. Maybe she can change his ways. The woman agrees and the parrot goes back with the vicar. As soon as he is put in the female parrot's cage, his awful behaviour begins.

"C'mon girl, let's get to it, let's get a bit of screwing done."

Lo and behold, before the vicar or the lady can intervene, the female parrot replies, "At long bloody last, my prayers have been answered."

★ ★ ★

TWO mates are out walking when one suddenly rushes behind a bush to have a pee. Unfortunately there's a snake hiding in the undergrowth and when Jack gets out his penis the snake bites it. Hearing Jack's screams, Bob rushes over and seeing what has happened rushes off to the doctor's.

"You'll have to hurry, otherwise your friend will die," says the doctor. "Cut a small incision in the wound and suck out all the poison, but be quick."

Bob goes back to his mate who's looking very pale and weak.
"What did the doctor say?" he whispers.
"I'm sorry mate, you're going to die."

★ ★ ★

A MAN comes home from work one day to find a rat shagging the backside off a cat in the garden. The next evening he returns home to find the rat doing the same thing to a bull terrier. Unable to believe his eyes, he takes the rat into the house to show his wife but as soon as she sees it she screams, "Aahh, get that sex maniac out of here."

★ ★ ★

THREE dogs meet up in the vet's. The Alsatian tells the other two he's being put down for biting his next door neighbour. "Same here", says the second dog - a Rotweiler - "I've scared too many children at the local school."
The third dog, a Great Dane, says, "I'm here because yesterday my gorgeous blonde owner got out of the bath, bent down to dry her feet and without a second thought I mounted her and did what comes naturally."
"So you're being put down as well," ask the other two dogs.
"Oh no, I'm here to have my nails cut."

★ ★ ★

A FEMALE elephant is having an awful time with flies who keep biting her on a part of her back too far away for her to shoo them off with her tail. When a little blackbird sees this he quickly lands on her back and within a minute has eaten up all the flies.
"Oh thank you so much!" cries the elephant. "If ever you need a favour doing, please don't hesitate to ask."
"Well, actually," stutters the bird, "I did often wonder what it

would be like to shag an elephant. Would you mind?"
The elephant gives her permission and the blackbird gets on
with the business. Suddenly a bunch of bananas fall off a tree
and hits the elephant on the head. "Ouch!" she yells.
"Oh sorry," replies the bird. "I didn't mean to hurt you."

★ ★ ★

THIS is the story of the three bears. One of them married a giraffe.
The other two put him up to it.

★ ★ ★

A MAN goes into a bar with a giraffe and they both get horribly drunk until the giraffe collapses in a dead faint on the floor
and the man gets up to leave.
"Hey," says the bartender. "You can't leave that lying there."
"It's not a lion, it's a giraffe," he replies.

★ ★ ★

THREE friends are sitting round the fire talking about their dogs.
The first one tells them his dog is called Woodman.
"Let me show you why. Woodman, go boy."
At that, the dog takes a log from the side of the fire and carves a
beautiful statue of a bird. Then the second explains why his dog is
called Stoneman.
"Go boy, go." Immediately the dog jumps up, takes part of the
stonework away from the front of the fire and trims it into a stone
carving of an Indian.
Finally, the third friend says, "My dog's called Ironman. Watch
this." The man heats the fire tongs until they are blisteringly hot
and then tells his mates,
"I'll just touch him on the balls with this and you watch him make
a bolt for the door."

"HEY, does your dog bite?" asks the man sitting down next to a guy with a dog at his feet.

"No", he replies. But a moment later, the dog takes one almighty bite out of the man's ankle.

"Heh, I thought you said your dog didn't bite," he says angrily.

"That's right, but this here's not my dog."

★ ★ ★

TWO men are sitting on a park bench watching a dog licking its balls.

One says, "Boy, I wish I could do that."

The other replies, "I think you'd better start by petting him first."

★ ★ ★

THE elephant keeper at the zoo was grooming his animal when a man stopped to ask him the time. The keeper got down on his knees, swung the elephant's balls to and fro and replied "Half past four."

Amazed, the man caught up with his friends and urged them to return with him to see this extraordinary occurrence. They agreed and all went back to the keeper. "Excuse me, do you know the time, please?" said one of the friends. Again the man got on his knees, gently handled the elephant's balls and replied, "Four forty five."

After the party moved on, the first man's curiosity got the better of him and he returned to the keeper.

"I'll give you £50 if you show me how you can tell the time."

"If that's what you want" said the keeper. He beckoned the man to get down on his knees also, then moved the elephant's balls to one side and said, "You see that clock tower over there?"

ON safari in darkest Africa, a hunter got separated from his party and came face to face with a huge lion. Knowing his gun was empty the hunter got down on his knees to say a last prayer and was amazed to find the lion praying.

"Thanks be to God!" exclaimed the man joyously.

"Quiet!" roared the lion, "I'm saying grace."

⋆ ⋆ ⋆

A GOOSE goes into the local job centre and joins the back of the waiting queue. When his turn comes he goes up to the interviewer and asks what's on offer.

"My goodness!" gasps the interviewer. "You can talk."

"Well, of course," retorts the goose. "I'm not bloody stupid."

"OK, let me see, come back on Thursday and I'll have something for you."

After the goose has gone, the man rings the circus and persuades the owner to take on the goose, with 5% of the profits coming to him.

Thursday arrives and in waddles the goose.

"So what have you got for me?" he asks.

"Well, I've got you a great job in the circus," he enthuses. "Good money and full board."

"No, that's no good to me" says the goose. "I'm an electrician."

⋆ ⋆ ⋆

"WHAT are those marks on your knees?" one girlfriend asks another.

"Oh, that's from making love doggie style", she replies.

"It looks painful to me, don't you know any other way?"

"Oh yes, I do but my dog doesn't."

IN YOUR BAD BEHAVIOUR

A MAN fishing off the end of the pier is suddenly amazed to see an old wizened woman in a wheelchair hurtling down towards the edge. To his dismay he realises she is determined to go over, so just in time he stops her and asks what's wrong.

The old woman, who's wrinkled, half bald and toothless, starts to cry and tells him she's nearly 90 and has never been kissed. The man looks at her, hides his repulsion and gives her a kiss, although it's almost too much to stomach when she sticks her tongue down his throat. However she goes away happy. But a couple of hours later he sees her again, hurtling down towards the pier's edge.

"What's wrong now?" he asks.

Tears streaming down her face, she tells him she has never been hugged. So he closes his eyes takes a deep breath and just manages to give her a big hug. The man returns to his fishing and after another hour he manages to catch a very big fish which he has trouble reeling in. At that crucial moment the old woman returns, hurtling down the pier, and losing concentration for a moment he loses his prize catch.

He turns to the tearful old hag who, this time, tells him she's never been fucked. So the man gently lifts her out of the wheelchair, and smiling toothlessly at him she tells him to lie her on the sand under the pier where they won't be disturbed. The man agrees, takes up two loose planks from the floor of the pier and drops her through to the sand below. The woman laughs excitedly, again saying, "I've never been fucked before."

Well you will be now," replies the man. "The tide comes in in 15 minutes" and with that he walks away.

★ ★ ★

THREE men are discussing how best to drive women wild. The first says he nibbles their ears and their toes and it really turns them on. The second says he kisses them all over and it drives them mad. The third says that after he's made love to them he wipes himself on their curtains - now that really does drive them wild!

* * *

I KNOW a man who's got a great trick. He goes to posh resorts and registers as an unmarried doctor.

* * *

A BOY rushed into his friend's bedroom unannounced to find him lying face down on a life-size Arena poster of a vivacious starlet. "Ben, what the hell are you doing?"
His friend looks up breathless and flushes.
"It's alright, Martin, I've got the charwoman underneath."

* * *

"IT'S about time you got married, son."
"But why, dad?" he replied, "Why should I buy a book when there's such a good lending library in town?"

* * *

NURSING one almighty hangover, Lady Ponsonby decided to get a breath of fresh air and take a walk around the grounds. After a few minutes she met her husband's manservant and casually mentioned to him that she was feeling under the weather after last night's riotous hen party and couldn't remember getting to bed.

"I helped you, madam" replied the manservant. "I took off your dress and hung it up so it wouldn't get creased."

"But I woke up totally naked," she replied.

"That's right, madam, I removed your underclothes because I thought they might be a little uncomfortable."

"Gosh, I can't remember anything," she said, "I must have been tight."

"Not after the first time, Your Ladyship."

★ ★ ★

A YOUNG floozy was washing her hair when the phone rang and it was answered by her flatmate.

"It's an obscene phone call for you," she called out.

"Take down the number, tell him I'll call him back soon," came the reply.

★ ★ ★

"IF you want an extra bit of sport in bed," one male said to the other, "mount her from behind and whisper in her ear. This is how I do it with your best friend." Then try and stay on for 10 seconds."

★ ★ ★

TWO men fell overboard when they were out at sea and only Jim could swim.

"Jump on my back, John and we'll try swimming for shore," he said.

For the next 2 hours Jim swam towards land. Twice he was ready to give up but urged on by John they eventually made it.

"Bloody hell, I'm fucked," panted Jim as he crawled up the sand.

"Yes, sorry about that," said John "It was the only way I could hang on."

I SAYS to my mate, "I like your hair, how do you get it like that?"

He replied, "My girlfriend strips and I rub my head between her tits and my hair goes like this. Try it."

"I will."

Next day, we meet up and he says, "Did you try it?"

"Yeah," I says. "And you've got a lovely house as well."

★ ★ ★

LEFT stranded after falling off her horse some miles from home, a young cattleman's daughter was rescued by an Indian who brought her back to the ranch on his mount. When the father heard the sound of hooves he went out to meet them and helped his daughter down from the back of the horse.

"How did you manage to stay on?" he asked her.

"Well, it was difficult at first but then he told me to hold on to the saddle horn."

"Oh my darling daughter, don't you realise, Indians always ride bareback."

★ ★ ★

A BOY and girl stop for a kiss while walking through the park. "Mmm, you smell nice," says the girl. "What have you got on?"

He replies, "I've got a hard on but I didn't realise you could smell it."

★ ★ ★

THREE men are discussing what to buy their wives for their birthdays.

"I'm going to get my wife some sexy underwear and a pair of

Italian shoes, then if she doesn't like one, hopefully she'll like the other."

"That's a good idea," says the second man.

"I'll get my wife two presents as well and maybe one of them will be alright. Let's see - I think I'll get a gold necklace and an evening dress."

"What about you Jack?" they say, turning to the third man who has remained morosely quiet.

"Oh, I know what I'm getting Doreen, a mink coat and a dildo. If she doesn't like the coat she can go fuck herself."

★ ★ ★

INTO a bar comes a man grinning all over his face. He says to the bartender, "I'll have three rums, one bourbon and two gin and blackcurrant, please."

The drinks are lined up before him and he downs them all straightaway.

"Hey, what's the big occasion?" asks the bartender.

"I've just had my first blowjob," replies the man.

"Oh right, was it OK?"

"Not too bad but even now I can still taste it."

★ ★ ★

FOR quite some time this man has been living next door to a beautiful young girl and they have never done more than just say hello on meeting.

One day, however, the girl comes out wearing a flimsy dressing gown and invites him over to her door. It's obvious she's making out to him and he becomes very hot under the collar. All of a sudden she urgently whispers to him, "Let's go inside, I hear someone coming..."

He blindly follows her indoors and once inside she drops her dressing gown to the floor and stands there stark naked.

"So honey," she coos, "what do you think my best attribute is?"

The man stutters, "It's, er.... It's got to be your ears."

"My ears!" she gasps. "Why? Have you ever seen such flawless skin, have you ever seen such beautiful breasts, have you ever seen such a firm backside? Yet you say my ears!"

"Well, it's like this" he explains. "When we were outside and you said you heard someone coming.... Well, that was me."

★ ★ ★

A CONFIDENCE trickster bought a pet shop and put an advertisement in the window saying he had a very special dog, ideal for spinsters.

Sure enough, the ad attracted a lot of attention and one woman came into the shop asking for more details.

"It's a big alsatian, miss," he said, "and it keeps women warm on cold nights - if you know what I mean." (wink wink)

The woman bought the dog but a few days later rang the pet shop complaining that the dog had done "Nothing special!"

The man went round to the woman's flat and found her in bed while the dog was asleep on the floor.

"Come on, Rover," he said, taking his clothes off, "How many more times do I have to show you!"

★ ★ ★

EVER since the new cook had arrived at camp, he had been treated miserably. They'd thrown away his clothes, turned his bed upside down and hidden his post. Eventually, however, they grew bored and told him there would be no more tricks.

"You really mean that?" he said.

"Yes" they assured him.

"OK, good, then I'll stop pissing in the soup."

DID you hear about the girl who swallowed a razor blade? The doctor decided to let it come out naturally but during the time it took for that to happen, it gave her an appendectomy, badly lacerated her husband, cut out the tongue of her next door neighbour and damaged the hand of a casual friend.

★ ★ ★

"I'M really fed up with my wife's slovenly ways," complained Bob. "This morning, I went to piss in the sink and it was full of dishes!"

★ ★ ★

"TWO men talking over a pint.
"I'm glad to see you and your wife are on better terms. Solved the eternal triangle problem, did you?"
"Oh yes," replied the other. "We ate the sheep."

★ ★ ★

WHEN he showed her his big one, she exclaimed, "But if we have oral sex, won't you lose respect for me?"
"Not at all," he replied, "as long as you're good at it."

★ ★ ★

DID you hear about the man who entered his dog in the local pet show?
He got three months.

★ ★ ★

THE beautiful blonde bimbo whispered to the handsome doctor. "Oh kiss me again, please kiss me again."

"It's ethically wrong you know," he said. "I shouldn't really be fucking you in the first place."

★ ★ ★

A VERY famous Member of Parliament was walking through the park when he suddenly got a huge erection and had to dash behind a tree to relieve himself. Unfortunately, a passer-by caught him in the act and took a photo of him. Extremely alarmed at the bad publicity this would bring, he offered to buy the camera and film from the stranger. It took a great deal of haggling but they finally agreed on £500. Walking back to work a little later with the camera slung over his shoulder, the MP met one of his colleagues.
"Is that a new camera?" he asked. "How much did you pay for it?"
"£500".
"My goodness, he must have seen you coming."

★ ★ ★

A MISERLY old woman was always trying to find ways of saving money and came upon the idea of feeding her husband cheap dog food. It took a few days for him to get used to it but when she insisted it was the best minced steak he had no reason to be suspicious. Three months went by when one afternoon she received a phone call from the local hospital to say her husband had been brought in following an accident. She arrived at casualty 20 minutes later and asked the doctor on duty how he was and what had happened.
"Just a few broken bones, nothing too serious. An odd accident, though. It seems he was hit by a car when he suddenly sat down in the middle of the road and tried to lick his backside."

THE rush hour train was packed to capacity and standing pressed up against a pretty young girl was a creepy looking man.

"Will you stop pushing that thing at me," she whispered angrily.

"It's only my wallet," he replied.

"Well, you must have a bloody good job, you've had three rises since we left Waterloo."

★ ★ ★

A MAN out walking with his dog is amazed to see his doctor down on all fours with his fingers halfway down a rabbit hole. As he continues to watch, the doctor withdraws his hand and a moment later a rabbit pops his head out. The doctor knocks it out and puts it in his bag. After watching him catch ten rabbits this way he goes over and asks what the secret is.

"It's very simple," replies the doctor. "Before you come out put your hand between a woman's legs; then when the rabbits smell it they can't help come up for more. That's when you get them."

"I can hardly believe it," says the man. "Are you sure?"

"Of course, you can trust me, I'm a doctor."

The man ponders the doctor's words on the way home and when he sees his wife bending over the oven he quickly puts his hand between her legs. Without looking round, his wife says, "Hello doctor, off rabbit hunting again?"

★ ★ ★

THREE hikers stop for a rest in the Yorkshire Dales and looking over into an adjoining field they see some sheep.

"Hey, I think that sheep's smiling at you," jokes one of them.

"I wish it was Cindy Crawford."

The second says, "I wish it was Sharon Stone."

The third says, "I wish it was dark."

AN Australian DJ on one of the local radio stations decides to launch a new competition. He asks people to ring in with a word used in everyday speech but not found in the dictionary. If they're successful, they win a prize. It's not long before a man rings up with the word 'goan'.

"Well thanks for that word, I'll just check it's not in the dictionary .... no, it's not. So how would you use this word?"

"Goan fuck yourself," came the reply.

Lost for words, the DJ quickly puts on some music.

An hour later, he gets another call and this time the word is 'smee'. He looks it up and it's not there.

"So how would you use this word?" he asks the caller.

"It's smee again; go fuck yourself."

★ ★ ★

THREE blokes were talking in a pub in Wales about the best way to shag a sheep.

The first two agreed it was the back legs down the wellies and the front legs over the wall. But the third said, "No, it was the back legs down the wellies and the front legs over the shoulders."

"Doesn't that make it difficult?" said the other two. "Why don't you do as we suggested?"

"What! And miss out on all the kissing?"

★ ★ ★

"YOU look happy this morning Jack" said his mate.

"Yeah, I came into some money last night - a girl with gold caps on her teeth."

★ ★ ★

"YOU will still love me now we're married, won't you?" asked

the newly wed girl.

"Oh, even more," he replied, "I've got a thing about married women."

⋆ ⋆ ⋆

A POOR simple young girl went to the doctors and was told she was pregnant.

"But how can that be?" she said. "I haven't been with a man."

Patiently, the doctor explains the birds and bees to the young girl.

"Oh no," she gasped, "the first aid teacher told me it was artificial respiration."

⋆ ⋆ ⋆

JACK and Flo had a distant cousin staying with them and one night when she was taking a bath, Flo went in to give her some more towels and noticed she didn't have any pubic hairs.

"Really," said Jack, when Flo told him about it later. "That's very odd, you must be mistaken."

"No, I'm not," said Flo angrily. "You can see for yourself."

Flo told him that the cousin usually had a bath on his darts night. As they had a bungalow, he could nip back, look through the window and see for himself. The darts night came around and sure enough the cousin went for her bath. A little later, Flo walked in and this time felt compelled to say something.

"Why haven't you got any hair on your fanny?" she asked.

"I didn't know I was supposed to," said the naive girl.

"Oh yes, look I'll show you," And with that Flo lifted her skirt, pulled down her knickers and showed the girl her thatch.

Jack came home 30 minutes later in a very angry mood. "What the hell were you doing exposing yourself like that," he shouted.

"Oh don't be silly Jack, you've seen me hundreds of times."

Maybe, but the bloody darts team haven't."

HAVE you heard about the two spinsters in the shower?
One said, "Where's the soap?" and the other replied, "Yes, you're right, it does."

★ ★ ★

LUCY'S mother looked so young that many people mistook them for sisters. Now it just so happened that Lucy was court- ing a local dairyman but, unknown to her, the dairyman was also seeing her mother. One day, Lucy came home in tears "What's wrong?" asked her mother.
"William and I stopped seeing each other a month ago because I'm sure he was being unfaithful. But I've just seen him in the High Street and I still love him!" she cried.
"Never mind, you'll find someone else. You'll just have to for- get about him. Did you return all the presents he gave you?"
"Yes I did and what's more I put tiny pinpricks in all his con- doms - that'll teach him .... Oh Mother, you've gone pale, are you alright?"

★ ★ ★

WHAT two other purposes have hill farmers found for sheep?
Wool and meat.

★ ★ ★

HOW can you tell if a woman is wearing pantyhose?
When she farts her ankles swell up.

★ ★ ★

"AND another thing Terry," said the macho man, "masturbation is a waste of fucking time."

A YOUNG man was meeting his future in-laws for the first time at their large mansion in the country. They sat down to lunch and the first course went by without incident but just as the young man was about to tuck into the roast, he was unable to stop a small fart escaping.

"Jasper!" exclaimed the hostess to the dog.

Unfortunately, less than five minutes later, another, larger fart began to build up until he was unable to contain it any longer. Again, the hostess shouted, "Jasper!"

Feeling pleased that the dog was getting blamed, the young man relaxed but in doing so he let out a rip roarer that fairly rattled the crockery. "Jasper, get the hell over here quickly before that bugger dumps on you."

★ ★ ★

A BLOKE was walking home late one night when he was set upon by two muggers who beat him up and stole his wallet. They also managed to break his top set of dentures. Lying on the ground battered and bruised, he was found by a kindly gentleman and helped to his feet.

"You look as if you could do with a stiff drink," said the gentleman. "My house is just round the corner, you're welcome to come and sit for a while until you're feeling better."

So some time later and two large whiskies later, the man started to recover and in doing so realised his dentures were broken.

"Wait a minute," said the gentleman, "I think I can help you out." He disappeared for a few minutes and came back with a selection of different dentures. "See if any of these fit."

After trying on six different pairs he found one that seemed to be perfect.

"I can't thank you enough" he said. "You rescue me from the pavement, help me to recover my wits and on top of all that you're a dentist as well."

"Oh no," said the gentleman, "I'm not a dentist, I'm an undertaker."

★　★　★

"HEY, Bob," they said laughing. "What's the difference between your sister and a Porsche?
Most of us haven't been in a Porsche."

★　★　★

A MAN got on a very crowded train and the only seat available was occupied by a dog.
"Excuse me, madam, can you move the dog so that I may sit down?"
"Bugger off!" she said. "Go and find somewhere else to sit."
But there was nowhere else and as the train slowed down at the crossing he picked the dog up and threw it out of the door.
The woman jumped up shouting. "Did you see that, did you see him molest poor Fou Fou? What a bad thing to do."
"You're right there madam," said a voice from the back. "It really was a bad thing to do, he threw out the wrong bitch.

★　★　★

DID you hear about the girl who said she'd do anything for a mink coat?
Now she can't do it up!

★　★　★

"YOUR kisses really burn."
"Sorry, perhaps I ought to put my cigarette out!"

★　★　★

WHY do Australian men come so quickly?
Because they can't wait to get down to the pub to tell their mates.

★ ★ ★

WHAT does a prat call his best friend's wife?
A really good fuck.

★ ★ ★

THE Head of State would just like to say in defence of the sexual harassment charge against him, that the woman must have been slightly deaf. What he did say was, "Hold my calls and sack my cook."

★ ★ ★

THE man was so drunk, he slipped and fell as he came out of the pub causing one car to swerve out of his way and plough into the back of a bus which caused a two-mile tailback. As the drunk was helped to his feet, one of the crowd asked him what had happened. "I don't know," he slurred "I've only just got here myself."

★ ★ ★

WELL, I've stuffed the goose. All we need to do now is kill it and buy some apple sauce, and we'll have a great Christmas dinner.

IN YOUR BEDCHAMBER

"WHY are you taking so long?" complained his wife.
"I'm trying really hard," he replied ,"but I can't think of anyone."

★ ★ ★

DID you wake up grumpy this morning?
No, I let him sleep.

★ ★ ★

THE best way to drive your husband mad is to smile in your sleep.

★ ★ ★

THE small guest house was full, but taking pity on the stranded traveller the owner agreed to the man sharing a bed with his daughter. However, when the man tried some hanky panky she replied, "Stop that at once or I'll call my father."
Some time went by and he tried again but got the same reply: "Stop that or I'll call my father."
Then to his amazement, third time lucky, she agreed and they spent a passionate 20 minutes bonking.
Five minutes later she tapped him on the shoulder and asked for more. He obligingly agreed and away they went. Exhausted afterwards, he was just about to go to sleep when she tapped his shoulder again. This was repeated half the night until he was so knackered he turned to her and said, "Stop that or I'll call your father."

★ ★ ★

HOW does a French girl hold her liquor?
By the ears.

★ ★ ★

WHAT'S the macho man's idea of foreplay?
A tap on the shoulder and "Are you awake?"

★ ★ ★

A WIFE with a large sexual appetite calls to her husband.
"Guess what I have hidden in my hands and I'll reward you with a
full night of passion."
The poor harassed husband replies, "An elephant".
"Not quite," she says, "but it's close enough."

★ ★ ★

A YOUNG girl tells her devoted father she wants to get mar-
ried. He's a bit shocked at one so young and decides to sit her
down and talk to her about the birds and the bees. He also tells
her that if her husband asks her to roll over she doesn't have
to.
"Oh father," she says, "I know all there is to know, you don't
have to worry."
A year goes by and one night in bed her husband asks her to
roll over.
"Oh no," says the girl "I don't have to if I don't want to."
"But darling, what's wrong, don't you ever want to get preg-
nant!"

★ ★ ★

IN a recent survey it was discovered that 15% of men liked women with thin legs, 10% liked women with fat legs and the rest liked something in between.

★ ★ ★

ONE night as they were going to bed Mabel asked her old husband how they would manage when he could no longer work. "Just look out of the window," said Bill. "I own those two shops and three houses."
Mabel wanted to know how he'd managed to do that on such a low wage.
"From the moment we were married I put 50p under the mattress every time you let me have my way and if you hadn't been such a frigid old cow, we'd have had two supermarkets and three pubs by now."

★ ★ ★

IF you suffer from insomnia, have sex. It won't help you sleep but you'll have more fun while you're awake!

★ ★ ★

THERE'S a shop next door that sells strobe lighting for the bedroom. It makes it look as if your wife is moving during sex.

★ ★ ★

LOOKING through an open bedroom window one night, a Peeping Tom came upon a young couple playing a rather kinky game. Stark naked, they were sitting in opposite corners of the room, a bag of marbles besides the man, and a pile of hoops besides the woman. As he watched the woman threw a hoop and it landed on the man's erect penis.
"Hooray!" she said "One to me".

Then the man rolled a marble straight between her legs and cheered "Now it's one all."

The next day the Peeping Tom's wife was going shopping and asked him if there was anything he needed.

"Yes," he replied with a secret grin on his face "A bag of sprouts and a packet of polo mints."

★ ★ ★

NOW I know why my wife closes her eyes when we're making love. She hates to see me having a good time.

★ ★ ★

HAVE you heard about the ideal couple? He's got a premature ejaculation problem and she's got a short attention span.

★ ★ ★

ONE night, unsure if his wife would respond to his amorous advances, Ken suddenly had a great idea. As he got into bed he handed his wife 2 paracetamol and a glass of water.

"What's that for?" she asked.

"For your headache."

"But I haven't got a headache."

"Good, then let's fuck."

★ ★ ★

AFTER many years of making love in the dark, the wife turns the light on one night to find her husband using a dildo on her.

"What's going on?" she cries horrified. "What's the meaning of this?"

"I can explain," he says, "but first you tell me how we got the kids."

DID you hear about the absent-minded shop assistant? At night after making love to her husband she'd say, "Will that be all, sir?"

★ ★ ★

OLD proverb: You can't take sex with you, so you might as well exhaust it down here.

★ ★ ★

"MY darling, will you love me always?"
"Of course, sweetheart, which way do you want to try first?"

★ ★ ★

HAVE you heard of the new style in women's nightdresses?
They have fur hems to keep a man's neck warm.

★ ★ ★

"DARLING, do you think we might try making love doggie style?" said husband to wife.
"OK, but not on a street where someone might come along who knows us," she replied.

IN YOUR BITTERNESS

A BITTER woman who buried her husband on the Monday returned with his headstone on the Thursday. On it she had inscribed, "Here lies my husband, stiff at last."

★ ★ ★

A BITTER old lady turned to her neighbour and said, "I see Edith's buried her tenth husband. Now at last they're together again."
"What d'you mean, her husbands?"
"No, silly, I'm talking about her legs."

★ ★ ★

WHAT'S the difference between a whore and a bitch?
A whore sleeps with everyone; a bitch sleeps with everyone except you.

★ ★ ★

A BITTER old woman turned to her friend and said, "If it wasn't for orgasms that old tart over there wouldn't know when to stop screwing."

★ ★ ★

A MAN who had done so much for his village was complaining about the lack of respect he had received from the rest of the inhabitants.

"For instance," he said "See all those beautifully mown lawns, the abundance of flowers, the avenue of trees? I did all that, but do they call me John the Horticulturist? No, they bloody well don't. And look at the stunning new village hall and the ornate wall around the church. I did all that but do they call me John the Builder. Not bloody likely! But just one, just one bloody sheep ..."

★ ★ ★

WHEN the bitter woman was asked what the meaning of life was she replied, "It's like a bed of roses - full of pricks."

★ ★ ★

DID you hear about the bitter old nurse?
On the night her husband got married again she put anaesthetic in the lubricating jelly.

★ ★ ★

TWO women, who were at school together, bump into each other 10 years later. The first one is a bit of a show-off.
"Yes, I can't complain. I went for a job on an estate just out-side Henley and ended up marrying the Lord of the Manor. Ha Ha."
"Oh, how nice" said the second.
"And Jack darling encouraged me to start a stud farm and we've now got one of the best in Southern England."
"Oh, how nice."
"We've got two lovely boys .... at Eton of course ...."
"Oh, how nice."
"Anyway, listen to me blathering on! What happened to you?"
"Me? Oh, I went to finishing school after we left, and learnt how to say, 'Oh how nice' instead of 'fuck you'."

OVERHEARD on the top deck of a bus:

"I'm knackered, Bill; it's been a hell of a day at work, You know, compared to us, women have it so easy. Why, they even sit down to take a piss."

★　★　★

WALKING round the art gallery, Bob is stopped by one of the local artists.

"I'm sorry to bother you, but I must say you're wife is quite stunning and I would deem it an honour to paint her portrait."

"Oh yes?" said Bob, watching his wife flirting with yet another local dignitary. "Yes, you're right, she reminds me of the Venus de Milo."

"How extraordinary," said the artist, looking closer at Bob. "In what way?"

"She's beautiful alright, but not all there!"

IN YOUR CHEEKINESS

IT was too late for Bob to drive home, so he was invited to stay the night at his mate's house.

"We've only the one bed," said Bob's mate "so you'll have to share with me and the wife."

They all went to bed and soon the husband was snoring. Then Bob got a nudge from the wife inviting him over for a bit of shagging.

"I can't do that, your husband will wake up at the noise" he whispered.

"Don't worry, there's no chance of that, but if you're worried pull out one of his pubic hairs and see if he wakens."

Bob did but the husband never moved a muscle and just went on snoring. So Bob and the wife got down to it and enjoyed a very pleasant 30 minutes. It wasn't long before she was nudging him again and this went on half the night, each time Bob plucking the husband's pubic hair out before he started. However on the twelfth time, the husband turned to Bob and said, "Listen mate, I don't mind you shagging my wife, but bloody hell, I do mind you keeping score on my arse."

★ ★ ★

A MAN travelling home late from work falls asleep on the train and ends up at the terminus. There's a taxi outside but the driver refuses to take him because he hasn't enough money for the fare and the driver won't let him pay the balance on getting home. The poor man ends up sleeping rough. A few days later, having plotted his revenge, he stays on to the terminus and sees 4 taxis waiting, the last one in the line being the driver who refused him last time. He goes up to the other 3 taxis in turn, asks how much the fare is, says he can't pay but offers to give them a blow job. Each driver in turn tells him to bugger off. He then goes up to the fourth taxi, asks how much the fare is and gets in. As they pass the three waiting taxis he looks out of the back window, smiles and gives them the thumbs up.

★ ★ ★

DO you know what the heaviest thing in the world is?
The body of a woman you no longer love.

★ ★ ★

MY wife's got long black hair running down here back. Wish it were on her head.

★ ★ ★

A FEMALE put-down.
I bet when you climax you call out your own name.

★ ★ ★

I'LL never forget the first time we met - but I'm trying.

★ ★ ★

HOW do you know when your girlfriend is putting on weight?
When she sits on your face and you can't hear the radio.

★ ★ ★

PORTER to man, "Can I carry your bag, sir?"
"No, let her walk."

DO you know what a constipated greeting is?
It's when you ask someone "How are you?" but don't give a shit.

★ ★ ★

HE'D like to get into her knickers but there's an asshole there already.

★ ★ ★

"MY darling," whispered the naive young man, "Will I be the first man to sleep with you?".
"You will be if you doze off," she replied.

★ ★ ★

"YOU are the world's worst lover!" yelled his wife.
"Get away," he replied "That really would be too much of a coincidence."

★ ★ ★

THE butler was summoned to the master bedroom to find her lady-ship lying naked across the bed.
"There you are Edward" she said. "Are you a good sport?"
"I believe so, ma'am," replied the startled butler.
"And are you a good fuck?" she continued!
"Yes, I believe I am."
"Well, in that case, fuck off, it's April Fools Day."

★ ★ ★

THERE were mixed reactions when Lady Godiva rode side-saddle through the town. Those on the right cheered, shouted and whistled, those on the left were strangely quiet.

MY wife saw the dustbin lorry leaving our house.
"Am I too late for the rubbish?" she asked.
"No," they answered. "Jump in."

★ ★ ★

A YOUNG man takes refuge in an old couple's house when his car breaks down on the moor.
"We've only got two bedrooms, young man, one for us and the other for our spinster daughter, but you're quite welcome to sleep on the sofa."
In the middle of the night it turns bitterly cold, so the old woman pops downstairs to see how the man is doing.
"I hope you're not too cold, would you like our eiderdown?"
"Good gracious, no thanks," he replied. "She's been down three times already."

★ ★ ★

"WELL I never!" cried outraged mother when she walked into the front room to see her daughter and boyfriend having it away on the sofa.
"Oh mother," replied daughter, "Of course you did."

★ ★ ★

AS Jack drew up at the lights a car screamed to a stop behind him and out jumped the driver and rushed over.
"I've been trying to get your attention for the last three miles" he said.
"Didn't you realise your wife had fallen off when you took that sharp bend?"
"Oh, I am relieved" said Jack. "I thought I'd gone deaf."

★ ★ ★

WHAT makes taxi drivers the world's worst lovers? They never check to see if you're coming before they pull out.

★ ★ ★

DID you hear about the dwarf who was expelled from the nudist colony?
He was always poking his nose into other people's business.

★ ★ ★

"BUT darling you're only saying I've got a beautiful body to get me into bed," she said.
"No, no, that's not true," he replied. "It's not just me that thinks that. I took some secret shots of you in the shower, showed them to my mates and they all agree. You really do have a beautiful body."

★ ★ ★

"LISTEN mate," said one man to another in the local bar. "Do the same as me, after sex when you're knackered and she's not, record your voice and keep the machine under your pillow so you can switch it on and make her think you're still talking to her."

★ ★ ★

HOW can you tell a short-sighted man in a nudist colony?
It isn't hard.

★ ★ ★

DID you hear about the blind man who went to a nudist colony? It was a touching sight.

WHO'S the most popular man in a nudist colony? The one who can carry two teas and ten doughnuts all at the same time.

★ ★ ★

DOCTOR, do you agree with eating everything raw?
No, always keep your clothes on.

★ ★ ★

A NUDIST never has to hold his hand out to see if it is raining.

★ ★ ★

A YOUNG man, finding himself stranded in the middle of nowhere, comes upon a little cottage. On knocking, the door is opened by a Chinaman who allows him to stay the night as long as he goes nowhere near his daughter. Disobey and the three most horrible tortures will be inflicted upon him.
However, the young man is rather stupid and when he sees the Chinaman's beautiful daughter he forgets all about his promise. That night when everything is quiet he steals into the daughter's room and they enjoy a night of non-stop rollicking, before he creeps back to his own bed at dawn.
A couple of hours later he wakes to find a boulder on his chest and pinned to it is a little note which says, "Beware, large boulder on chest - torture 1."
The young man is arrogant enough to dismiss the whole thing and he throws the boulder out of the window. As he does so he notices another note which says, "Beware boulder tied to left testicle - torture 2."
Quickly thinking that the lesser of two evils was to break a few bones jumping out of the window, he did just that before the rope tightened. However as he fell to the ground another sign

was waiting for him. It read "Beware, right testicle tied to bed-room door - torture 3."

⋆ ⋆ ⋆

A MAN walks into the local hotel and sees a pretty girl drinking by herself at the bar.

"Do you mind if I join you?" he asks.

At that she screams at the top of her voice "No, I will not go up to your room!"

Everyone stops talking, looks at him as he turns a bright red and slowly shuffles away.

A few minutes later she walks over to him, apologises and explains that she is studying human behaviour and people's reactions to embarrassing situations.

The man listens quietly to her explanation and then shouts at the top of his voice "£150, you've got to be joking."

⋆ ⋆ ⋆

WHAT is the difference between erotic sex and kinky sex? For erotic sex you use a feather, during kinky sex it's the whole chicken.

⋆ ⋆ ⋆

"WHAT'S wrong mate? You look tired."

"I am," said Bob. "I think I pulled a muscle this morning."

"It's odd that it should make you so tired."

"Not really, if you pull it 450 times."

⋆ ⋆ ⋆

A WOMAN walked into the menswear department and asked the wizened old assistant whether he fitted trusses.

"Indeed we do," came the puzzled reply.

"Well, in that case, wash your hands thoroughly and serve me with some of those gentlemen's cigars," she demanded.

★ ★ ★

A DIVORCED couple still remained good friends and would often meet in the local pub to catch up on all the gossip. So it wasn't surprising that when he broke a leg skiing she would go round to his place to help him out. One day, she was lifting him out of the bath when she noticed he had an erection.

"Oh look, Bob," she remarked. "He still remembers me."

★ ★ ★

DRIVING down a very busy high street, the man's car suddenly stalled and nothing he did would get it going again. Feeling more and more flustered, his temper eventually boiled over when a man behind him repeatedly beeped his horn. Out got the man and strode up to the car behind, opened the door and pushed his fingers down on the horn.

"Here, we'll do a swap. I'll blast your horn while you go and start that bugger up."

★ ★ ★

A 'DIRTY old man' picked up a beautiful young girl in the local pub and invited her out for dinner. To his surprise she accepted and they went off to the most expensive restaurant in town where she ordered all the most expensive food and drink on the menu. Astonished, the man asked her if she always had such a big appetite.

"Only when someone wants to get into my knickers," she replied.

★ ★ ★

HAVE you heard about the miserly man? He always stays in with his dates and plays snap. It's cheap on wining and dining; the only expense is the elastic.

★ ★ ★

"ACCORDING to the latest MORI poll 50% of male adults sing in the bath - the rest are wankers. And do you know what they sing?"
"No."
"I didn't think so."

★ ★ ★

WALKING along the seashore, a man finds a bottle washed up on the sand and when he opens it, a genie pops out. As thanks for setting him free, the genie grants the man one wish.
"Er... I wish I was always hard and had lots of arse" he says.
So the genie turns him into a toilet seat.

★ ★ ★

DO you know the difference between a woman trying to slim and a virgin? One's trying to diet and the other's dying to try it.

★ ★ ★

"I'LL tell you what eternity feels like," said the unscrupulous woman. "It's the time it takes between you coming and him leaving."

★ ★ ★

"SWEETHEART," said the young man to his girlfriend. "What I'd really like is a little pussy."
"Me too," she replied. "Mine's as big as an elephant's."

A SALES rep was staying overnight at an hotel and took a great fancy to the waitress but when he tried to entice her up to his room she flatly refused.

"I'm not that sort of girl" she said "Besides, I don't like sex very much."

"Oh come now! Do you realise I'm a shoe salesman. You may like to see some of the latest and most fashionable shoes on offer if you come upstairs?"

In the end the girl relented and it wasn't long before he was on top of her in bed. Much to his surprise she reacted very enthusiastically, wrapping her legs around him and twisting and turning quite vigorously.

"There, I knew you'd find me good," said the arrogant man.

"Oh no," she replied. "I'm just trying on the shoes."

★ ★ ★

A VERY large lady visits the doctor complaining of a sore throat. The doctor shines a light down her throat and after a few moments says to her, "Would you like to take all your clothes off and then get down on all fours?"

This the fat lady does.

"Very good," says the doctor. "Now would you please crawl over to the wall behind the door."

So the fat lady does as she's told.

"Mm Mm, yes, I see. Right now, will you please crawl to the wall between the lampstand and the glass fronted cabinet. Good ... excellent. OK, you may get dressed now."

When the fat lady is dressed and sits back down she asked him what is wrong.

"Oh you have a sore throat, I'll give you a prescription for it."

"But why on earth did you have me crawling around the room on all fours with no clothes on?" she asks impatiently.

"Ah, well you see, tomorrow I'm having a pink sofa delivered and I was just trying to find the best place to put it."

WHAT'S the difference between an ugly girl and rubbish? Rubbish gets taken out once a week.

★ ★ ★

HE bought an apple for the teacher and she kissed him. So the next day he took a cantaloupe melon.

★ ★ ★

HER husband was so ugly, every time he went to the zoo he had to buy two tickets - one for going in and one for getting out.

★ ★ ★

"I CAN'T go out with you tonight, I'm getting married."
"OK. How about tomorrow night then?"

★ ★ ★

"FATHER, I have something to confess. My girlfriend is pregnant and I need £150."
The man hands over the money. Then a few days later the other son arrives home with similar news.
"How much do you need?"
"£170."
Time passes and one day the daughter comes to see her father.
"I'm sorry, but I am pregnant," she says.
"Never mind," he says smiling. "It's about time we were on the receiving end."

★ ★ ★

A YOUNG punk rocker gets on the tube and sits opposite an old man who stares at him constantly. The punk has spiky red, blue and orange hair, rings in his nose, his eyebrows, lips and ears, and long dangling feather earrings. After 10 minutes, the punk can't take any more of the staring and shouts at the old man, "What are you looking at, you old fart, didn't you do anything crazy when you were young?"

"Yes," replies the old man. "When I was young and in the navy, I shagged a parrot when I was on shore leave. I thought maybe you were my son."

★ ★ ★

"HOW dare you tell that dirty, filthy joke before my wife!"
"I do apologise, I didn't know she wanted to tell it herself."

★ ★ ★

A VERY attractive woman walks up to the bar in a local pub and, smiling seductively, signals for the barman to come close to her. When he does, she starts to run her fingers through his hair and whispers, "Are you the landlord?"

"No, I'm sorry, he's not here at the moment" And he gasps with delight as she brings her fingers down through his hair and begins to gently stroke his beard.

"Is there anything I can do?" he whispers.

"Yes, will you please give him a message?" By this time, she's put her fingers in his mouth and he's sucking on them sexily.

"Will you please tell the landlord that there's no toilet paper in the Ladies."

★ ★ ★

TWO burglars broke into a house in the village, tied up the old spinster and ransacked the rooms. The boss turned to his mate and said, "Before we go, I think I'll give her one to remember me by."

"I don't think we've got time, Boss. Let's get out of here before someone sees something and calls the police."
"Now hold on a minute," said the spinster. "Just who's in charge of this robbery?"

★ ★ ★

A MARKET gardener and his daughter went into town to sell their produce and pick up some supplies for the following month. They made a healthy profit on the vegetables and spent some of it on buying onion sets, seed potatoes, and the like, for the coming Spring. However, on the way back, they were attacked by a gang of thieves who took everything they had.
"Oh dear, our Josie!" said the distraught man. "How are we going to manage to live without any money?"
"Don't worry, father, I've saved the money."
"But how, they searched you thoroughly."
"I hid it in that place that women have."
"Oh my goodness, if your mother had been here, we could have saved half the supplies as well."

★ ★ ★

HAVE you heard about the miserly man who keeps a crate in the boot of his car?
He's filling it up with all the small furry animals he runs over in the road so when he's got enough, he'll get it made up into a fur coat for the wife.

★ ★ ★

DUE to engine trouble, a scheduled flight from New York to London had to be cancelled and the airline staff were left to try and re-book all the passengers onto other flights. The queues were enormous, but one angry, pompous man strode to the front and interrupted the booking staff mid-conversation.

"Now look here, I have to be on the next flight, and I have to travel first class," he said forcefully.

"We will do all we can to help you, sir" replied one of the staff. "If you will just get back in line while I finish attending to this gentleman here."

Annoyed at being fobbed off, the man replied loudly so that everyone could hear, "Young lady, do you have any idea who I am?"

She smiled and picked up the microphone for the public address system.

"All passengers in the airport terminal, may I have your attention please. I have a passenger here at Gate 5 who does not know who he is. If anyone can help in this matter, please come to the gate as soon as possible. Thank you."

★ ★ ★

AFTER doing his rounds in a remote part of the Lake District, the doctor stops off at Bill Higgins' house to see how he is since his wife died.

"Thanks for asking," he says. "I do feel a bit lonely now she's gone but she's never far from my thoughts. I buried her in the garden face down with her bum in the air."

"My goodness, why?"

"Well, it's somewhere to park the bike."

★ ★ ★

A PASSING motorist sees a man fishing in a flower bed next to the mental institution. He thinks he'll have a laugh, so he sticks his head out of the window and shouts,

"Have you caught many?"

"Just three apart from you," he replies.

IN YOUR CHURCHYARD

THE Reverend James was taking his usual morning walk through the woods when he met a frog that was looking very unhappy.

"I wish you could talk and tell me what is wrong" said the Reverend.

"I can," said the frog. "I used to be a choirboy but an evil old crone turned me into a frog and the spell can only be reversed if someone takes me home, looks after me and let's me sleep in their bed." Being such a caring soul, the Reverend did as the frog requested and the next morning the frog turned back into a choirboy.

"And that, your honour, is the case for the defence."

* * *

THE local vicar is on his parish rounds when he comes to a house playing very loud music. Knocking at the door it is opened by a young lad smoking a cigarette, holding a bottle of scotch and accompanied by two young girls.

"Excuse me, son" says the vicar, "is your mum or dad in?"

"Does it fucking well look like it?" replies the boy.

* * *

THE vicar was doing his parish rounds when he came upon a house that had eight children, from ages two to 12, playing in the garden. He knocked at the door but couldn't get any reply, so he peeped through the window. To his horror he saw a couple going hammer and tongs on the dining room carpet, so he beat a hasty retreat, and went to the house opposite.

"Your neighbours across the road love having children, don't they?" he commented to the man.

"They sure do, vicar. His wife is in hospital at the moment having another baby, so my wife's popped over to see if there's anything she can do."

★ ★ ★

A YOUNG woman and a clergyman found themselves to be the only ones in the tea-rooms. So to be polite, the clergyman said, "That's a lovely baby you have there."

The woman explained that it had taken six years of marriage before conceiving. She had almost given up hope.

"Yes, indeed," replied the clergyman. "Persistence is the answer. Look at me, I breed pigeons, but for years never won a race. Now I'm winning gold cups all the time."

"Indeed," replied the woman, "and why's that?"

"Oh, I changed the cock," he said.

"Yes, that's what I did."

★ ★ ★

A VERY pretty young girl was just about to walk into the church in a topless dress when the vicar turned towards her.

"I'm afraid you can't come into church dressed like that" he said.

"But I have a divine right," she replied.

"My dear, I agree," nodded the vicar "You have a divine left as well but I still can't let you into church."

★ ★ ★

THE vicar returned to the rectory complaining bitterly that someone had stolen his bicycle while he'd been out on his parish calls.

"I've got an idea," replied the verger. "This Sunday in church

make the Ten Commandments the theme of the sermon and when you get to "Thou shalt not steal" watch their faces carefully for any tell-tale signs."

So that Sunday the vicar began his sermon but halfway through suddenly dried up and finished early.

"What happened?" asked the verger later.

"Well, I was going to do as you suggested but when I got to 'Thou shalt not commit adultery', I suddenly remembered where I'd left my bicycle."

★ ★ ★

A YOUNG man and a bishop were sharing a railway carriage. The bishop spent the journey doing *The Times* crossword but after some time began shaking his head muttering.

"Can I help you sir?" asked the young man.

"Well, I'm having trouble with one word - the clue is 'Essentially feminine' - four letters, the last three UNT."

"Why sir that'll be aunt."

"Of course" said the bishop "Do you have a rubber, by any chance?"

★ ★ ★

A CHURCHMAN, staying overnight at an hotel, strikes up an acquaintance with the receptionist and at the end of the evening invites her up to his room for a bedtime drink.

One thing led to another and it wasn't long before they were having it away in bed.

"I'm not sure I should be here," said the receptionist, "After all, you are a man of the church."

"It's alright," he replied "I read about it in the Gideon bible here on my bedside table."

"Oh where?" she asked.

"Here, on the front cover," he replied. "Look it says, 'You're onto a winner with the receptionist downstairs.'

★ ★ ★

A MAN was taken seriously ill and the vicar was summoned to come as soon as possible. Now this puzzled the vicar because he knew the man was not of his parish and indeed went to a different church. However, he rushed around to the house and on knocking, the door was opened by a small child.

"Hello," he said "Isn't it nice that your father thought of me at this time?"

The child replied, "Well, we thought it might be catching, so we didn't want to take any risks."

★ ★ ★

THE Mother Superior was late getting up and had to rush her morning prayers before visiting the young nuns at their work.

"Good morning, Sister Veronica, how are you? Those tomatoes are coming along very well."

"Thank you, Reverend Mother. Yes, I'm fine, though I'm sorry you got out of bed the wrong side this morning."

Puzzled, the Reverend Mother moved on.

"Good morning, Sister Mary, what a lovely day."

"It is indeed, Reverend Mother; it's a shame you got out of bed on the wrong side this morning."

Even more puzzled, the Mother Superior approached Sister Elizabeth and asked cautiously, "Sister, do you get the impression I got out of bed the wrong side this morning."

Sister Elizabeth blushed, "Yes, Reverend Mother."

"Why?"

"Because you're wearing Father O'Neal's slippers."

THREE nuns went to confession. The first said, "Forgive me, Father, for I have sinned. I looked at a man's private parts."

"Then go and wash your eyes with holy water" replied the priest.

"The second nun went into confession. "Forgive me, Father, for I have sinned. I touched a man's private parts."

"Then go and wash your hands with holy water."

The third nun went in and after a short while came out saying, "Won't be long sisters, I've just got to go and gargle."

⋆ ⋆ ⋆

A NUN and a priest are travelling through the desert when suddenly the camel collapses on the sand. It is the hottest time of the day and the nun realises they must have shelter or they will collapse as well. So she takes off her clothes to make a shelter, and on seeing a nude woman for the first time in decades the priest gets a huge erection.

"What's that?" asks the nun.

"It's the giver of life," he replies.

"In that case, stick it up the camel's arse and see if we can get to the next town."

⋆ ⋆ ⋆

EVERY week before Bob and his two mates went out on the town, Bob would pop into the local church for confession.

"Father, forgive me, for I have sinned with a woman."

The priest replied, "Was it Rosie from the Frog and Toad?"

"No, Father."

"Was it Cute Kate from the Cosie Cafe?"

"No, Father."

"Then it must have been whoring Helen from the Greasy Spoon."

"However, I'll give you your penance and think carefully about what you have done."

"Thank you, Father, I will."

Then Bob would rush back outside and say to his two mates, "I've got the names of three little ravers tonight lads."

★ ★ ★

TWO monks who belonged to a silent order spent the day fishing together. Nothing was caught until the very end of the day, when one of the monks caught a mermaid. He looked at the beautiful naked creature, fondled her enthusiastically and then threw her back in. Unable to keep silent, the other monk shouted, "Why?"

"How?" he replied.

★ ★ ★

IT was a young priest's first time at hearing confession and the old priest said he'd sit at the back to see he did it right.

When it was all over, the young priest looked quite pleased with himself.

"That didn't seem to go too badly," he said.

"No, not too bad, but maybe next time a little less of the Wow! Really! and a bit more tut tutting."

★ ★ ★

"IS there a Roman Catholic priest on the train?" called a man, walking along the aisle from carriage to carriage. A little while later he was back, shouting, "Is there an English Catholic priest on the train?" but still no response.

Then a man got up and tapped him on the shoulder.

"Excuse me sir, can I be of any help? I'm a Methodist minister."

"No, thanks," replied the man "I'm just looking to borrow a corkscrew."

LATE for church, a woman says to the man at the door, "Is mass out?"

"No," he replies "but your hat's on crooked."

★   ★   ★

FIRST night in the Garden of Eden and Adam warns Eve, "You'd better stand back a bit, I don't know how big this thing gets."

★   ★   ★

WHO was the world's first bookkeeper?

Adam, he turned over a leaf and made an entry.

★   ★   ★

MOSES came down from Mount Sinai and addressed the waiting Israelites.

"I've got good news and bad news. The good news is I've got them down to ten, but the bad news is that Adultery is out."

★   ★   ★

WHY don't men believe in the return of the Messiah?

A second coming is beyond their understanding.

★   ★   ★

"FATHER, I had it off with two voluptuous blondes last night," confessed the young man.

"Tut, tut, that's not the way a good Catholic man would behave," replied the priest.

"But, I'm not a Catholic" he said.

"Then why are you telling me?"
"I'm telling everyone" came the reply.

★ ★ ★

A YOUNG and very shy vicar was out on his parish rounds for the very first time. His first call was at the house of an old lady living on her own. She invited him in and made a pot of tea while he sat there frantically trying to think of something to say.

"Um... winter draws on then, Mrs Hubbard," he finally stammered.

"In fact, I did put them on this morning," she retorted. "But it's got nothing to do with you."

IN YOUR COURTING

A YOUNG man had a special party piece where he would put two fingers in his mouth and give a whistle that could be heard half a mile away.

This man started courting and one night took his girl out into the country where they spent a couple of enjoyable hours. However, their fun made them late back and as they got to the bus stop the last bus was moving off.

"Quick, stop him, whistle," she said, The man put his two fingers to his mouth, paused and said, "It's a lovely night, let's walk, it won't take long."

★ ★ ★

A COUPLE go out on their first date, get on really well and go back to his place.

When they get there the girl tells him she has something to confess. The fact is she's got no tits, she's wearing falsies.

Hearing this, the man tells her he also has something to confess. He's got a cock like a baby. The evening progresses and as passions are aroused they strip off. She takes her falsies off and he drops his trousers. On seeing his cock she gasps, "Oh my God."

"Well, I told you it was like a baby, 7.5 lbs!" he replied.

★ ★ ★

PARKED down Lover's Lane, but failing to get into the right kind of mood, the man finally disentangles himself from the girl, saying, "You've got no tits and your hole's too tight."

She replies through clenched teeth, "Get off my fucking back."

★ ★ ★

AFTER a moment of passion in the back seat of the car, he turned to her and said, "If I'd known you were a virgin, I'd have taken more time." She replied, "If I'd known you had time, I'd have taken my tights off first."

★ ★ ★

A YOUNG couple were snogging on the sofa with the lights turned down very low. The girl's father, becoming worried, called downstairs, "Tracy, is that boy there yet?" She replied, "No, but we won't be long."

★ ★ ★

**A COUPLE are getting down to business in Lovers Lane when the boy suddenly sees a policeman approaching.
"Oh God, Fuzz."
"Well, what did you expect?" she retorted. "An Afro?"**

★ ★ ★

"MY blind date was so boring," said the girl to her friends, "that in the end I had to sit on his face just to keep him quiet."

★ ★ ★

MAISIE took her new boyfriend home to meet the folks but when they saw him they were rather disappointed and taking their daughter aside said, "He's not exactly young is he? In fact he's old, fat and bald," they whispered. "There's no need to whisper," she said, "he's deaf as well."

AS the man got more and more passionate he whispered to his date, "Sweetheart, am I the first man you've ever made love to?" "Of course" she replied, "Why do men always ask the same stupid question?"

* * *

A MAN with a good line in chatting up asked his latest girl-friend, "Shall we have breakfast together in the morning?" "That might be nice," she replied.
"Well, shall I ring you or just give you a nudge?"

* * *

IT'S Lovers Lane and a passing policeman goes up to a parked car, looks through the window and says, "What's going on here, then?" "Just a little necking" replies the man.
"Well, put your little neck back in your trousers and drive out of here."

* * *

AFTER an evening in a Newcastle nightclub, a local girl who'd been chatted up all night by a rather attractive man, suggested they go back to her place.
They were sitting on the sofa when the bloke's hand started to wander up the girl's thigh. Suddenly she slapped his face and shouted indignantly, "Where's yer manners, like? Tits first."

* * *

A GIRL turns to her friend and says, "Do you prefer watching TV or going out with your boyfriend?"
"There's not a lot of difference" she said. "Either way, I get a lot of interference."

A YOUNG couple on their second date found themselves alone in the house. It wasn't long before passion got the better of them and they were soon upstairs, naked on the bed. However when the man started making love to her, she suddenly stopped, looking a bit uncertain.
"What's wrong darling? Shall I take it out?" he said.
"Mmm" she murmured. "Yes take it out, then put it in a few times until I make up my mind."

★ ★ ★

THE best people to have sex with are schoolteachers.
They make you do it time and time again until you get it right.

★ ★ ★

DID you hear about the young girl who failed her driving test? When the car stopped, she automatically got into the back seat.

★ ★ ★

OUT on their first date, a young man drove his girlfriend out into the country in his old sports car. However, after labouring slowly up a steep hill, the car suddenly made some strange noises, and came to a halt.
"Shall we get out and push it up?" he said.
"OK, but will it be alright to leave the car here?"

★ ★ ★

A YOUNG courting couple went out into the countryside and after some passionate kissing she sat astride him as he lay on the grass.
Suddenly they heard someone coming so she remained where

she was but quickly covered him up with hay.

"Well, hello" said the local doctor. "What brings you out here?"

Quickly thinking, she replied, "I was just looking at my uncle's farm. When he goes, it's promised to me so I'm going to build a new barn there." She wriggled around and pointed east, "A new house there." she wriggled around and pointed west, "And turn that piece of land into a garden centre," and she wriggled around again to point south.

"Hmm, that's very interesting, and what's more interesting is that I recognise that pair of boots as belonging to my son."

"Thanks a lot, dad," came a muffled voice, "And due to your bad timing she'll need to build a nursery and somewhere to keep the pushchair as well."

★ ★ ★

I NEVER wear gloves when I go out on a date.
I feel better without them.

★ ★ ★

THE snow was thick on the ground when May and her boyfriend, Tom, got stranded miles from anywhere with engine trouble.

"Don't worry," said Tom. "I know about cars, I'm sure I can fix it."

After tinkering around with the engine for a few minutes he got back into the car and put his hands between her legs saying, "My hands are so cold I can't work on the engine properly, so I'm just warming them up."

A few minutes later he got back out and continued to mend the car but every so often got back in to warm up his hands between her legs.

When some time had passed and he got in the car again she turned to him and said, "It's a pity your ears never get cold."

★ ★ ★

"MAY I have some talcum powder?" said the young girl to the bandy-legged chemist, "Certainly, Miss, please walk this way."
"If I could walk like that I wouldn't need talcum powder," she replied.

★ ★ ★

WHAT is the definition of a nymphomaniac?
A girl who trips you up and is underneath you before you hit the ground.

★ ★ ★

A COURTING couple in Lover's Lane have been kissing feverishly for quite some time when the man, unable to contain himself any longer, sticks his todger in the girl's hand. She immediately gets out of the car shouting loudly, "I've only two words to say to you - Piss Off!"
In agony, the man screams back, "And, I've only got two words to say to you - Let go!"

★ ★ ★

TWO old men sitting in the park. One says to the other, "When I was young I never made love to my wife before we got married. Did you?"
"I'm not sure" said the other. "What was her maiden name?"

★ ★ ★

"FATHER, I'm pregnant."

"Bloody hell, who's the father?"

"It's no good asking me, you've never let me go steady."

★ ★ ★

A COUPLE were fooling around in the back of the parked car. She said, "Do you mind taking your ring off? It's uncomfortable."

"That's not my ring," he laughed. "That's my wristwatch."

★ ★ ★

CHAT up lines:

Why don't you come over here and sit on my lap and we'll talk about the first thing that pops up.

That dress would look really nice on the floor next to my bed.

★ ★ ★

A YOUNG couple had nowhere to go to have sex until the girl came up with an idea.

"If you come round to my house after tea we'll have it to ourselves as my parents will be off to church. And don't forget to bring some condoms."

The boy arrived early the next day and the door was opened by her father.

"We're off to church" he said.

"In that case, I'll come with you," said the boy quickly.

As soon as she could, the girl whispered to him, "Why didn't we stop at home. You didn't tell me you went to church."

"No" he replied, "and you didn't tell me your father was a chemist."

★ ★ ★

YOU know something's wrong if, on your first date, she asks you if you want sex and you're not sure.

★ ★ ★

"BUT Heinz," he said. "No wonder it was a disaster. It's not a good idea on a first date to take her back to your place, strip off completely and ask her if she'd like a delivery of German sausage."

★ ★ ★

FIRST man to second:
"How did your date go last night? Did you have a good time?"
"Yes great. Funny thing is she likes it in her ear," he replied.
"Are you sure?"
"Oh yes, 'cos when I tried to put it in her mouth, she kept turning her head."

★ ★ ★

JACK can't wait to get Maisie into bed. In no time at all they are going at it like a couple of steam trains when Jack notices that every time he goes in and out, Maisie's toes curl up. After they've finished, Jack mentions this to Maisie, who replies, "That usually happens when someone forgets to remove my pantyhose."

★ ★ ★

"BUT darling," said the distraught man, "what do you mean, it's all over?"
"I'm sorry, it is," she replied. "You're no good in bed."
"Oh come on," he argued. "How can you tell after 20 seconds?"

"WHAT would you say if I stole a kiss, my darling?" said the shy man.

"The same thing I'd say to any prat who had a chance to steal a car and only took the wheels," she replied.

★ ★ ★

IT was a four-berth cabin on the overnight ferry and on one of the upper berths was a travelling salesman who sold planks of wood, and across the aisle was a frisky young blonde. They soon struck up a conversation and it wasn't long before he was asking her to join him in his berth.

"But how will I get across?" she asked.

"That's no problem. I've got something long and hard here, you can get across on that."

Suddenly the voice of an old lady in one of the bottom berths interrupted.

"Be careful, my dear, how do you think he's going to get you back!"

★ ★ ★

"MY darling," whispered Jack in Flo's ear, "it's only a week before we get wed; can't we fool around a bit?"

"Now, Jack," she replied. "We said we'd wait till we were married; can't you just wait another seven days?"

"Oh Flo, it's going to be the longest seven days of my life. Can't you just give me a hint of what's to come? How about unbuttoning your blouse and letting me have a quick feel of your boobs?"

"Oh Jack .... I suppose so, if you're that desperate."

So she unbuttoned her blouse and Jack had a quick feel. He was barely able to contain himself.

"Oh Flo, just one other little thing, please, please let me have a quick sniff of your pussy. I promise I won't touch. Go on, there's only a week to go."

So Flo relented, dropped her knickers and let Jack have a quick sniff.

"Golly, Flo," he said "Are you sure it's going to last another week?"

★ ★ ★

A YOUNG girl left home for the first time and took a flat in the city.

"Whatever you do, don't let a man into your flat, you must promise me that."

"I won't," she promised.

Some weeks later they were talking on the telephone and the girl was telling her mum about her new boyfriend.

"You haven't let him into your flat, have you?" she asked.

"Oh no, I wouldn't do that! I go round to his place."

★ ★ ★

"DARLING, what would you say if I asked you to marry me?"
"Nothing. I can't speak and laugh at the same time."

★ ★ ★

"WHO was that bird I seen you with last night?"

"It's not, I seen, it's I saw."

"OK, who was that eyesore I seen you with last night?"

IN YOUR DAYS ON THE GAME

AFTER a long time at sea, the old captain comes ashore and goes straight down the whorehouse. He's taken upstairs by one of the girls, they agree a price and he gets to work. Pleased with his performance, he says to the girl, "How's it going? I'm not too fast am I? How fast am I going?"
The girl yawns and says, "You're doing about three knots. You're not in, you're not stiff and you're not getting your money back!"

★ ★ ★

A HUSBAND and wife went to London, he to a meeting and she to the shops. The meeting finished earlier than planned, so he went into Mayfair to look for a "quickie". He met a high-class girl but she gave him the push when he said he only had £20, and her rate was £200. So the man left, met his wife and they went off to a restaurant. At the next table sat the 'high class lady' he'd approached earlier. When she saw him she leant over and said, "Serves you right, that's what you get for twenty quid."

★ ★ ★

A MAN travelled all around London looking for a prostitute with the pox. Finally, one of them agreed to help.
"There's only one girl I know who has the pox ...."
"Oh thank you, thank you, please take me to her and I'll pay her and you well."
"But why?" she asked.
"Let me explain. If I catch the pox I can go home and give it to the

dairy maid, who'll give it to the gardener, who'll give it to my mother, who'll give it to my father, who'll give it to the Mayoress, who'll give it to the headmaster - and that's the bugger I'm after."

★ ★ ★

DID you hear about the man who was so tight with his money he rang up a hooker and asked her what night she was free?

★ ★ ★

A BUSINESSMAN goes to a brothel, pays £150 and proceeds to make mad passionate love to one of the girls. In fact he is so good, she offers a screw on the house. Again it is so fantastic the girl says she'll pay him £150 if he will do it a third time. However, although the mind is willing the body is weak and as she looks down at his shrivelled penis he says to it, disgustedly, "You're good at spending money, but when it comes to earning some!!"

★ ★ ★

A BROTHEL is like a circus, except that a circus is a cunning array of stunts.

★ ★ ★

THE local Soho police have just raided the local whorehouse and lined the girls up along the street ready for taking down the Nick. At that moment an old woman comes along and when she sees the queue, asks the girl at the end why they are all there.
"We're queueing up to get a nice juicy ice lolly," replies one of the girls sarcastically. The old woman takes it literally and joins the end of the queue. Time passes as the coppers question each of the girls and when one sees the old woman he says, "You're a bit old

for this sort of thing aren't you?"

"Indeed not," replies the old woman angrily, "I may not have any teeth but I can still suck."

★ ★ ★

A MAN with both his arms and legs in plaster knocks at the door of the local brothel.
"I'm looking for a woman," he says when the Madam opens the door.
"And what can you do in that state?" she asks.
"I knocked on the door, didn't I?"

★ ★ ★

AN old man goes to the local brothel and asks the price. Madam tells him prices start at £50.

"You're putting me on!" he exclaims.

"OK," she replies, "that'll be an extra £10."

★ ★ ★

"WHEN I grow up I want to be a prostitute," said a young lush girl to the Reverend Mother. The Reverend Mother threw up her hands in horror "What did you say?"
"I said I want to be a prostitute."
"Oh praise the Lord!" replied the Reverend Mother. "I thought you said a Protestant."

★ ★ ★

NEGOTIATIONS are still continuing over a new pay deal for the Soho girls. They are demanding more money on the table, even more money on the floor and danger money on top of the piano.

A MAN went up to town and engaged the services of a young
lady. After doing the business she asked for £75.
"Good gracious, you're expensive."
"Well, haven't you heard of me? I'm Polly, the best in town."
"Did you say your name was Polo?"
"No, Polly. Why?"
He replied, "Because you've definitely got a hole with a mint in
it."

★ ★ ★

"HEY dad," teenage son says to his father. "I've got this homework
problem. I've got to show the difference between possible and
real."
"Well, son, here's what you do. Go and ask your mum if she would
sleep with Mel Gibson for a thousand pounds. Then go and ask
your sister if she would sleep with Leonardo di Caprio for a thousand pounds and come and tell me the answer."
Son goes off to his mother, who replies she would (but keep it to
himself) and to his sister, who's wild about the idea. He then
returns to his Dad and says, "I see what you mean. We are sitting
on a possible £2,000 but in real terms we are living with a couple
of whores."

★ ★ ★

"SON, if you ever go to a whorehouse you will die. They are
terrible places of sin. Be warned." But the son's curiosity got
the better of him and he ended up at the local brothel and was
taken upstairs to Fifi's room. On entering he saw her lying
naked on the bed and suddenly his father's warning came back
to him.
"Bloody hell, dad was right, I can feel myself going stiff
already."

AN old man of 95 went to a brothel and told the woman on the door he wanted a big, buxom girl. The old man was very shaky on his legs and looked as if he would collapse any minute. Seeing this the woman replied, "Listen, grandpa you've had it."

"Oh bugger," he said, looking confused, "How much do I owe you?"

★ ★ ★

A MAN invited a prostitute back to his hotel bedroom and with only a few words spoken, immediately got her down on the bed and started giving her a good seeing to. After a good hour of very energetic sex he suddenly got up and said, "Just one moment, please" and walked into the bathroom. He returned a moment later, jumped in the bed and began again. Another hour of passion went on, when he suddenly got up again and disappeared into the bathroom, only to return a moment later and begin again. Hour after hour went by and the prostitute was feeling very knackered and needed a breather. She jumped up, saying, 'Won't be a moment' and going into the bathroom she found the man's three brothers.

★ ★ ★

WHAT did the nymphomaniac say after having sex? "So which football team do you guys play for?"

★ ★ ★

A MAN landed up in a very seedy part of town where the whore houses were the lowest of the low. Knocking at one of the doors, he shouted, "Come on, let me in." And a voice replied, "Put £50 through the letter box first."
He did this but nothing happened.

"Hey," he bellowed, "I want to be screwed."
"What! Again!" he heard her reply.

★ ★ ★

A MAN was very surprised that on visiting a foreign whorehouse he was given £500 on leaving. Unable to believe his luck, he returned the following day and again on leaving was given £500. However on the third day he left without anything and disappointed, asked why.
"We're not filming today, sir," came the reply.

★ ★ ★

A GOOD time girl went into the DIY store to buy some hinges. When she was paying the storekeeper asked, "Need a screw for those hinges?"
"No, but how about a blow job for the shelves over there?"

★ ★ ★

A PANDA goes down to the local brothel and demands sex with their best girl. It's a bit unusual but business hasn't been very good, so they agree and choose Big Rose to see to him. However, just as they're about to go upstairs the panda requests something to eat. Anything to please the customer, so Big Rose prepares a snack for him - after all she'll put it on the bill - and then they get down to the main business. After an hour of strenuous bonking the panda gets up and heads for the door.
"Hold on a minute, haven't you forgotten something. I'm a prostitute and that means you pay me for all the favours I've given you over the last hour."
"So what?" replies the Panda. "You should know by now that the definition of a panda is an animal that eats, shoots and leaves. Goodbye."

"HI, my name's Martini" said the prostitute. "Anytime, any-place, anywhere."

★   ★   ★

"HOW much will it cost?" the man asked the streetwalker.

"£15 up the alley, £120 if we spend the night in a comfortable hotel."

"OK, here's £120."

"Good, it's cold out here tonight. I could do with a nice hotel room."

"Not bloody likely!" replied the man. "I want it eight times up the alley."

★   ★   ★

THOR, the mighty God of War, is on his holidays and decides to come down to earth and sample some of the local talent. He stops off at a brothel and demands the services of their best girl. For two days he shags her unmercifully and is just about to leave when he realises he never told her his name.

"I'm Thor."

"You're sore! Bloody hell, I can't even walk!" she complains.

★   ★   ★

AN old couple living off a small pension find themselves down to the last few pennies and unable to pay their bills. In one last desperate attempt to keep the bailiffs from the door the old girl decides to go on the game. She takes her curlers out, puts her teeth in and struggles into a mini skirt before disappearing into the night.

Just before dawn, she staggers home to her husband who asks her how much she's made.

"£120.50," she replies.

"Bloody hell, who was the prick who gave you only 50p?"

"They all did," she cries.

★ ★ ★

A MAN goes into a brothel and tells the Madam that he's only got £5, what can she offer him? The Madam gives him a duck and off he goes to one of the rooms where he shags it for 25 minutes. The following week, he goes back but this time he's got £10 - he can afford something better.

The Madam shows him into a room where there are a line of blokes looking through peepholes. He takes his turn and through the peephole he sees three women and one man up to all sorts of things on a trapeze.

"It's good this, isn't it?" he says turning to the bloke next to him.

"Yes" replies his neighbour, "but you should have been here last week, there was a man shagging a duck."

★ ★ ★

A HUGE, 6'6", 18 stone man was having great trouble finding anyone who would have sex with him because one look at his gigantic penis frightened the girls away. The poor man roamed London seeking satisfaction but with no luck. He ended up sitting in a boozer looking sadly into his beer.

"What's up, mate?" said a man sitting down opposite. "You look as if you've got the problems of the world on your shoulders."

The big man told him of his fruitless search.

"I know just the answer" replied the newcomer. "If you come with me I'll take you to Madam Cyn, she's got girls who've seen and done everything."

They arrived at the whorehouse door and the big man explained his problem.

"Just how big is it?" Madam asked.

"Five inches" he replied.

She laughed, "Five inches long! Goodness, that's a lot of fuss about nothing."

"No, Madam, five inches thick."

★ ★ ★

THREE men are walking around Soho looking for a screw when they see a prostitute hanging round the street corner. The first man goes over and asks her what she can do for a tenner. She beckons him into an alley where they stay for ten minutes before he rejoins his mates on the street.

"What did she do, what did she do?" they urged.

"It was wonderful" said the man with a big grin on his face. "She put this doughnut on the end of my knob and then slowly ate it off."

This really got the other two men going. So the second went over to her and asked what she could do with £20. Again, she took him into the alley and he reappeared 20 minutes later full of smiles.

"Wow, she really knows how to turn you on!" he said. "She put two doughnuts on the end of my knob, sprinkled them with sugar and then slowly licked them off."

By this time, the third man couldn't wait to have a go, but he didn't tell the others he had £50 on him. However, after only a few minutes he was back looking very pissed off.

"What's wrong, mate? That was quick," they said.

"Well, she had these four doughnuts which she put over my knob, covered them with raspberry jam, sugar, chocolate, whipped cream and amaretto."

"Go on, what happened?"

"Well it looked so good, I ate it myself."

"I'VE met some disgusting people in my time but you are the worst ever. You're a dirty, dreadful old man," said the prostitute to her client.

"Listen, I've paid you, haven't I? So I'll ask you to keep a civil tongue in my arse."

★ ★ ★

A COLONEL-IN-CHIEF arrives back home after spending six months on a distant outpost and heads straight for the local brothel. Once inside, he goes upstairs with one of the girls and into a bedroom where she starts to fiddle with his flies.

"Now, now," he says, as he pushes her hand away, "Any more of that familiarity and the fucks off."

★ ★ ★

"MY dear, what would your mother say if she saw you?" said the kindly social worker to the street corner prostitute.

"She wouldn't say anything. She'd kill me. I'm on her patch."

★ ★ ★

A SOLDIER, on weekend leave, goes into the nearest town looking for a bit of sex. He ends up staying the night at one of the seedy brothels and next morning, when he wakes up, he groans, "Bloody hell, I feel terrible, you haven't got AIDS, have you?" he says to the girl.

"No", she replies.

"Thank goodness, I wouldn't want that again."

★ ★ ★

A MAN visited a brothel in the middle of an African Jungle and a sign inside the door advertised a special 'Jungle Roulette'.

"What's that?" he inquired.

"Well, it's a special service where six girls offer to give you a blow job and you can choose up to three of them."

"Wow, that sounds good. What's the catch?"

"One of the girls is a cannibal."

★ ★ ★

THE President's housekeeper was horrified to see the family parrot escape from his cage and fly out of the window. Feeling partly to blame, she rushed down to the local pet shop to buy another that looked exactly the same.

"I've only one like that," said the man, "but it's a bit risky because this parrot has come from a whorehouse and has picked up some foul language."

"Never mind, I'll just have to take a chance."

Later on in the day, the President and his family arrive home and as they enter, the parrot speaks.

"Too young," he says as the daughter comes in.

"Too old," he says of the wife.

Then, as the President enters, he squawks excitedly, "Hello big boy, long time no see."

★ ★ ★

WHY don't prostitutes vote?

Because they don't care who gets in.

IN YOUR DESERT ISLAND DAYS

A MAN is abandoned on a desert island. After six years, a beautiful, shapely blonde in a wet-suit gets washed ashore, and they get into conversation.

"How long have you been here?" she asks.

"Six years," he says.

"That's a long time. Would you like a drink?"

"I'd love one."

With that she unzips a pocket in her wet suit and gets out a bottle of Scotch. The blonde then asks if he would like a cigarette.

"Yes, please," he replies and she unzips another pocket to produce a packet of cigarettes and a lighter.

"How long did you say you'd been here?" she asks again.

"Six years."

"Ah... then would you like to play around?"

He was astonished. "Don't tell me you've got a set of golf clubs in there as well."

★ ★ ★

ONLY two people survived the sinking of the luxury liner and separately they managed to make it to a desert island. The man who had been travelling economy class couldn't believe that his companion was none other than one of Hollywood's most famous starlets.

At first they remained on platonic terms but as the weeks passed natural desires took over until one night they tore each other's clothes off and went at it like the clappers.

The next day he turned to her and asked whether she would mind doing him a favour. Would she dress up in some of his clothes? He had a pair of trousers and a shirt.

Puzzled, she agreed and when they met up later he patted her on the back and boasted, "Hello mate, you'll never guess who I fucked last night."

* * *

A MAN was stranded on a desert island with a sheep and a dog. After some months, he became romantically attached to the sheep but every time he tried to get near to her the dog would start barking. Then one day his prayers were answered when a beautiful girl was washed ashore. He looked after her until she'd recovered her strength and in gratitude she asked him if there was anything she'd like him to do.

"In fact, there is," he said. "Would you mind taking the dog for a walk while I shag this sheep?"

* * *

A BLOKE found himself stranded on a desert island with six women. To keep it fair, it was decided he would service a different woman every night and have Mondays free. After a few months the man was exhausted, realising how tiring it was to perform constantly every night except one. Then one day to his joy, he found a man washed up on the beach who would be able to take some of the workload from him. However, his hopes were shattered the first words the man said were, "Hello pretty boy, you've a big one."

Oh fuck, thinks the man, there goes my Mondays.

* * *

A MAN was stranded on a desert island and one day found a bottle washed up on the beach. Inside the bottle was a genie, who was so grateful for being let out that he said he would grant the man one wish. After some thought the man said he had always wanted to visit the Far East, so could the genie build a road from the island to the Great Wall of China.

"My goodness", replied the genie. "I'm not sure I can do that. Imagine all the work involved in building across oceans, and mountainous landscapes, all the materials .... no, I don't think that's such a good idea."

"OK", said the man. He thought for a moment and said, "Another thing I've always wanted is to understand women. I want to know what makes them laugh, why they get so angry, why they cry ...."

At this the genie replied, "Now about this road, do you want a dual carriageway or a motorway?"

★　★　★

AFTER two months of being shipwrecked on a desert island, the man sees a barrel floating towards the shore and holding onto the barrel is a stunningly beautiful naked woman. As he rushes down to meet her she says, "I think I have something you want."

The man's eyes light up "I don't believe it," he gasps. "You've got beer in that barrel."

★　★　★

THE man had been stranded on a desert island for two years. One afternoon, looking out to sea, he shouted excitedly to himself, "Oh boy, oh boy, a boat's coming and there's a beautiful, young, voluptuous blonde on board, and she's stark naked ... and she's waving to me, blowing me kisses and rolling her hips..."

By this time, he had a mighty erection which he suddenly grabbed with both hands.

"Fooled you, fooled you," he laughed. "There ain't no fucking boat."

THREE men had been marooned on a desert island for three months when one day a man-made raft was washed ashore, carrying a beautiful young girl.

"She's mine," said the Frenchman. "Look, she's got a red, white and blue blanket covering her." He pulled the blanket away, only to reveal a pair of tartan knickers.

"There," said the Scotsman triumphantly. "She was made for me." And he pulled them off.

"Aaah!" said the Indian, falling to his knees. "Behold, the sacred beard of our Holy prophet...."

IN YOUR DOTAGE

THREE old men were discussing who had the worst health problem.

The 80-year-old said, "Every morning I get up to take a pee but I have to stand there for half an hour because it trickles out so slowly."

The 85 year old said, "That's nothing, every morning I go for a shit and have to sit there for two hours because of my constipation, it's terrible."

The 90 year old said, "I wish I had your problems. Me, every morning at 7.30 I piss like an elephant and shit like a pig. Trouble is .. I don't wake up 'till nine."

★ ★ ★

AN old widower of 80 married a young girl of 26 and not long after astounded the vicar by telling him he would soon be needed for a christening. Recovering from the news, the vicar congratulated the old man and asked him if this was going to be the first of many.

"Oh no vicar, you see my eldest son is going abroad."

Of course the vicar thought the worse but said, "I don't understand. What's your son got to do with it?"

"Well, you see, he used to lift me on and off."

★ ★ ★

A FEISTY spinster reached 100 years old and attracted the attention of the press.

"How's your health?" asked one.

"Let me tell you, I've never been to a doctor in my life," she replied.

"That's incredible - do you mean to say you've never been bedridden in your life?"

"Of course I have, young fella, in fact table-ended as well, but there's no need to put that in the paper."

★ ★ ★

ONE resident at the Green Fields retirement home is sitting outside enjoying the early afternoon sun. Every now and again he leans over to the left and immediately a care helper rushes over and straightens him up. Later that day his son comes to visit and the son asks his father if the home is treating him well.

"Yes and no," comes the reply. "The beds are comfortable, the food's tasty, but they won't let me fart."

★ ★ ★

HE has such a bad memory, the only thing to stay in his head for longer than 12 hours is a cold.

★ ★ ★

YOU know you're getting old when you bend down to tie up your shoes and look around to see if there's anything else needs to be done while you're down there.

★ ★ ★

AN old man stopped to comfort a little boy who was crying on a park bench.

"What's wrong, son?" he said.

"I'm crying because I can't do what the big boys do."
So the old man sat down and cried too.

★ ★ ★

TWO old ladies in the Pastures Green retirement home.
"Did you hear old Ben had a massive stroke?"
"He always did," came the reply. "That's why he was always so
popular with the ladies."

★ ★ ★

GETTING old is when you don't comb your hair, you just start re-arranging it.

★ ★ ★

GRANDMA was 102. She didn't have wrinkles; she had pleats.
(Dennis Wolfering)

★ ★ ★

HE'S so old that when he asks for a three-minute egg, they ask for
the money up front.

★ ★ ★

"I DON'T understand," said the young widow's friend.
"You say your husband was killed by the bells. What does that
mean?"
"Well my husband was 75 and he would save up all his
strength for us to make love on a Sunday to the rhythm of the
church bells. He would still be here today if it hadn't been for
that blasted ice cream van going past."

AN old man of 85 was sitting hunched up over his pint, crying his eyes out.

"What's wrong?" asked a fellow drinker.

"I got married two weeks ago to a beautiful curvaceous young red-head who's a gourmet cook, a wonderful conversationalist and fantastic in bed," replied the old man.

"That's wonderful; you're a very lucky man. I don't understand why you're so upset."

"I can't remember where I live!" he cried.

★ ★ ★

IT'S good to exercise. My grandpa started walking 5 miles a day when he was 60. Today he's 95 and we don't know where the hell he is.

★ ★ ★

FIRST prize at a fancy dress party for nudists went to a young girl who wore black gloves and black shoes and went as the five of spades.

The second prize went to a 98-year-old man for the best dried fruit arrangement.

★ ★ ★

YOU know old age has overtaken you when the phone rings and a sexy voice at the other end says, "Do you know who this is, lover?" And you say "No" and put the phone down.

★ ★ ★

YOU know it's old age when you try to straighten out the wrinkles in your socks and realise you're not wearing any.

YOU know you're getting old when the phone rings on a Saturday night and you hope it isn't for you.
(Ogden Nash)

★ ★ ★

THEY say life begins at 40. But so does lumbago, rheumatism, deafness and repeating oneself more than three times to the same person.

★ ★ ★

TWO old men sitting on a park bench. One turns to the other and says, "Do you remember when we used to chase the girls down the street?"
The other replied, "Yes, I remember chasing them but I can't remember for the life of me why."

★ ★ ★

AN old spinster sees a sign offering three cucumbers for 50p.
"Well, I can always eat the other two," she says.

★ ★ ★

AN old lady went to the doctor complaining of constipation.
"I sit there for hours," she said.
"Ah yes, but do you take anything?" asked the doctor.
"Oh yes, I take my knitting."

★ ★ ★

TWO old men meet on a park bench and one says to the other "Hello Bob, I haven't seen you around for a few weeks. Where have you been?"

"In jail," came the reply.

"Never! What happened?"

"Well, I just happened to be walking down the street when this beautiful curvaceous blonde rushes up to me with a policeman in tow and accuses me of sexually assaulting her. I was so flattered I didn't deny it."

★ ★ ★

FOUR very old ladies were walking through the park when a man approached and flashed at them. Two of the ladies had strokes but the other two weren't quick enough.

★ ★ ★

"ARE you sure it's a good idea to marry such a young, energetic girl?" said the doctor to his elderly patient. "You know, such energetic sex could prove fatal."

"Oh well", said the old man, "if she dies, at least she dies happy."

★ ★ ★

A VERY old man went to the doctor's to find out if he was fit enough to have sex.

"Let me see your sex organs, please," replied the doctor, so the man stuck out his tongue and held up his index finger.

★ ★ ★

OLD man looking at his withered penis:

"We were born together, we've lived through childhood together, had adventures together, known marriage together, even played together. So now, why now, did you have to die first?" he sighed.

A MAN getting on in years visited his doctor complaining about his poor love life. The doctor's advice was to give up smoking, stick to one pint of beer a day and take up jogging. Build up to running about an hour a day. Four weeks later the man rang his doctor to let him know how it was going.

"Thank you, doctor, I feel so much better. I've done all you've said and there's been a great improvement."

"Well, that's good to hear," replied the doctor "and how's your love life?"

"I've no idea", he answered. "I'm 200 miles from home now."

★ ★ ★

WHAT is the similarity between men and old age? They both come too soon.

★ ★ ★

A RICH old man of 88 married a beautiful young girl of 23 and it wasn't long before she was expecting a baby. Overjoyed at the news, the old man was taken aside by his kindly doctor, who had known his patient for a long time and was concerned for his well-being.

"Listen, Jack, it's about the baby. Let's see if I can explain what I mean. There was a big game hunter who'd spent all his life in Africa but was now really too old to last the distance. He decided to go out one last time but being so absentminded, instead of his gun, he took his walking stick with him. Some time went by when suddenly a man-eating lion confronted the man. He lifted his stick and shot the animal dead."

"But, that can't be!" cried his patient, "Someone else must have shot it."

"Absolutely," replied the doctor. "That's what I'm trying to tell you."

AN old woman is walking along the road when she comes upon a frog.

"Excuse me, Miss", says the frog. "If you pick me up and kiss me I'll turn into a Robert Redford look-alike and I'll stay with you for-ever."

The old woman picks up the frog and puts it in her handbag and continues on her way.

Puzzled, the frog calls from her bag, "Excuse me, aren't you going to kiss me then?"

"Oh no", replies the old woman. "At my age, it's far more exciting to have a talking frog."

★ ★ ★

THE interfering old busybody from next door was complaining that her neighbour's old husband was chasing all the young girls.

"I think it's disgusting," she said.

"Oh, there's nothing to it," replied the wife calmly. "After all, you've seen dogs chasing cars many times but have you ever seen them catch one, and even if they did, I doubt whether they could drive."

★ ★ ★

ROSIE was bored. In her younger days she'd been known as 'Good time Rose', but since moving to the retirement home there was nothing to do. Then she had a great idea and on the door of her room pinned a notice saying, "The Good Times are back. £30 in bed, £10 on the table."

Nothing happened for a couple of days and then one night there was a knock on the door and old Alfred was standing there.

"I've got £30 here" he said.

"OK, hop into bed."

"Not bloody likely, I want three on the table."

★   ★   ★

THE DUTY Officer answered the phone at the police station.
"Hurry please, I want to report a burglar trapped in the bed-
room of an old spinster."
"We'll be right round," said the policeman, "Who am I talking
to?"
"The burglar," he answered frantically.

★   ★   ★

AN old retired colonel was invited to a reunion dinner and halfway
through the proceedings he rang his wife.
"Agnes, this reunion is turning out to be more than I bargained for.
They've got naked girls dancing on the table and then giving their
favours to anyone who's interested. What do you think I should
do?"
She replied, "If you think you can do anything you'd better get
home straightaway."

★   ★   ★

IT'S the old man's 100th birthday and as a special treat, all his
mates pay for a naked lady to come over and do the business.
The doorbell goes and when he opens the door she's standing
there in her coat which she lets fall open to reveal that she's
totally bare underneath.
"Hello, darling," she says seductively. "I'm here for
'Supersex'."
"I'll just have the soup, thanks," says the old man.

★   ★   ★

JACK and Flo went to stay for a weekend with his parents. There wasn't much room in the tiny flat so Jack ended up sleeping with his dad. In the middle of the night he got an elbow in the ribs.

"Jack, Jack," whispered his dad, "I'm going next door to give your mum a good rogering!"

"What! Dad, it's the middle of the night and you're 75 years old."

"Yes, but I've got such a mighty fine erection - the first for 15 years - and I don't want to waste it, son."

"Well, in that case, I'll have to come with you," said Jack. "You're holding my cock."

★ ★ ★

A WOMAN knows when she's getting old.
It's when her girdle pinches, but her husband doesn't.

★ ★ ★

"NOW, remember, Bert, let that bald man go ahead of you in the toilet. I've heard that hair loss and incontinence usually start at the same time in men over 50."

★ ★ ★

A MAN of 75 retires to a golfing community and spends every day out on the course. But as time passes, he realises he can't see where the ball is going after a particularly long tee shot, so he goes to visit the eye doctor. The doctor examines him and says, "There's nothing wrong with your eyes except the fact that you're getting on in years. It may be a good idea if you hired a caddy who could spot the ball for you."
The old man follows the doctor's advice and places an ad in the local newspaper. Early the next day the doorbell rings and standing there is a man of 85.

IN YOUR DOTAGE ★ 107

"I've come about your ad in the local paper," he says.

"Gosh!" says the golfer. "Are you sure you'll be able to see the ball at such long distances?"

"No problem at all, I've got the eyes of a hawk," he replies.

So the next day they go out onto the course and the golfer tees off, sending the ball flying down the fairway.

"Did you see where that went?" asks the golfer.

"Sure did," replies the old man.

"Good," says the golfer. "Where?"

"I forget," he replies.

★ ★ ★

AN 85-YEAR-OLD man married a young girl of 25 and the event made headline news on the local radio. The old man was interviewed and asked about his sex life.

"Oh, it's nearly every night," he replied. "Nearly on Monday, nearly on Tuesday ...."

IN YOUR EMPLOYMENT

THREE girls arrive at the hotel to be interviewed for the job of a chambermaid. The manager asks each of them in turn what they would do if they found a £10 note.

The first said, "Finders keepers."

The second said she would hand it in and after three months, if it had not been claimed, would take it herself.

The third answered the same as the second except that with the money she would buy everyone who worked in the hotel a drink and then give the rest to the local hospice.

Now ... which girl got the job?

The one with big tits, of course.

★ ★ ★

TWO businessmen travelling home on the train. One turns to the other and asks how his business is doing.

"Very well, very well indeed, ever since I've taken on this new salesman. Sadly there's just one problem. He's seduced both my wife and my daughter and made two of the office girls pregnant."

"Good gracious, what are you going to do?"

"Don't worry, I'm watching him very closely and if he tries to fiddle the books, I'll sack him on the spot."

★ ★ ★

IT is the conference season and three dentists and three bankers find themselves together at the railway ticket office. The dentists each buy a ticket but the bankers buy one between them.

"How are you all going to travel on one ticket?" ask the dentists.
"You'll see" they reply.

On boarding the train the dentists take their seats but the bankers all cram into the one toilet. The conductor comes round shouting "Tickets please!", knocks on the toilet door and a ticket is passed to him. The dentists are impressed and decide to do the same on the return journey. They only buy one ticket but to their amazement the bankers don't buy a ticket at all.

"How come?" ask the dentists.

"You'll see," the bankers reply.

They all got onto the train, the three dentists crammed into one toilet, the three bankers get into another.

A few minutes later one of the bankers leaves his toilet, knocks on the other toilet door and shouts, "Tickets please!"

★ ★ ★

A MAN goes for an audition as a pianist in a local night-club. He starts by playing a stunning blues number which has everyone stopping work to listen to it. When he's finished the club owner is delighted and asks him about the music.

"I wrote it myself" said the man. "It's called 'I want to shag you long and hard'."

After a stunned silence, the owner asks him to play something else and this time it's a funky jazz number. Absolutely superb, there are cheers all round the bar. The man tells them he also wrote it and called it, "Give me a blow job and I'll show you what for."

After some embarrassment the owner comes to a decision.

"You've got the job, on one condition; you never ever tell the audience the titles of the music you play."

Although not too happy about it, the man agrees. After all, the pay is good.

Some weeks go by and the club's popularity goes from strength

to strength. People come from miles around to hear the pianist and his reputation spreads like wildfire. The night after a particularly successful session, the pianist staggers off to the toilet. He's been given free drinks all night by the admiring public and is feeling a bit the worse for wear. In fact he's so far gone he forgets to do his flies back up. On the way back to the stage a lady taps him on the shoulder.

"Excuse me, do you know your fly is open and your dick is hanging out?"

He replies, "Bloody hell, I do, I wrote it."

★ ★ ★

A SILLY young man lived for his work, nothing else mattered. Every night and all weekend he would bring papers home to work on. Then one day he left some important papers at home and in a panic rushed home to get them. As he was leaving his spare room he saw his wife and boss in bed together.

Later that day he mentioned what he had seen to a colleague.

"Why, that's appalling, are you going back tomorrow to try and catch them at it?"

"Good gracious no, it was lucky he didn't see me this time."

★ ★ ★

A MAN went for a job in an undertaker's and was found to be ideal for the job apart from the fact that he kept winking.

"Mr Smith, I'd like to give you the job but in these sad situations, it would be very callous to keep winking at the bereaved customers."

"Oh that's no problem", replied the man. "I just need to take a paracetamol and the winking will immediately stop."

The man looked for the pills in his briefcase which, to the undertaker's astonishment, was full of an amazing variety of condoms.

"Good gracious," gasped the undertaker.
"I'm surprised you've got any time left to work. Your leisure time must be very tiring?"
"Oh no," smiled the man. "I've got a lovely wife at home. But have you ever tried to buy a bottle of paracetamol from a chemist, winking all the time?"

★ ★ ★

IT was the day of the inspector's visit to the local bakery and as he was doing his rounds he came upon a man pressing down the outsides of the fruit pies with his thumb.
"Hey, haven't you a tool for that?" asked the inspector.
"Yes," said the man, "but I use that for putting holes in the doughnuts."

★ ★ ★

UNABLE to get any answer when he knocked on the door, the postman went round to the back of the house, only to find a beautiful young woman sunbathing stark naked in the garden. Now the young lady was very strong willed and determined to outstare the man. Their eyes locked for a good long minute in the hope that she could shame him into looking away.
It worked. All of a sudden the postman yelled,
"What the bloody hell are you looking at. Haven't you seen a postman before!"

★ ★ ★

THE two handsome delivery boys carried the woman's box of groceries into her kitchen.
"That will be £15, please," said the first one.
At this, the woman let her dressing gown fall open to reveal she

was stark naked underneath.

"Perhaps, there's some other way we could settle the bill," she said smiling.

"Just a moment, then," said the second. "I'll have to see if it's alright with our driver. This morning we've already screwed away two orders, one on Beech Street and the other on the High Street."

★　★　★

THE taxi was hurtling down the road at such a tremendous speed that the man tapped the driver on the shoulder, saying, "Why are you going so fast?"

"Well, I heard someone say 'faster, faster'!" said the cabbie.

"Yes, but she wasn't talking to you, so slow down, please."

★　★　★

THE phone rang and a voice at the other end said, "Mr Smallman? We have one of your employees staying at our hotel. He has run up quite a large bill and I'm checking to see that it will be paid."

"How much is it?" asked Mr Smallman.

"£550," came the reply.

"What?" he spluttered. "For three days! That's impossible."

"I've got the chits here," said the hotel man.

"You've got the chits! What do you think I've got?"

★　★　★

A SUCCESSFUL company is taken over by three business whizz kids and its time for them to decide on the management structure. The first one says, "I've got 42% of the shares, so I'll be Chairman."

"I've got 37% of the shares, so I'll be Managing Director" says the second.

"What about me?" says the third man. "You needed me to buy

the other 21% but you've carved the power up between your-selves."

After a moment's consultation the other two turn to him and say, "You can deal with sexual matters."

"What the hell does that mean?"

"When we want your fucking advice, we'll ask for it."

★　★　★

'SIMPLE Sam' is the local odd-job man in the village, not too bright but always willing to have a go. One day, he hears there are vacancies going in the local sawmill, so he goes along in the hope of getting a job. Reluctantly, the boss takes him on, emphasising how dangerous the job is and how he must always think 'Safety.' However, only two hours into the job and Sam stumbles over a plank of wood, puts his hands out to save himself and gets all his fingers and thumbs sawn off by a giant blade. There's no one else about, so he runs off in shock to the local hospital, where he faints on the doorstep. Later, as he regains consciousness, he hears the doctor's voice.

"Sam, Sam, if only you'd brought your fingers in with you we might have been able to sew them on before it was too late."

"I would have" cried Sam, "but I couldn't pick them up."

★　★　★

A WOMAN went into a butcher's shop and asked for a Norfolk Turkey.

"Just a moment," said the assistant, and he disappeared into the backroom and came back with the bird, which he showed to the woman.

Immediately she put her fingers right up its backside and after a minute exclaimed, "This isn't a Norfolk Turkey, this is a Shropshire. How dare you try to trick me?"

Astonished at her outburst, he apologised profusely and returned to the backroom where he picked up another turkey. On returning, the woman shoved her hands up its arse, smiled and said, "That's better. Wrap it up, please."

After she had left the shop, the butcher came out of his office and asked what all the commotion was about. When the assistant recounted the incident the butcher said, "It's no good trying to fool that old biddy, she knows her turkeys. You should know them too by now. Where have you been?"

Fed up with the butcher's jibes, the assistant turns round and sticks his bum in the air.

"You're the expert, you tell me!"

★ ★ ★

"JENKINS, what on earth do you think you are doing?" said the boss to his employee when he found him in the toilets masturbating. Jenkins thought quickly and said, "Oh that! It's not what it seems."

"Really, then what does it mean?"

"Well, sir, I've got ESP and I'm just bonking my girlfriend in Bristol."

★ ★ ★

A BIG strapping boy went up to the big house for a job as a handyman but returned home very disappointed.

"Oh, dad, I'm so ashamed, I really made a cock up."

"How come, son?"

"The lady was very nice, she asked me lots of questions, seemed pleased with what I had to say, I told her I was a hard worker but then right at the end she asked to see my testimonials .... that's when I lost it!"

THE business is doing badly and one of two people from middle management will have to go. It's not an easy decision, as both Doreen and Jack have been there a long time and they're both very good. The first one to leave work tomorrow will get their cards, decides the Personnel Manager; that's the only way he can think of doing it. The following evening, 30 minutes before she usually leaves, Doreen tells Jack she has a bad headache. It could be a migraine coming on, so she's going to go home early. As she gets her coat, the Personnel Manager spots her and decides to take immediate action. He goes over to her and says, "There's something I have to say to you, Doreen. I'm going to have to lay you or Jack off."

"Jack off!" she retorted angrily. "I've got a bad headache."

★ ★ ★

WHAT'S the definition of a faithful servant?
One who carries out his master's wishes when he's told, "Drive over that cliff, Jenkins, I've reached the end of my tether."

★ ★ ★

A MAN walking along a country road comes across a shepherd with a huge flock of sheep. He says to the shepherd, "I will bet you £150 against one of your sheep that I can tell you the exact number in this flock."

There's a pause for a moment while the shepherd thinks it over but he feels quite confident because the flock is so big.

"OK," he says. "You're on."

"964," says the man.

"Good gracious!" splutters the farmer. "You're absolutely right. You'd better take one of the sheep."

The man picks one up and begins to walk away, when the shepherd cries, "Hold on a minute, will you give me a chance to get even?

Double or nothing, that I can guess your occupation."

"OK," replies the man.

"You are a government economist," says the shepherd.

"I'm amazed," responds the man. "That's absolutely right, but tell me, how did you deduce that?"

"Well," says the shepherd. "Put down my dog and I will tell you."

★　★　★

AS the man parks his Rolls Royce in the car park, a local businessman approaches.

"That's a lovely car you have there; how much did it cost?"

"About £200,000."

"Blimey, how much petrol does it take?"

"29 gallons."

"And how many miles does it do to the gallon?"

"About two miles. I work for Cunard you know."

"Well, I work fucking hard as well, but I still can't afford a Rolls Royce" he retorts.

★　★　★

THE new assistant is being shown round the lighthouse and given a grand tour of all the facilities.

"It's not a bad life," says the keeper. "There's not much time to get bored, we've got something on most nights. On Monday, we have the local chef in from one of the top hotels round here and he puts on a sumptuous banquet. Then on Tuesday, we have the casino, and Wednesday, a visit from some of the call girls. That's a real passionate night, eh?"

He looks at the man who seems to be shaking his head.

"Oh dear, you're not a poofter, are you? Cos you'll hate Thursdays."

IN YOUR FARMYARD

IT was market day in the small town and towards the end of the day a vet approached one of the old farmers.

"Have you ever considered artificial insemination for your herd of cows, Mr Woodall?"

"No thanks, I'll stick w'old fashioned way, if it's all the same to you."

"OK, but if you change your mind, give us a ring and we'll take it from there."

On the way home, the farmer pondered the man's words but couldn't imagine how a cow could be served without a bull. His curiosity eventually got the better of him and he rang the man asking for his cow to be served as soon as possible.

"OK", replied the vet. "If you can get a few things ready. Wash down the cow's backside, put down some clean straw and have a bucket of hot water and a stool ready."

When all was ready, the vet arrived.

"Have you done everything I asked?"

"That I have" replied the farmer. "I've even hammered a nail in the door for you to hang your trousers on."

★ ★ ★

A FARMER was getting less and less eggs from his hens and decided he would have to replace the old rooster who wasn't carrying out his job properly. So he bought a new rooster. Later in the henhouse the old rooster turned to the new rooster and said, "Look, let's make a deal. Let me just have three of the hens and I'll leave the rest to you."

"No way" came the reply. "This is all mine now."

"OK," said the crestfallen rooster, "but let me have some pride. If we have a race across the farmyard and back, the winner takes all."

"Alright," said the new rooster, thinking there was no way he was going to lose to this tired old bird.

They set off, but just as the new cock was about to overtake, the farmer burst out of his house and shot him dead.

"Bloody hell, that's the third queer rooster I've bought this month."

★ ★ ★

OVER a pint in the local pub a farmer was telling his neighbour about the trouble he was having with his chickens. They weren't laying, they weren't breeding. On this his neighbour told him not to worry because he had a cockerel that was forever on the job, in fact he'd worn his chickens out, so he was quite happy to sell him. The transaction took place and the rooster went home to the new farm. In no time at all he was servicing all the chickens with amazing results, and not only that the ducks were looking a lot livelier, as were the geese. The farmer was overjoyed.

However, two days later the farmer couldn't find his prize rooster anywhere and it took a lot of searching before he was eventually discovered behind the barn, lying stiff with his legs in the air.

"Oh no," said the farmer, "my poor bird, all that work has killed him."

"Don't be daft, you fool" whispered the rooster "I'm just trying to entice that hovering vulture down."

★ ★ ★

A SHAPELY young farmer's daughter took a cow over to the neighbouring farm to be serviced by their bull. The farmhand opened the gate and it wasn't long before both animals were well away.

"Oh my!" said the farmhand, breaking out in sweat. "I wish I was doing that."

"OK, do," she said, "I'm not stopping you."

"Thanks," he said, "but maybe the cow wouldn't like it."

★ ★ ★

A MAN taking his driving test is asked to make a U turn.

"Fetch me my wellies, I'll make his eyes water."

★ ★ ★

A MAN'S car broke down in the middle of nowhere and he ended up seeking refuge at a farmer's cottage.

"Well, we've only got two bedrooms," he said, "but you can share a bed with my daughter as long as you don't bother her." The man agreed and not wanting to disturb her, slipped into bed without turning the light on. In the morning he thanked the farmer for his hospitality and commented on how cold his daughter was.

"Oh yes," replied the farmer sadly. "We're burying her this morning."

★ ★ ★

A VENTRILOQUIST was being shown around a farm by a local yokel.

As a joke the ventriloquist made the bull look as if he was saying, "Hello there."

The yokel did not react. So he then made the hen say, "This man has been stealing all my eggs."

At which point the yokel got very flustered and said, When we get to the sow, don't believe a word she says."

A FARMER stopped work to have a midmorning snack and as he sat there he watched the cock chasing the chicken around the farmyard.
Having finished, the farmer threw his scraps on the ground and immediately the cock ran over to gobble them up.
"Bloody hell!" he said, "I hope I never get that hungry."

★ ★ ★

AT the summer fayre, Farmer Brown has brought along his favourite horse and is making a lot of money by taking bets on anyone who could make him laugh.

One cunning-looking local comes up and takes up the bet. He whispers something in the horse's ear and the animal starts to laugh uncontrollably.

Not to be outsmarted the farmer offers him double or nothing if he can make the horse cry.

The local goes round to the other side of the horse, out of sight of onlookers, and after a moment the horse starts to cry uncontrollably.

As the farmer pays up, he asks the man how he managed to make the horse laugh and then cry.

"Well, first I told him my knob was bigger than his, and the second time I showed him."

★ ★ ★

FINDING himself lost, a motorist stops to ask a farmer for directions and as they are talking he notices a pig with a wooden leg.
"Why's that pig got a wooden leg?" he asks.
"Oh, that pig is a real hero. Do you know he's been a life saver. About four months ago our barn caught alight and if it hadn't been for that pig alerting us by his noise, we'd have lost all our horses."

"Very good," replies the motorist, "but why has he got a wooden leg?"

The farmer continues, "And do you know, not long after that I fell into a fast flowing river and he saved my life by running for help."

"Yes, I see, but that doesn't explain why he's got a wooden leg."

"Oh come on, sir, after all that pig's done for us, we couldn't bear to eat him in one go."

★ ★ ★

BACKING out of the farmyard on his milk float, the man drove over and killed the prize rooster. Feeling very bad about it, he sought out the farmer's wife to tell her the bad news.

"Excuse me, madam, I'm so sorry but I've run over your prize rooster and I would like to replace it."

"Well, that's fine with me," she said. "You'll find the chickens behind the barn."

★ ★ ★

HOW can you stop a rooster from crowing on Monday morning?

Eat him for Sunday lunch.

★ ★ ★

A LOCAL crop dealer is on his way to visit a farm out in the middle of nowhere. It's a long distance to travel, so he puts his foot down and is going at 60mph when he's passed by a three-legged chicken that soon disappears into the distance. He gets to the farm, carries out his business when he suddenly remembers the chicken and asks the farmer about it.

"Oh yes, that's our three-legged chicken. We raised them ourselves. You see there's me, my wife and our John and we all like the legs but it was a waste when we had to kill two chickens for our Sunday lunch."

"And are they tasty?" asked the crop dealer.

"I don't know, we still haven't caught one of the buggers yet!"

★ ★ ★

A LITTLE girl was walking along the street pulling a cow by a rope. She passed the old village busybody, Mrs Seebad, who said, "My dear child, where on earth are you going with that animal?"

"I'm taking it to the bull," she said.

"Oh fancy asking you to do a thing like that. Can't your dad do it?"

"Oh no, it has to be the bull," she said, smiling sweetly.

★ ★ ★

"DON'T worry about the cow," said the vet to the farmer. "It just needs a pessary up its backside. Take this tube, simply insert it in the cow's bum and blow."

When the farmer returned to his farm, he explained the method to his cowman and left him to it. Half an hour later, the cowman came looking for him.

"I'm sorry, Mr Brooks, I can't seem to blow the damn thing up."

Farmer Brooks went back to the cow shed, took the tube out, turned it round and re-inserted it. He then blew the pessary up first time.

"Mr Brooks, why did you turn the tube round?" asked the cowman.

"I didn't want to suck the end that had been in your dirty mouth!" he replied.

THE vicar's out for his morning constitution when he sees the local farmer in the field, shagging a pig. He walks further on and sees the farmer's son, shagging a sheep. Then just behind the barn he spots the grandfather tossing off. Unable to contain his anger, he goes up to the farmhouse and knocks loudly on the door. When the wife opens it, he yells, "It's absolutely disgusting, your husband's shagging pigs, your son's shagging sheep and then what do I see behind the barn but your father tossing himself off!"

"I know," she says sadly, "but, you see, dad's too old to go chasing the animals anymore."

* * *

AN Australian tourist travelling through Wales sees a farmer with the back legs of a sheep stuck down his wellingtons.

"Are you shearing that sheep?" he asks.

"No bloody way, catch one of your own," comes the reply.

* * *

THE old farmer wasn't a very friendly man; in fact, most of the time he was downright rude. One day a travelling salesman stopped by and as they were talking a fly landed on the man's chin.

"Is there something on my chin?" he asked.

"Ay," said the farmer. "It's a fanny fly - you usually find them on cows."

"Are you trying to infer that my chin looks like a fanny?" he demanded.

"I ain't saying that at all," said the farmer and then added, "but you can't fool the fly."

* * *

A MAN knocked on the door of a farmer's cottage and said, "I happened to notice you had some canary grass down in that bottom meadow, would you mind if I picked myself a few canaries?"

"Go right ahead, but you won't get any canaries" replied the farmer.

A little while later, the farmer spotted the man heading for home and was flabbergasted to see he had a cage full of canaries. Some weeks later, the man returned.

"Would you mind if I took a walk down towards the stream. I've seen some toad flax and would like to collect a few toads."

"That's OK," said the farmer, "but you won't get any toads from toad flax."

An hour later the farmer couldn't believe his eyes when he saw the man had a bag full of toads. The following week the man knocked at the door again.

"Good morning, I've just noticed that you have some pussy willow near those woods...."

"Just a moment, sir, I'll get my boots, I'm coming with you."

IN YOUR FILMS

A SLEAZY young man went to the cinema and sat next to a pretty girl. As the film started, he put his hand on her leg but she slapped him away. A little later, he tried again and put his hand on her knee, only to be pushed off again. Then when he put his hand on her thigh, she turned to him angrily and said, "You've got no chance. You're just wasting your time. I'm Picasso's daughter and what you're looking for is on the back of my neck!"

★ ★ ★

DID you hear about the film at the Soho sex club?
It must have been very emotional, there wasn't a dry fly in the place.

★ ★ ★

AT long last the Cisco Kid is captured by the Sioux Indians, who bury him up to his neck in the sand to face a long and painful death. Out of respect for the 'Kid' the Indians grant him one last wish and he asks them to free his old trusty horse.
So the horse is freed and the Cisko Kid, whistles him over and whispers in his ear. The horse then runs away but appears an hour later with a beautiful girl on its back. The girl gets off, comes over to the Cisco Kid and lifts her skirt to show she has no knickers on. She then sits on his face and wiggles around.
As the Cisco Kid comes up for air he shouts to his horse, "You silly bugger, I said go and get me a posse."

★ ★ ★

IT was a glamorous Hollywood party and a beautiful, curvaceous blonde came up to one of the show business agents and said, "Wow, you really turn me on, let's go somewhere less busy and I'll make mad, passionate love to you all night."
The agent replied, "I don't know, what's in it for me?"

★ ★ ★

LITTLE Red Riding Hood is walking through the woods when she spots the big bad wolf hiding behind a tree.
"Come out, come out, I can see you, Mr Wolf" she shouts.
"How can you see me?" he asks.
"I saw your big bushy tail sticking out."
Mr Wolf turns and disappears deeper into the woods but a few minutes later, Little Red Riding Hood shouts, "Come out, come out, Mr Wolf, I can see you behind the rocks."
Out comes the wolf and asks, "How can you see me?"
"I saw your big ears sticking out" she says.
Once again the wolf runs off further into the woods but again he hears her shouting.
"Come out, come out Mr Wolf, I can see you behind that bush."
"How did you see me this time?"
"I saw your long nose sticking out."
"Just who are you anyway?" asks the wolf angrily.
"I'm Little Red Riding Hood."
"And what are you doing in here?"
"I'm going to see my grandma."
"Well fuck off and go and see her because I'm dying for a shit!" he yells.

★ ★ ★

TWO girls are watching a film in the local cinema when one turns to the other in panic.

"Tracy, the man next to me is masturbating."
"Well, just ignore him."
"I can't, he's using my hand."

⋆ ⋆ ⋆

DID you hear why Snow White was asked to leave Fairyland?
She was found sitting on Pinocchio's face saying, "Tell a lie, tell the truth, tell a lie, tell the truth...."

⋆ ⋆ ⋆

AN usherette in the local cinema was known to be an 'easy going girl' and one night she gave her favours to the cinema manager. After an hour of humping, he was about to leave when he gave her two passes to the film premier of a much advertised new drama. But instead of being grateful, she complained, "This isn't going to put food in my childrens' mouths."
"If it's food you wanted, you should have fucked a grocer," he retorted.

⋆ ⋆ ⋆

THE film had only been on 20 minutes when a woman came rushing out into the foyer of the cinema looking very upset.
"I've been interfered with," she complained to the manager. He eventually managed to calm her down and took her to another section of the cinema. However, a short time later another woman ran out complaining of the same thing.
This was too much for the manager, so he took his torch and went to investigate. Lo and behold the torch picked up a bald-headed man crawling along on all fours.
"What's going on?" he demanded.

"I've lost my hairpiece" said the man. "I put my hand on it twice but it got away."

★ ★ ★

A REPORTER from the Hollywood gutter press was interviewing one of the industry's hottest starlets.
"Will you be telling all in your memoirs?" he asked.
"Oh yes, but the book won't be published until after my death."
"Oh great, I hope it's soon."

IN YOUR HARD TIMES

A TRAMP was roaming the streets when he suddenly came across a £10 note lying on the pavement. Picking it up, he looked down at his old worn out shoes and said, "Feet, I'm going to get you some new shoes." A little later he looked at his tattered clothes and said, "Legs, I'm going to get you some new trousers." A little later he noticed his willy had grown into a right big stonker." "Oh, oh," he said. "Who told you we'd come into money."

★ ★ ★

A FRUSTRATED young lady heard that men with big feet also had big members, so when a tramp came to the door with the biggest feet she'd ever seen he was invited inside. After wining and dining him, she then took him to bed. The next day, as he was leaving, she called out crossly, "By the way, in future try and wear shoes that fit you."

★ ★ ★

A COUPLE of old tramps who haven't eaten for many days suddenly come upon a dead dog. The first tramp cries out "At last, food", and he starts to eat the dog. "Don't you want any?" he asks his mate, who replies, "No thanks mate, not at the moment."

When the first tramp has finished, they go on their way but after a few minutes the tramp that ate the dog groans in pain and vomits it up.

"Oh great!" exclaims the second tramp. "At last, just what I've been waiting for - a hot meal!"

WALKING down the street, a man is approached by a tramp who begs him for some money.

"Let me give you a drink," said the man.

"I don't drink," replied the tramp.

"Then let me give you a cigarette."

"No thanks, I don't smoke."

"How about this betting slip for the 2.30 at Cheltenham tomorrow."

Again the tramp refused, saying, "I don't gamble either."

Suddenly the man had an idea. "Why don't you come back with me and I'll cook you a 3-course meal with all the trimmings?"

"Look," said the tramp. "Wouldn't it be just easier to give me the money."

"Maybe, but I want my wife to see what happens to someone who doesn't drink, smoke or gamble."

★ ★ ★

TWO down-and-out alcoholics had run out of money and were unable to buy any more grog. It was sending one of them completely round the twist, so his mate came up with a great idea. They just had a few pence left, enough to buy a sausage, which Bert shoved in Dick's flies.

"OK, Dick, now watch this." The two men went into a bar, ordered drinks which they soon polished off, and when the barman asked for the money Bert got down onto the floor and started sucking the sausage.

"Why, you disgusting buggers!" shouted the barman, "Get out of here or I'll have the law onto you."

All day they repeated the trick and drank freely until they were sozzled.

"You know, Dick, my knees are bloody sore from kneeling on the floor so often."

"That's nothing," replied Bert "I lost the sausage after the second pub."

⋆ ⋆ ⋆

DID you hear about the two old tramps at Christmas?
Not able to buy turkey and stuffing, they bought two budgies
and a pair of chest expanders.

⋆ ⋆ ⋆

A TRAMP, wearing only one boot, was shuffling down the street when he was stopped by a busybody woman.
"Do you realise you've lost a boot?" she said.
"Oh no," he replied. "I've just found a boot."

⋆ ⋆ ⋆

TWO tramps are so hungry, they haven't eaten for days and are beginning to get quite desperate.
"John," said one, "I've got to have a crap; I'll just go behind that bush." So off he goes.
Meanwhile, John remains where he is and he suddenly hears a very strange noise.
"Bob, what's that funny noise I can hear? It sort of goes oh.. oh.. oh.."
"How should I know, I can't hear anything." And he squats down again.
"Bob, Bob, it's that noise again. Look, I'll have to come round and see what it is."
So John goes behind the bush trying to locate the noise 'oh.. oh.. oh.. oh..'
"Oh, I see," he says triumphantly, "it's just your arse eating the grass."

AN old tramp walks into Social Services with a pig on a lead.
"Can you find somewhere for me and my pig to live?" he asks.
"Just a bed if that's all you've got. My pig can sleep underneath it."
"But what about the smell?" asks the official.
"Oh, the pig don't mind."

IN YOUR HONEYMOON DAYS

THE honeymoon couple couldn't wait to get to their bridal suite. As soon as the door closed they tore their clothes off and dived into the bed. But suddenly the bride began to shake.

"I caaaan't help it."

She explained she had a curious ailment which only happened once a year but it meant she had uncontrollable shakes.

Quickly, the bridegroom had an idea. He rang for room service and asked them to send up four waiters. When they arrived he got them each to take either an arm or a leg and hold her down on the bed. Then he inserted his todger and shouted,

"OK lads, let her go!"

★ ★ ★

IT was decided that the newly weds would spend their honeymoon night with her parents. But the walls were very thin and mum and dad were disturbed by all the humping noises.

"I know," said the father, "every time they do it, we will do it." After an hour, the honeymooners went quiet and everyone fell asleep. But two hours later they started again and after 45 minutes, quiet was restored and the parents fell into an exhausted sleep. However, around dawn activity began again and the father was forced to shout out, "Stop it, you're killing your mother."

★ ★ ★

A YOUNG hillbilly returns alone from his honeymoon and when asked where his new wife is, replies, "I found out she was a virgin, so I shot her."

"Quite right," comes the reply. "If she wasn't good enough for her family then she sure ain't good enough for ours."

★ ★ ★

"OH sure," said the frustrated wife. "My husband's a winner all right! When it comes to lovemaking, he always finishes first."

★ ★ ★

AFTER a wonderful first night of their honeymoon, the man came down to breakfast in the hotel dining room. Looking through the window at the magnificent scenery one of his fellow guests greeted him warmly.
"Good morning, a delightful spot sir."
"Oh yes," replied the man, "and so well concealed."

★ ★ ★

A YOUNG couple got married but on the first night of their honeymoon quarrelled about politics - she's Liberal, he's Conservative. Sometime later, having turned their backs on each other, she said "Sweetheart, there's a split in the Liberal Party and I think it's a good time for the Conservative Party to get in."
"Well, it's too damned late. The Conservative stood as an Independent and now he's lost his deposit."

★ ★ ★

ON the morning after their honeymoon night, the husband came down to breakfast to see a lettuce, and only a lettuce, on his plate. "What's this?" he asked puzzled, "I just wanted to see if you ate like a rabbit too," she replied.

A MIDDLE-AGED couple went to Las Vegas for their second honeymoon but unfortunately lost all their money gambling and didn't have enough left to pay the hotel bill. Feeling quite desperate, they happened to pass a poster advertising a visiting rodeo. Enormous prizes could be won for staying on the bucking bronco. The husband decided to have a go even though many had gone before him and all had fallen off. To the amazement of the onlookers he managed to stay on and won 30,000 dollars.

The wife was dumbfounded.

"How did you manage that? You've never been on a horse in your life."

"I know, but don't you remember when we went on our honeymoon and you had that dreadful cough?"

★ ★ ★

TWO friends get married at the same time and go on honeymoon together. They decide to have a bet on who would perform the most times on the first night. They would put the score up outside the bedroom door.

John performed three times and notched up 111 outside the door.

Next morning, when Bill staggered down after seeing John's score, he said, "Well done, mate, a hundred and eleven, you beat me by two!"

★ ★ ★

A YOUNG newly wed couple were staying with his folks but when they went to bed that night they were unable to allow their passions to erupt for fear of making too much noise and waking them up.

"Let's go to a hotel," he suggested.

So they packed the suitcase but had trouble closing the lid.

Next door, the father heard her say, "Let me sit on it" and a moment later he heard his son say "Let's both sit on it." Amazed, the father jumped out of bed and rushed to the door saying, "I've just got to see this!"

★ ★ ★

THE night before they are due to get married, the intended groom suffers a very bad accident and the part of his body most affected is his willy.

When the doctor realises the man's getting married the next day, he bandages up the injured member as carefully as possible and surrounds it with little splints.

The following night in the bridal suite his wife starts to strip for him. She takes off her top, exposes her boobs and says, "These have never been touched by any other man."

Then she takes her knickers off and says, "And no man has ever seen this."

At that point the man opens his dressing gown and says, "Well, look at this. It's still in the original packaging."

★ ★ ★

"DARLING, what's wrong?" asked the newly wedded husband of his tearful wife.

"Didn't you like last night?"

"Oh yes," she sobbed, "but look at it now, we've used it all up."

★ ★ ★

A 90-YEAR-OLD man and his 19-year-old wife came back from their honeymoon and the man was asked if he'd had a good time. "Not bad, I suppose," he said. "Trouble is, have you ever tried putting a marshmallow into a child's piggy bank?"

A GIRL married a quiet, humble man and after one week, he came home rather flustered.

"When I got to work this morning, I found a pencil tied to my willy."

"That's right," she said. "I thought if you couldn't come, at least you could write."

⋆ ⋆ ⋆

A COUPLE on their honeymoon ask for a suite in the local hotel. The clerk asks them if they want the bridal.

"No, that's alright," replies the groom. "I'll hold onto her ears until she gets the hang of it."

⋆ ⋆ ⋆

A 75-YEAR-OLD man and 19-year-old girl get married. On their wedding night he gets into bed and holds up four fingers. Surprised, the girl says, "You want to do it four times tonight?"

"No, no," replies the old man. "I meant pick a finger."

⋆ ⋆ ⋆

IT is a special honeymoon hotel and on the big night three men find themselves stranded on their balconies.

"Bloody hell," complains the first man. "She's pushed me out here and locked the door just because I slapped her on her backside and said she had a beautiful big arse."

"Same here," groans the second man. "I just said my wife had great big tits."

They look over at the third man and one of them says, "I guess you've put your foot in it as well?"

"No," retorts the man, "but I sure as hell could have."

ON their honeymoon night, he stripped off and his wife exclaimed, "Oh, what a cute dinky winky!"

"Doreen," he said sternly, "that's no dinky, winky, that's my cock."

"Oh no," she replied, "a cock is big and fat and long."

★ ★ ★

HAVE you heard about the miserly man who got married and went to Cornwall for his honeymoon, on his own? His wife had been there before.

★ ★ ★

IT was their honeymoon night. The Reverend Johns and his new wife retired to the honeymoon suite and he disappeared into the bathroom to get ready. When he came out, his wife was already in bed.

"Oh Mabel, I thought you'd be on your knees," he said.

"Oh we can do it that way later. For the moment, I just want to see your face," she replied.

★ ★ ★

A FIVE times divorced woman is convinced that the only way she will be happy is if she marries a man who has had no sexual experience with women. For three years she searches the country and eventually finds a strapping young man in Wales.

After a short courtship, they get married and retire to the honeymoon suite. She disappears into the bathroom to make herself as sexy as possible and when she returns, she's astonished to find all the furniture has been moved over to one wall.

"What's going on?" she asks astonished.

"I don't know what it's like to shag a woman but if it's anything like a sheep, I want as much room as possible", he replies.

IN YOUR JUGDGEMENT

A MAN is up before the courts for walking down the High Street completely naked.

"Is it true that you didn't have a stitch on?" asks the Judge.

"That's right, Your honour."

"Well, have you no shame? Are you married?"

"Yes, Your Honour."

"And how many children do you have?"

"16, your Honour."

"Release this man, he was only in his work clothes."

★ ★ ★

"YOU have been brought before this court to answer the allegation that you stole a young woman's bicycle. How do you plead?"

"Not guilty m'lord," said the young man. "I was walking down the lane when this lady cycled by, stopped when she saw me and asked me to kiss her. Then she took all her clothes off and said I could have anything I wanted. Well, your Honour, I don't wear ladies clothes, so I took the bicycle."

★ ★ ★

"MRS Mopps, you are up before the court for beating your husband black and blue. Do you have anything to say for yourself, before I pass sentence?"

"Yes, m'lud. Our Jack came home so drunk I locked him out of the house because of his disgusting behaviour. But he was hammering on the door, and said he was sure I'd open up if I knew what he was knocking with. So I opened the door m'lud and he gave me a box of chocolates. That's when I hit him."

★ ★ ★

JUDGE to husband, "I'm awarding your wife £300 a month." "Well, that's very generous m'lud, I'll try and chip in a couple of pounds myself."

★ ★ ★

"MADAM, you are up before this court for driving on the wrong side of the road. Do you have anything to say in your defence?" "Yes m'lud, the other side was full."

★ ★ ★

WHEN a witness was asked if a certain event had surprised him, he replied, "Why, you could have buggered me through my oilskins." The Judge leaned over to the Counsel and said, "I think he means he was taken aback."

★ ★ ★

A YOUNG girl was in the witness box giving evidence against her boss for his sexual advancements towards her. "And what did he say?" asked the barrister. At this point, the girl was too embarrassed to repeat it, so it was suggested that she write it down for the jury and the judge to read. First it was passed to the Foreman, who read, "Get your knickers off and meet me in the basement." The Foreman then handed it to Miss Wantin, an elderly spinster who had fallen asleep and had to be woken up. She read the note, gave Fred a wink and a toothless smile, and put the note in her pocket.

★ ★ ★

A POLICEMAN, his dog and a policewoman were on night duty. It was very cold and the policewoman shivered.
"Are you alright?" asked the policeman.
"Yes," she replied "I just forgot to put on my black woollen knickers before coming out."
"Don't worry," said the policeman "My dog's well trained. Let him sniff between your legs and we'll send him back to the station to get them."
Some time passed before the dog reappeared with part of the sergeant's hand between his teeth.

★ ★ ★

POLICE have announced that they would like to interview a man wearing high heels and black lace knickers, but the Chief Constable has stated they must wear their uniforms instead.

★ ★ ★

LAST week, a policeman stopped me driving the wrong way up a one- way street.
He said, "Didn't you see the arrow?"
"No", I replied. "Honestly, Officer, I didn't even see the Indians."

★ ★ ★

"GOOD morning, I'm a criminal lawyer," said the man to his new client.

"Oh well, at least you're not ashamed about describing yourself," came the reply.

* * *

A POLICEMAN on night duty thought he heard a noise up an alley and when he shone his torch he saw a woman with her blouse undone and her knickers round her ankles, eating a packet of mints.
"What's going on?" he asked.
"Blimey, has he gone?" she replied.

* * *

A CRAFTY barrister was defending a beautiful, shapely blonde accused of fraud and in his final address he turned to the all-male jury and said. "Gentlemen, are we going to see this poor, very friendly woman spend the next few years in jail or should she return to her private and secluded flat at 48 Green Walk, telephone number 491 7360?"

* * *

"BEFORE I pass sentence have you anything to say?" demanded the judge.
"Fuck all," came the reply.
The judge turned to one of the court officials and said, "I didn't hear that; what did he say?"
"He said fuck all, m'lud" whispered the official.
"Oh, that's odd. I was sure I'd seen his lips move."

* * *

DRIVING home from the pub one night a couple were stopped for speeding.

"You were doing 40mph in a 30mph zone," said the officer.

"Oh no, you're wrong," said the driver.

"I assure you, Sir, that my instruments are very accurate and that you were driving much too fast."

At that point his wife leant across and said to the officer. "It's no good arguing with him now, not when he's had a drink."

★ ★ ★

A MAN was up before the court on a charge of vagrancy. He had lost his job, house and family and fallen on hard times.

The judge found him guilty as charged and looking down at him said, "Young man, it is drink and drink alone that has brought you before this court today."

On hearing this, the young man cheered up considerably.

"Oh thank you m'lud, everyone else says it's my fault."

★ ★ ★

A MAN was up in court on a charge of soliciting. He had approached one of the principal bass singers in the local opera company, the judge was told.

"If that's so, then case dismissed" replied the judge. "I've heard the singers and in my opinion they all need fucking."

★ ★ ★

A YOUNG boy of 12 was in court charged with being the father of a new born baby.

In his defence, counsel asked the boy to show the court his penis.

"There," he said triumphantly. "Such a small, limp exhibit."

And taking it in his hand he tossed it from side to side, saying, "Consider, members of the jury, whether this immature penis

could possibly ever have fathered a child."

At this point, the young boy tapped his defence counsel on the shoulder and whispered, "If you don't let go, we're going to lose this case."

★ ★ ★

WHEN the man was found humping his girlfriend in the railway carriage he was charged with having a first class ride in a second class carriage.

★ ★ ★

"JOHN Smith and Mary Owen - you are up before the court today for seriously causing a breach of the peace and very nearly forcing the number 49 bus off the road. Have you anything to say in your defence?"

"Yes, Your Honour. We're very sorry for our behaviour but we were the victims of circumstance. Mary collapsed in the middle of the road and I knelt down to give her mouth to mouth resuscitation, but before we knew what was happening, passion took over and away we went. All of a sudden, I was coming, she was coming, and the bus was the only one that had brakes."

★ ★ ★

A WOMAN got a divorce on the grounds that her husband's penis was too big. Two years later she was up before the same judge, this time requesting a divorce because her husband's penis was too small. Her divorce went through but as she was leaving court the judge gave her a few words of warning.

"Madam, this court will not look too favourably upon you if you appear before us again with a third husband. We have more important things to do than sort out the right fitting for you."

★ ★ ★

THE judge addressed the defendant, a sickly 65-year-old man. "You have been charged with kerb crawling on September 4 of this year; how do you plead?"

"Guilty, Your Honour," said the man going into a coughing spasm.

"You are also charged that on September 21, you were found in an illegal club watching pornographic films; how do you plead?"

"Guilty, Your Honour," replied the man suffering another bout of bad coughing.

"And finally, last week you were found with a prostitute in a compromising position in a dark alley; how do you plead?"

During a bout of coughing that shook the man's whole body, he replied, "Guilty, Your Honour."

In a sudden moment of compassion, the judge said.

"Look, before I pass sentence, would you like to suck a fisherman's friend?"

"No, thanks. Don't you think I'm in enough trouble already?"

★ ★ ★

"YOUNG man, you are up before the court for bad behaviour towards Penny Ball, our celebrated referee's one and only daughter. You are fined £100 for handling, bad tackling and pulling off the jumper."

IN YOUR LEARNING YEARS

"MUMMY, the milkman's here. Are you going to pay him or shall I go out to play?"

★　★　★

SWEET little Sally-Anne goes into the garden to play, only to see her beloved cat lying stiff with his legs in the air. She runs in crying to daddy, who comes out and has to tell her that poor little Fluffy is dead.
"But why are his legs sticking up in the air" she asks.
For a moment, he is lost for words but quickly recovers and tells her it is so that Jesus can grab the legs easier and take Fluffy to heaven.
Sally-Anne seems to accept her pussy-cat's death, but a week later daddy comes home from work to find her crying her eyes out.
"Oh daddy, mummy nearly died today."
"How?" he stammered, very shocked. "What happened?"
"Mummy was lying on the kitchen floor with her legs in the air shouting, "I'm coming, I'm coming!" and if it hadn't been for Mr Brown next door holding her down, Jesus would have taken her away."

★　★　★

A WOMAN was walking along the street with her little daughter when they came upon two dogs humping. When the daughter asked her mother what they were doing, embarrassed mum did some quick thinking and replied, "The dog on top has hurt itself so the one underneath is carrying it."

"Well, isn't that just the truth?" said the little girl. "You try and do someone a good turn and all they do is turn round and fuck you."

★ ★ ★

"MUMMY, mummy, I didn't know birds were made of metal."
"Why do you think that, son,"
"Because I've just heard dad telling his friend he would like to screw the arse off the bird next door."

★ ★ ★

A LITTLE girl in a convent school asks her teacher, an old nun, who came first, Adam or Eve.
"Adam," replied the nun, "but then men always do come first."

★ ★ ★

"MY dad's got two of those," said little Tommy as he watched his grandfather urinating.
"No, you're mistaken there," replied grandfather.
"I'm not," replied the little boy, "he has one for weeing with and a great big purple one for cleaning the au pair's teeth."

★ ★ ★

WHEN she was a baby, she was so shy, she used to pin her own nappies.

★ ★ ★

A LITTLE boy went unannounced into his mother's bedroom when she was dressing.

"What big balloons you have," he said.

"Why Johnny, why do you call them that."

"Well, I saw father blowing up the maid's yesterday, when you went out."

★ ★ ★

LITTLE boy goes to his mum looking confused. He asks, "Mum, is it bad to have a willy?"

"No, dear," replies mum.

"Then why is daddy in the bedroom trying to pull it off?"

★ ★ ★

I ALWAYS knew my parents really hated me.

My bath toys were a kettle and toaster.

★ ★ ★

"MUMMY, mummy, the au pair is in bed with a strange man. Ha ha, got you! April fool. It's only daddy."

★ ★ ★

A FATHER was very upset about his young son's betting habits, so went up to school to talk to the boy's teacher, who promised to have a word with him.

"Maybe if he lost heavily on a bet, it would cure him," she suggested. That night after school she asked the boy to stay behind and confronted him about the bad ways he was getting into.

"It's not only me, miss," replied the boy. "You're a cheat; you pretend to be a natural blonde but you've got dark hair between your legs."

"I have not!" she blurted out without thinking.

"Oh yes you have, and I'll bet you my next month's pocket money."

The teacher was in a bit of a quandary. She had promised to help and this could be an expensive bet for him to lose. So she lifted her skirt and dropped her knickers. Having won the bet she rang the boy's father to tell him the good news.

"Damn, damn, damn!" he said, "This morning he bet me he'd see your bush before the day was out."

★ ★ ★

THE junior teacher decided to play a little guessing game with her class.

"Listen everyone, I'm going to turn around and hold something in my hand and you have to guess what it is. Here's a clue, it's yellow and you can eat it."

One of the children guessed a melon but another guessed a banana. "That's right," she said. "Now I'm holding something red in my hand, and this is also something you can eat." A little girl guessed apple.

"Well done, it shows all of you are really thinking." At this point a boy at the back asked if he could have a turn. With his back to the class he said, "I've got something in my hand that's long and has a little red tip.

"Now John, enough of that" said the teacher.

"It's alright miss, it shows you were thinking, but look," and he turned around to show a match.

★ ★ ★

LITTLE Billy peeped into his big sister's bedroom one day to see her rubbing her hands between her legs, saying, "I need a man, please, I need a man."

The next night he peeped into her bedroom again and was

amazed to find a man in bed with her. Later on that night if anyone had looked in Billy's room they would have seen him rubbing his hands between his legs, saying, "I need a Playstation, please, I need a Playstation."

★ ★ ★

A WOMAN who lost the top half of her bikini in the sea was running back up the beach with her arms across her breasts when a little boy stopped her.

"Please, miss," he said "If you're selling those puppies, can I have the one with the pink nose?"

★ ★ ★

A LITTLE girl said to her mummy, "Mummy, mummy, now I know how babies are made. I looked in your bedroom last night and saw daddy stick his willy in your mouth."

Mummy replied, "No dear, that's not how babies are made, that's how mummy gets her new jewellery."

★ ★ ★

"MUMMY, mummy, why do fairy stories always start, 'Once upon a time...'?"

"They don't always sweetheart, sometimes they start "Had to work late again... or even "Damn traffic, it took ages..."

★ ★ ★

"MUMMY, mummy, Bobby's got something I haven't got." said the upset little girl, pointing between her legs.

"Oh don't worry about that," said Mummy relieved, "as long as you've got one of these you'll always be able to get one of those."

LITTLE girl goes into her parents' bedroom to find her mummy sitting astride her daddy.

"What are you doing?" she asks.

"It's alright, my love, I'm just flattening daddy's tummy."

"Don't bother," replies the little girl, "because as soon as you go out the au pair blows it up again."

★ ★ ★

"DADDY, daddy, are you still growing?"

"Why do you ask, son?"

"Because the top of your head is coming through your hair."

★ ★ ★

ONCE a week the boy would travel across town to pick up child support money from his father and take it back to his mum. This money had come regularly for 16 years but on the boy's sixteenth birthday his father told him it was the last payment and to tell his mum he wasn't the father anymore.

"OK dad," replied the boy. "Mum says you never were."

★ ★ ★

THE children go back to school after Christmas and are asked by the teacher what they received from Father Christmas.

"I got a brmm brmmm," says one little boy, but the teacher is quite angry and tells him he's not a baby and should use the right names.

"Sorry, Miss, I got a car."

"Well done, Bobby, and how about you, Tracy?"

"I got a woof woof," she said.

Again the teacher had to remind the class to use proper words.

"I got a puppy, Miss," she replied.

"Jason, what did you get?"

The little boy hesitated because he didn't want to get it wrong and make teacher cross with him.

"I, er... got a book," he stuttered.

"Well done," smiled the teacher. "And what was it called?"

"Winnie The Shit, Miss."

★ ★ ★

"NOW try and get to sleep, son. Dream about what you would like for Christmas."

"I want a watch, daddy," he replied.

"Well, you can't," retorted Dad. "Now get to sleep."

★ ★ ★

"SHALL we make love tonight?" says husband to wife.

"Jack, please don't talk like that in front of the children; instead, when you're in the mood just say, 'Can I use your washing machine, please'?"

So a couple of nights go past when wife turns to husband and says, "Jack, do you want to use my washing machine tonight?"

"No thanks love, I didn't want to bother you, so I did it by hand."

★ ★ ★

A WOMAN was breastfeeding her baby in the park when a young boy sat down next to her.

"What does the baby have to drink?" asked the boy.

"Just milk and orange juice," she replied.

After a few moments thought the little boy asked, "Which one is the orange juice?"

★ ★ ★

"MUMMY, mummy, you can go to bed now because dad's locked up for the night."

"I don't think so, sweetheart, he isn't home yet."

"But it's true mum, the police have just been on the phone to tell you."

★ ★ ★

"PLEASE miss, I've hurt my finger," said little Rosie to her teacher. "Have you got any cider?"

Puzzled, the teacher asked her why she wanted cider.

"Because I heard my sister telling her friend that when she gets a prick in her hand she always put it in cider."

★ ★ ★

THE parents were so proud when their son John went away to University but all he did was constantly write home for money to spend on books, trips, membership fees and so on. Then halfway through the term he wrote to tell them he had a lead role in the University play but needed money for the costume. All this money was beginning to really annoy the parents but they did as he asked and it was a month later when he wrote again to say thanks.

"Everyone thought I looked a real count in the costume" he wrote. On seeing this, the father retorted, "Bloody hell, I gave him all that money and he still can't spell!"

★ ★ ★

A LITTLE boy walks into an off-licence and asks the woman behind the counter for a packet of fags and a bottle of cider.

"Now, now, sonny, do you want to get me into trouble" she says.

"Nah, I'm not interested in sex, just give me what I asked for, please."

MUM arrived back from staying overnight with her mother and asked her daughter if everything went alright.

"Oh yes," said little Anne. "Dad took me to the fair and I had some candy floss and an ice cream. It was great. But last night, I had a tummy ache, so I went to look for daddy and he was in the au pair's room and he was in her bed and...."

"Stop," said mum angrily "I want your daddy to hear this."

When dad came in, Anne repeated her story while Mum looked on, beside herself with rage.

"Tell us what they were doing?" she demanded.

"The same thing that you and the man from next door were doing last week, mum," she replied.

* * *

MAROONED in the middle of the Yorkshire Dales, a man finds overnight accommodation with a local farmer, who tells him he can share a bedroom with his young son. That night, just before retiring, the young boy kneels down at the bottom of the bed and the man is so impressed he kneels down as well.

"What are you doing?" asks the boy.

"The same as you."

"Gosh, my mum's going to give you hell. There isn't one where you are."

* * *

"GRANDPA," said the little boy. "What position do you play in football?"

"I don't play football son, why do you ask?"

"I heard dad telling mum that when you kicked off, we'd be able to afford a holiday."

* * *

A LITTLE girl was found wandering down the crowded High Street, crying her eyes out. When the policeman asked her what was wrong, she told him she'd lost her father.
"What's your dad like?" he asked.
"Football, beer and fishing," she replied.

★ ★ ★

"MUMMY, do babies come out of the same place that boys put their willies into?"
"That's right."
"So if I have a baby, will it hurt my teeth?"

★ ★ ★

WHEN their small son wanders into the bedroom to find mum astride dad, they decide to pretend it's a game so as not to upset him.
"Can I join in, dad?" he asks.
"Of course, son."
The boy climbs aboard, jumping up and down on his dad as if he was a horse. As the climax draws near, the movements get faster and faster, and the little boy shouts to his mother.
"Hang on, Mum, this is where me and the au pair usually fall off."

★ ★ ★

A LITTLE boy was out walking with his mother when they met the new vicar.
"Good morning" he said, and looking down at the young boy he continued, "And who do we have here?"
"I'm Mr Coles son" said the little boy.
Later, his mother corrected him on his answer.
"You don't say that" she said. "You say, I'm Billy Cole."

A few days later, the little boy was stopped by the local head-master.
"You're Mr Cole's son aren't you?"
"I thought I was, but mum says I'm not," he replied.

★　★　★

IT was halfway through the English lesson when Miss decided to test her class on spelling.
"I want everyone to tell me what their fathers do for a living and then spell it out to me."
"Johnny, what does your Dad do?"
"He's a farmer, Miss."
"OK, spell that, please."
"F-a-r-m-e-r."
"Well done Johnny. Now Bob how about you?"
"He's a police constable, Miss."
"Very well, please spell that out."
"P-O-L-I-C-E C...U..."
"No, try again."
"CCC-U-S-"
"No, no, you'll have to think carefully about this, go and practise in your book."
"Who's next? Oh yes, Colin, what does your father do?"
"He's a bookmaker, Miss."
"Now can you spell that for me please?"
"No, Miss, but I can give you 5-4 on that Bob writes cunt in his book."

★　★　★

NEIGHBOUR to little girl:
"What's the name of your new baby sister?"
"I don't know; I can't understand anything she says."

"MUMMY, mummy, why has daddy put his willy in the biscuit barrel?"

"Take no notice, darling, he's fucking crackers."

★ ★ ★

"PLEASE Miss, I want a wee wee," said little Annie, holding herself.

"Annie, we don't use words like that in the classroom. When you want to go to the toilet just put your hand up and say you want to do number one," said her teacher.

Soon afterwards, Jason yelled out, "Miss, I got to go and do a poo poo."

"Now, Jason, when you want to do that, you say you need to go and do number two."

The rest of the lesson went without any interruption until five minutes before the bell when Gregory put his hand up and said, "Please Miss, I want to fart, would that be number three?"

★ ★ ★

A CONCERNED father knew his son's pet hamster was dying and felt he ought to try and soften the blow.

"Son, I know your little Brownie is like one of the family but eventually he will die and go up to heaven. We must try not to be too sad. He's had a good life with us, so we must celebrate the happy times and not get too upset when he goes."

"Dad, can we have a party?"

"Yes, that's a good idea. You can invite some friends round."

"Dad?"

"Yes, son."

"Can I kill it now?"

★ ★ ★

"PLEASE, Miss, I think I know where God lives."
"Where's that, Maisie?"
"At the corner of our street in number 47."
"Why's that?"
"On my way to school this morning I heard a lady in the room upstairs calling, 'Oh God, oh God....'!"

★ ★ ★

AT a family gathering, a young boy suddenly lets out a noisy fart. "Bobby, manners please, you shouldn't do that in front of your grandma."
"Sorry, dad, I didn't know it was her turn."

★ ★ ★

THE teacher turned to her class and said, "Today, children, we are going to find out how many of you know the meaning of certain words by putting them into sentences. The first word is 'definitely'. Who can do that one for me?"
"Please, Miss, the sea is definitely blue."
"That's a good try Tracy, but sometimes the sea is grey, or even green depending on the weather, so we can't be that definite."
"I have one, Miss" said John. "Apples are definitely red."
"Well done for trying, but apples can also be green."
"Yes, Tom, do you want to say something?"
"Please Miss, does a fart have lumps?"
"Good gracious Tom, no .... no, of course not."
"Then, Miss, I've definitely crapped in my pants."

★ ★ ★

"NOW, children, tomorrow I'd like you to bring in something connected with your father's work so that we can all learn a bit more about the different jobs people do," says the primary school teacher. The next day, little Jimmy brings in a bus ticket "cos my father is a bus conductor, Miss."

"Well done, Jimmy, and how about you Lucy?"

"I've brought in a betting slip cos my dad's a bookie, Miss."

"Fine....and you, Billy?"

"I've brought in a light bulb and a toilet roll. My dad works at the big car factory and this is what he brings home every night."

* * *

A GROUP of boys were getting a reputation around the neighbourhood for troublemaking so the clergyman agreed to have a few words and asked each of them in turn to come and see him. An 8-year old boy came in, sat down and was asked sternly, "Where is God?"

The boy did not reply and the clergyman repeated the question even more forcefully.

"Where is God?"

Again, he was met with silence, so he pointed his finger at the small boy and shouted, "Where is God?"

Terrified, the boy bolted from the room, ran all the way home and locked himself in the closet. His older brother followed him to the closet and asked, "What happened?"

He replied, "We're in really big trouble this time. God is missing and they think we did it."

* * *

THE teacher was called away to speak to the headmaster, so she told the class to make up a poem about Timbuctoo and she would hear them all when she got back.

The first child recited hers.

"When I was lying in my bed

I dreamt of a ship with funnels red
A beautiful ship, its hull was blue
I think it was going to Timbuctoo."

"Well done, Lucy. Now let's hear the next." During the morning all the poems were heard, the last one coming from young Billy, a rather disruptive boy.

"As we were walking down a road in Kent
We saw two ladies in a tent
I said to Tim, what shall we do?
Then I bucked one and Tim bucked two."

"Get to the headmaster!" roared the teacher.

IN YOUR LEISURE TIME

ON her way home from an all night party, the girl was stopped by the traffic cops and breathalised.

Looking at the results one of the policemen said, "You've had a few stiff ones tonight, Miss."

"How amazing" she said "I didn't know you could tell that as well."

★ ★ ★

A FELLOW went to a dance and as he was going round on the floor he said to the girl,

"You're name's Hyacinth."

"How did you know?" she said.

"By your scent."

Later he danced with another girl and this time guessed her name was Rose. Towards the end of the dance his new partner was overheard to say, "But how did you know my name was Fanny?"

★ ★ ★

JUST before Bobby Davro is due to appear on stage at a cabaret/dinner, a stranger comes up to him and says, "Hey, Bobby, you're the tops with me, I'm your biggest fan and tonight I've got a red hot date. I'd really like to impress her and wondered if you would pretend to know me and come over and say hello. My name's Jack and I'll be sitting on the first table."

And indeed Bobby Davro remembers the stranger's request and halfway through his act comes over to Jack's table.

"Hello, Jack, good to see you, hope all is well."
"Fuck off, Bob, can't you see I'm busy?" replied Jack.

★ ★ ★

AFTER a really wild party, two girls wake up the next morning and one says to the other, "Ugh, my mouth tastes like the inside of a bird's cage."
"Well, I'm not surprised" said the other, "You did have a cock or two in there last night."

★ ★ ★

A WOMAN in a very chic French restaurant suddenly sneezes and her boobs pop out of her evening gown.
Moments later, her waiter is berated by the Manager.
"Pierre, please remember this is a high class establishment, next time use warm spoons."

★ ★ ★

THREE sisters, named Flora, Fiona and Fanny lived in the same village in Yorkshire and were renowned for their beauty, although all of them had extra large feet. One evening, Flora and Fiona went to the local village bop and were soon chatting to some lads from the next village.
"By gum," said one of the lads. "Haven't you got big feet!"
"Oh that's nought" they replied. "You should see our Fanny's."

★ ★ ★

HAVE you heard about the girl who gave up 10-pin bowling for sex? She found out the balls were lighter and she didn't have to wear shoes.

A RATHER shy man was dancing with a very shapely redhead when suddenly one of her earrings came off and dropped down the back of her dress.

"Would you mind getting that for me?" she asked him.

"Of course," he said, but the earring had dropped down a long way.

"Er..." he said embarrassingly, "I feel a perfect arse."

"My tits are good too," she purred.

★　★　★

A WOMAN was being taught how to swim by the local swimming instructor, sleazy Sid, who was holding her up in the water.

With an astonished look on her face she said, "Are you sure I'll drown if you take your finger out?"

★　★　★

JACK was fanatical about his special racing bike and he would clean it mornings and evenings, rubbing a special lubricant over it to stop any rust.

One day, he was invited to dinner at his girlfriend's house and went round on the bicycle but was told he couldn't bring it inside, it would have to remain round the back of the house.

After the meal, the mother said she wasn't washing up, she'd done the cooking.

"Well, I'm not," said the daughter.

"And I'm not," said the father.

"Neither am I," said Jack. "It looks like rain and I've got to see to my bike."

They seemed to have reached a stalemate so the father shouted, "Right, the next one who speaks will do the dishes!"

It was so quiet you could hear a pin drop, but Jack was getting very agitated as he looked through the windows at the storm clouds gathering. He needed to get the lubricant on the bike. In sheer desperation to make someone speak he suddenly jumped on top of his girlfriend and rogered her there and then on the dining-room floor. The parents were utterly shocked but no word was said. So as he saw the first few spots of rain he jumped on the wife and gave her a good seeing to as well. But still no words were uttered.

As the rain started to fall Jack knew he had failed, jumped up and said, "It's no good, I've got to use the lubricant."

At which point the father shot out of the room saying, "OK, I'll do the dishes."

★ ★ ★

A MAN went for an audition at the local club.

"You'd better not be a hypnotist, they're not welcome here."

"No, I'm a singer," he replied, "but what's wrong with hypnotists?"

"Well, we had one here a couple of days ago. He had 12 people on stage in a trance when he tripped over the microphone wire and shouted 'Shit'. We've been clearing up ever since."

★ ★ ★

OVERHEARD at a fancy dress party:

"I'm a turkey," said the girl, "What are you?"

"Sage and onion," he replied.

★ ★ ★

I WAS dancing in a night-club with this girl.

I said, "Can I smell your fanny?"

"No, you can't" she said.

"Oh well, it must be your feet then."

THE lift was packed solid with people as the doors closed and the attendant called out, "Which floors please?"

A man standing at the back shouted out, "Ballroom!" and a lady in front of him cried, "Oh I'm so sorry, I didn't know I was crushing you that much."

★ ★ ★

IT was the church social and everyone was having a good time singing and dancing. Suddenly at a lull in the noise, Mrs Riddler shouted over to the vicar,

"What is it a man stands up to do, a woman sits down to do and a dog lifts up his leg to do?"

Blushing profusely, the vicar replied that he didn't know and amidst peals of laughter she cried, "Why, to shake hands of course!"

★ ★ ★

A YOUNG lad goes on a picnic with his Grandpa. After they've eaten, the old man opens a can of lager.

"Grandpa, can I have some?"

"Son, is your todger long enough to touch your backside?"

"No".

"Then you can't have a lager."

A little later Grandpa lights a cigarette.

"Grandpa, can I have one of those?"

"Is your todger long enough to touch your backside?"

"No."

"Then you can't have one."

On the way back to the house, they pop into the newsagents and pick up a couple of scratch-cards. The man wins nothing but the boy wins £10,000.

"Are you going to share that with me?" asks grandpa.

"Is your todger long enough to touch your backside?" asks the boy.
"Yes," said the man.
"Then go fuck yourself."

★   ★   ★

A RATHER toffee-nosed couple moved into the area and to show off their new house invited the neighbours in for a cocktail party. They sent their adolescent son to bed and told him not to bother them but he kept coming down on any excuse - stomach ache, thirsty, couldn't sleep. Eventually, one of the guests, a retired colonel, suggested he take the boy back up to bed and he would soon get him settled.

Ten minutes later, the Colonel reappeared and they had no more trouble for the rest of the evening. As the party was breaking up, the couple took the Colonel aside and asked him what the secret was.

"Oh, simple really. I taught him to masturbate."

★   ★   ★

"I'M sorry you can't come in here, you have to wear a tie" said the bouncer at the night-club.
The man goes back to his car but can only find a set of jump leads. He slings them round his neck and walks back to the club.
"Will this do?" he asks.
"OK, but don't start anything."

★   ★   ★

IT was the night of the grand fancy-dress party and on arriving, everyone was announced.

Shortly after 8pm, Jack arrived at the door wearing only his under-pants.

"What are you?" insisted the announcer.

"I'm premature ejaculation," replied Jack.

"What! I can't say that, there are ladies present."

"OK, well just say I've come in my underpants."

⋆ ⋆ ⋆

IT was a busy night in the Club and the crap table was doing a roaring trade. On one such throw a lot of money had been bet and as the dice landed, a beautiful brunette opened her coat to reveal she had nothing on underneath as she shouted, "I've won". She collected all the winnings and walked away.

"What did she throw?" asked the croupier afterwards.

"I don't know," everyone replied. "We weren't looking at the dice."

⋆ ⋆ ⋆

A COUPLE popped into the local hotel bar for a drink but when the man went to the gents he found it infested with flies. Returning to the bar, he complained to the barman, who said to him reassur-ingly, "Don't worry, sir, the bell for lunch will be rung in five min-utes."

"How will that help?" asked the puzzled man.

"They'll all come up to the dining room," he replied.

⋆ ⋆ ⋆

THE final of Mastermind is being held in Leeds next week. The three contestants will be:

1. Brian Rawlings on British Rail 1949-1969.

2. Cynthia Prescott, English Poetry 1828-1858.

3. Kevin Shuttelworth on Yorkshire suit lengths £10.99-£40.

A RATHER shy young man went along to the village dance and met up with a rather pretty girl. His chat up lines were sadly lacking, so in blind panic he said the only thing he could think of.
"You're Scottish, aren't you?"
"Ay, I am, how did ye know that?"
"It's the way you roll your R's."
"Oh no," she said. "It's these high-heeled shoes that do that."

★ ★ ★

"WAITER, I see on the menu that you have a chicken tarka. Shouldn't that be chicken tikka?"
"No, sir, it's like chicken tikka only a little 'otter."

★ ★ ★

A YOUNG man began courting a girl from a high-class family and one evening they invited him to join them at the opera. Worried about making a good impression, he calmed his nerves by downing a few pints beforehand. When it was time for the performance, they were shown to their seats - the first row of the balcony, but halfway through the first act the man needed to pee. The longer he sat, the more agonising it became, yet he was too embarrassed to disturb the whole row by getting out to go to the toilet. Eventually he hit upon an idea. Covering his lap with the programme, he slid out his dick and peed over the edge of the balcony. Such relief! But a moment later, a voice was heard from below:
"For goodness sake, wave it about a bit."

★ ★ ★

"HEY, Jack, would you like a ticket for the local policeman's ball?"
"No thanks, I can't dance."
"That doesn't matter. It's not a dance, it's a raffle."

IN YOUR LOCAL

A MAN goes into a bar with a cat and a heron and orders two pints of beer for himself and the cat, and a glass of wine for the heron. "That'll be £4.20" says the barmaid.

"You get these, heron," says the cat, so the bird pays.

A little later, they order another round and this time the cat says to the man, "Your round, mate," so the man pays up.

The three stay at the bar all night drinking heavily but never once does the cat pay for a round, always having some excuse. Eventually, the bemused landlord cannot contain his curiosity any longer and asks the man what he's doing with the cat and heron. Sadly, the man explains that one night in bed he was visited by a genie who granted him one wish and he asked for a bird with long legs and a tight pussy!

★ ★ ★

YOU know you must be drunk when somebody says, "Go fuck yourself" and you ask for the telephone number.

★ ★ ★

A BLOKE who's well known for challenging people to dares walks into a pub with an alligator. He picks up a bottle, hits it over the head of the alligator, which stuns the beast into slowly opening its mouth. At this point the man drops his trousers and puts his knob in the alligator's mouth, leaving it there for 10 seconds and removing it just as the jaws of the alligator snap shut.

"Now," said the man addressing the stunned onlookers. "Is there anyone here who will take on this dare?"

The room remains silent for a few moments and then an old lady stands up, saying, "I'll have a go, but please don't hit me too hard with the bottle."

★ ★ ★

EVERY day a man in the local bar would be surrounded by beautiful women - like bees round a honey pot.
"I don't understand it," said the barman. "It's not as if he has a lot of money or he dresses expensively, all he does is just sit there licking his eyebrows."

★ ★ ★

A MAN walks into a pub, orders a pint and is charged £1.80. A little later he orders another and hands over £1.80. But the third time, the barman gives it to him for free.
"How come?" asks the man.
"Well, the owner of this pub doesn't know that I know he's upstairs with my wife. So I'm doing to him down here, what he's doing to me up there."

★ ★ ★

A MAN walked into a bar with a tiny pianist on his shoulder. The pianist could only have been a foot tall. During the evening the pianist entertained the customers with his wonderful playing and eventually the barman asked the man where he got this wonderful entertainer.
"Well, I was walking in a wood and came across an old bottle. In the bottle was a genie who offered me anything I wanted, but she thought I said a twelve inch pianist."

★ ★ ★

A DRUNK staggered into the police station to report his car had been stolen.

"Where did you leave it, sir?"

"On the end of this key and now the bloody thing's gone."

The policeman was not in the mood for such nonsense.

"Look at you, you're a disgrace, you're so drunk you don't know what's going on. Why, you've even left your flies open."

"Bugger me!" said the drunk. "They've stolen my girlfriend as well."

★　★　★

WHAT a landlord!

I asked him for something cold, tall and full of gin and he introduced me to his wife.

★　★　★

A MAN thought up a clever way to make some money. His friend had an unusual anatomy in that he had three balls.

"We can make a fortune" he told him. "Come on, I'll show you."

They went into the local pub and the man got everyone's attention by standing on a chair and shouting, "I'll bet anyone in this bar that my friend and the barman there, have five balls between them."

People rushed forward and soon a lot of money had changed hands. At that point the man turned to the barman and said, "I hope you don't mind taking part in this bet."

"Not at all" replied the barman "It's amazing to find a man with 4 balls, you see I've only got one."

★　★　★

A LADY at the far end of the bar waves her arm in the air to get the attention of the waiter and in doing so shows a good hairy underarm.

Down the other end of the bar is a very drunk man.

"Hey waiter, get that ballerina a drink!" he shouts.

"How do you know she's a ballerina?"

"Well, no one else would get their leg so high."

★ ★ ★

A RANCH hand goes into the saloon and orders a shot of whisky. He drinks it down in one gulp, rushes outside, kisses his horse's arse and comes back in again.

Another whisky is ordered and drunk before he rushes outside and kisses his horse's backside again.

After he has done this half a dozen times, the bartender's curiosity gets the better of him and he asks the man why, after each drink, he rushes outside to kiss the horse's bum.

"Chapped lips," replies the man.

"Oh, does that cure them?" asks the surprised bartender.

"No, but it sure as hell stops me licking them."

★ ★ ★

A CRAFTY man goes into the pub and up to the bar where the bartender greets him.

"Good evening sir, what's your pleasure?"

"Well, I'll have a pint of bitter, please, and a packet of crisps.

"He puts 30p down on the bar. On seeing this, the bartender asks him what he's up to.

He replies, "That's for the crisps. I didn't want a drink but I thought it would be rude to turn down your generous offer."

"I was only being polite," explains the bartender but the man refuses to pay, so he's banned from the pub.

A few weeks later he comes into the pub again and is immediately recognised by the bartender.

"You're barred!" he shouts.

"But why? I've never been here before, I live overseas."
Puzzled, the bartender apologises.
"I'm sorry sir, you must have a double."
"Why thank you, and a packet of crisps, please."

★ ★ ★

I SAW this white horse standing behind a bar.
I said, "Do you know there's a whisky named after you."
He said, "What, Adrian?"

★ ★ ★

A MAN walks into a bar with a stoat on his shoulder.
"Hey, what's this all about?" asks the bartender.
"Let me tell you, mate, this stoat gives the best blow job ever."
"Give me a break, now get out and take it with you."
The man persists. "No, really. Why don't you take it out the back and see?"
A little while later, the bartender reappears.
"That was fantastic, I'll give you £100 for it."
"No, way" replies the man. They haggle for a while but the man eventually sells for £600. After closing time, the bartender takes the stoat home and finds his wife in the kitchen.
"Mabel, teach this stoat to cook and then get the fuck out of here."

★ ★ ★

A MAN is trying to decide what to call his new bar when he spots Lisa coming up the street. Now this man is really keen on Lisa, who's not only gorgeous looking but has legs that go on for ever. That's it, he thinks, I'll call my new bar Lisa's Legs.
The next day three men are waiting outside the bar when a cop

stops to ask them what they are doing.

"We're waiting for Lisa's Legs to open so we can go in and satisfy our needs," they reply.

★ ★ ★

A MAN walked into a pub carrying a red, long nosed, short legged dog.

"Ugh, that's an ugly dog", commented a man standing at the bar with his prize bull terrier at his feet.

"Maybe," replied the first man, "but she's a mean bitch."

"Oh yeah? Listen, I'll bet you £50 my dog will have chased her off in less than a minute."

"OK, it's a deal," and with that they lined the two dogs up. On the word 'Attack' the two dogs flew at each other and in no time at all, the bull terrier has been bitten in half.

"Bloody hell!" sobbed the owner, aghast. "What the fuck do you call that dog?"

The man replied, "Well, before I docked her tail and painted her red, she was a crocodile."

★ ★ ★

"SAME as usual, Jack" asks the bartender as he sees one of his regulars' walk up to the bar.

"No thanks, just an orange juice, please," replies the man dejectedly. Taken aback the bartender asks why.

"It's my wife. She says if I come home one more time legless and covered in puke, she'll pack her bags and leave."

The bartender tells him he has a way to get around the problem.

"Have a £10 note handy and when you arrive home in your usual state, insist it was someone else who threw up all over you. Show her the money and say he offered to pay for the dry cleaning."

Jack's well pleased with the idea and spends the evening drinking pint after pint until he's blind drunk. Sure enough, by the time he's got home, he's thrown up on himself but still remembers the little trick. As soon as his wife starts shouting at him he shows her the money and explains what happened.

"But that's a £20 note," she retorts.

"Er ... yes, that's right, the same guy messed in my pants as well."

★　★　★

A MAN walks into his local and finds a seat at the bar next to a drunk. For some five minutes the drunk looks at something in his hand and eventually the man's curiosity gets the better of him and he asks what it is.

"It's odd," replied the drunk. It looks like plastic but feels like rubber."

"Here, let me see" said the man.

He takes the object and begins to roll it between his fingers.

"You're right" he says "It does feel like rubber but looks like plastic. Where did you get it from?"

"My nose," replies the drunk.

★　★　★

A GIANT of a man, very drunk and very mean, throws open the doors of the pub and shouts loudly, "All you on the right side are cock-suckers and all you on the left are mother-fuckers!"

Suddenly a man runs from the left side to the right.

"Where are you going, wimp?" roars the drunk.

"Sorry sir, I was on the wrong side," he replies.

★　★　★

AFTER gulping down a Scotch in the local bar, the man bets the bartender £50 he can piss in the empty glass. Eager to

make some easy money, the bartender agrees, so the man drops his trousers and starts to piss everywhere - on the floor, the bar, the tables, even the bartender himself. But nothing goes in the glass. The bartender chuckles to himself and demands the £50.

"Just a second," replies the man who goes up to two guys sitting in the corner and comes back moments later with £200 in his hand.

"Here's your £50" he says and hands over the money.

Puzzled the bartender asks, "What was all that about?"

"Well you see, I bet them £200 that I could piss all over this pub, and over you, and you'd still be smiling at the end of it."

★ ★ ★

FOUR men in the pub were discussing what part of a woman they found most attractive.

The first said he went for the lips, full, pouty, curvy lips.

The second said he went for the eyes - dark and mysterious.

The third went for the hair - long, blonde, fragrant.

At that point, the fourth man interrupted.

"Listen lads, I feel like the rest of you. We all know what part of the female we find most attractive. It's just that I don't lie through my bloody teeth about it."

★ ★ ★

IT has just been announced that Bob Swillall has been elected Chairman of Alcoholics Unanimous. He will be notified of this as soon as he comes round.

★ ★ ★

A MAN goes into a bar and asks for a pint of bitter. The barman serves him and the customer drinks it very quickly and then says, "Do you have any brown ale?"

"Of course, sir." And he's served the drink.

A little later the man again asks, "Do you have any lager."

"Of course, sir. That's what pubs are for."

And a little later still he asks, "Have you got any stout?"

"Naturally," replies the barman.

The barman is pestered all night by these ridiculous questions until finally his temper snaps.

"Sir, this is a pub. We have everything you could wish for - dark ales, light ales, ciders, four kinds of beers, bottled drinks, red wine, white wine ... so please, enough of these stupid questions."

A moment goes by before the man asks, "Do you have shorts?"

"Look, fuck face, I've just said we have everything, so YES, we have shorts."

"Thank goodness for that," replied the man. "I'll have a pair in a large size, 'cos I've just pissed myself."

★ ★ ★

JACK was sitting at the bar gazing dejectedly into his beer. "What's up?" asked the barman.

"It was last night," he replied. "I got so drunk I don't remember what I did but when I saw a woman in bed with me I naturally gave her £50."

"Well, that's reasonable, even if you don't remember it," consoled the barman.

"It's not that," said Jack. "It's the fact that it was my wife and she automatically gave me £10 change."

★ ★ ★

EIGHT football hooligans walk into a bar and one of them orders nine pints of beer.

"There's only eight of you," says the barman politely, but for his trouble he gets thrown up against the wall and punched.

"Of course, sir!" he gasps and pulls nine pints. Each of his mates takes one and the ninth is taken over to a man sitting quietly in the corner.

"Here you are, mate, have this one on us, it gives me a good feeling to help someone who can't walk."

"Gosh! Thanks, but I can walk you know."

"Not for long, if you don't get the next round in."

⋆　⋆　⋆

A MAN walked into the pub with a dog.

"I'm sorry, sir, no dogs allowed in here."

"Yes, but he's a really intelligent dog, ask him to do anything and he will."

"OK," said the barman. "Tell him to go and get me a newspaper."

The man hands the dog £5 and off he goes. Two hours go by and there's still no sign of the dog, so the anxious owner goes looking for him. After roaming the streets, shouting his name, he eventually finds him in a back alley with a bitch, doing the business.

"What's all this about?" asked the owner. "You've never done this before."

"No, but I've never had so much money before," replied the dog.

⋆　⋆　⋆

A BLOKE goes into a pub and orders a triple whisky and a pint of beer. As soon as the barman puts them in front of him he drinks them all down in one gulp.

"I shouldn't be drinking all this," he says.

"Why's that?"

"Because I've only got 20p on me."

* * *

A GAMBLING man goes into a pub and bets the customers that he can smell any wood and tell them what it is, blindfolded. They take on his bet, blindfold him and get him to smell the table. After a moment he says, "That's mahogany."

Next, they get him to smell the top of the bar.

"Yes, I know that, it's oak" he answers confidently.

"OK, it's double or nothing."

They put a snooker cue under his nose. A minute goes by and then he replies, "I would say that's Canadian maple."

Feeling very dispirited, the regulars have one more trick up their sleeve. They get hold of old Meg - the village's oldest tart - lay her out on the table, pull down her knickers and get the man to smell between her legs. After a good sniff, he asks them to turn it over, which they do, and he has another good sniff.

"Can you just turn it back again?" he asks, and again he has a good smell.

This goes on for a couple of minutes with the regulars turning Meg over time and time again.

"OK, your time's up," they say at last.

"Right," says the man, "I would say it's a shit-house door made out of fish boxes."

* * *

A MAN walks into a wild west bar, itching for a fight. He takes immediate dislike to the piano player, so takes out his shotgun and shoots four holes in the man's ear. He then turns to the barman and asks for a shot of whisky. As he serves the man, the barman says, "Mind if I give some advice? If I were you I'd shave down the metal sight and grease the barrel well."

"Why? Will that make me shoot better?"

"No, but it'll be easier for you. The piano player's father is Big Jake, a man feared round these parts, and when he hears what you've done, he'll shove that gun right up your arse."

★   ★   ★

A MAN walked into a pub boasting that he could identify any drink blindfolded. Would anyone care to take up the challenge?

Half a dozen of the regulars agreed to the bet. They each put down £10 that he could not identify all six drinks offered to him. Along came the first. The man tasted it and said, "Yes, that's a famous brewery called Jenkins and it's their special bitter."

He was correct.

Another was put before him.

"This is a tequila and is Jose Revello."

Correct; and so it went on. Each time the man was able to name the drink and the manufacturer. By the time the sixth drink came along the punters were getting desperate. This time when they put a drink before him, he tasted it, spat it out and swore profusely.

"Bloody hell, this is urine, this is just plain piss."

"Yes," said a voice, "but who's is it?"

★   ★   ★

A MAN goes into a bar and asks the barman if it would be alright to tell an Irish joke.

"I think you ought to know," said the barman, "that my name's O'Riley and many of my fellow countrymen use this pub. That group over there is the local darts team - they're Irish. Those two

men over there are Irish, they work round the corner on the building site, and (lowering his voice) that big Irish bastard in the corner is the local hard man."

The newcomer thought for a moment and then said, "Thanks, it
would take too bloody long to explain the joke to you anyway."

★ ★ ★

**AN anti-drink campaigner walks into a local bar and calls for
the customers' attention.**

**"I would like to show you all something about drinking" he
announces and at that point he puts two jars on the table. One
he fills with whisky, the other with water. Then he produces
two earthworms and drops one into each jar. The one in the
whisky jar breathes his last and sinks to the bottom while the
other swims happily around in the water.**

**"So what does this show you about drinking?" asks the cam-
paigner and a voice at the back replies, "If you drink, you
won't have worms!"**

★ ★ ★

A MAN goes into a pub carrying an octopus.

"Sorry, mate, you can't bring that in here," says the barman.

"Hold on a minute" says the man, "this isn't just any old octopus,
this one can play every single musical instrument you care to put
before him. How about a small wager? If he can play all the instruments you can produce, I get free drinks for the night. If not, then
I'll buy everyone in here a drink."

The barman agrees and the wager begins. First, the octopus plays
the piano and it's beautiful, then it plays the trumpet - a superb
piece of jazz - followed by the double bass, violin and the harp. In
fact, the harp is so well played it brings tears to the eyes of the customers.

"I'm not beaten yet!" thinks the barman. He goes upstairs into the attic and finds his old bagpipes. They haven't been played for years but he dusts them down and hands them to the octopus. It looks at them, feels them but doesn't start to play.

"Gotcha," smiles the barman triumphantly. "Time to pay up."

"Just a moment," replies the man confidently. "When he realises he can't fuck it, then he'll play it."

★ ★ ★

A MAN walks into a bar with a toy poodle on a lead.

"No dogs allowed in here," says the barman. "Only guide dogs for the blind."

"But I am blind," insists the man.

"Well, that's not a guide dog."

"Why, what is it?"

"It's a poodle."

"Bugger, I've been conned."

IN YOUR MARRIAGE

A COUPLE had just got married and as they went upstairs to bed the groom turned to his new wife and told her to put his trousers on.

"But they don't fit," she said.

"Exactly. Remember that. I wear the trousers round here."

Inflamed, the new wife took her knickers off and threw them at him.

"OK" she said, "Put these on."

He replied, "I can't get into these."

"You're damned right you can't and you never will if you don't change your outdated attitude."

★ ★ ★

I KNEW my future mother-in-law didn't like me from the start, when she bit the groom on the wedding cake in half.

★ ★ ★

THE groom was so ugly he had to wear the veil!

★ ★ ★

ON the day of their marriage a man said to his new wife, "Everything I have is yours. You can do anything you like in the house but you must never look in the top right hand drawer of my desk."

27 years passed when one day during spring cleaning she couldn't resist opening the drawer. In it she found three golf balls and £10,000. When her husband came home, she con-

fessed she'd looked in the drawer and couldn't understand why he had never allowed her to look.

"I must be honest," he said. "I decided that if I was ever unfaithful I would put a golf ball in the drawer."

"Well, that's alright" replied the wife. "Only three times in 27 years."

"But I have to say that every time I got a dozen golf balls, I sold them" he said.

★　★　★

IT was their wedding night and they were spending it in a four-Star hotel. As she went upstairs to their room to prepare herself, he stayed downstairs for a final drink. However, as he thought of what awaited him upstairs he abandoned his drink and soon followed her up. But as he entered the room he found her stark naked on her back with the night porter fondling her breasts and the elevator boy down below.

"Darling, how could you!" he wailed.

"Oh come on, Ron, I always told you I was a bit of a goer," she said.

★　★　★

A DISAPPOINTED husband said to his wife, on seeing he put her bra on.

"I don't know why you bother, you've nothing to put in it."

She retorted. "Listen, you, I don't complain when you buy underpants."

★　★　★

"NOW listen, son, you'll look back on this time as the happiest in your life," confided the boy's father.

"But dad, I'm not getting married for another week."

"That's what I mean, son," he nodded sadly.

WHY did the one-legged man settle down and get married? He couldn't catch sheep anymore.

★ ★ ★

THREE couples get married on the same day and find themselves in the same hotel for their wedding night. When the girls have gone up to bed the men have one more drink before following them and they agree to swap stories of their night of passion the next morning after breakfast.

The next day they meet up and the first man describes the wonderful night he and his wife had.

"We made love five times, I can't wait for tonight."

The second man agrees.

"Neither can I, last night we made love seven times, every which way we could think of."

The third man was strangely quiet.

"How about you?" asked the other two.

"We made love once," he said.

"Once! What did your wife say?"

"It's nearly breakfast time, we'd better get some sleep."

★ ★ ★

A COUPLE went down to the registry office to arrange a date for their marriage.

"Names please," said the official.

"My name's Robert Smith and this is Jenny Smith."

"Any connection?" she asked.

"Only once," blushed the girl. "Behind his dad's barn last Sunday."

★ ★ ★

AFTER only one month of marriage, the tearful young girl confided in her friend that she was leaving her husband because he drank too much.

"But why did you marry him in the first place if you knew about his drinking?" she asked.

"Ah, but I didn't, not until he came home three nights ago sober."

★ ★ ★

MY wife is so neat, in the middle of the night I got up to get a drink and when I returned, the bed was made.

★ ★ ★

SHE can remember when she got married, and where she got married, but she can't for the life of her remember why.

★ ★ ★

A MAN came home from work early to find his wife bending down clearing out the cupboards. Quick as a tick, he lifted her dress, pulled down her knickers and took her from behind. When it was over he gave her two sharp smacks on her bare backside.

"You bloody sod," she said. "You have your wicked way and all the thanks I get is a good slapping."

"That's for not looking round to see who it was," he retorted.

★ ★ ★

DO you know what it means to come home at night to someone who gives you love, affection and understanding? It means you're in the wrong house.

★ ★ ★

A MAN said, "Was that your wife who answered the door?"

"Of course it was," replied the husband. "You don't think I've got an au pair that ugly."

★ ★ ★

MY wife gets so easily upset that she cries when the traffic lights are against her.

★ ★ ★

MOANING man:
"Is there anything worse than a wife who never stops talking about her last husband?"
"Yes - a wife who never stops talking about her next husband," his friend replied.

★ ★ ★

TWO mates talking about marriage.
One complained that his wife never felt like sex, but the other replied, "I know what the trouble is, you need a good technique. Tonight after supper open a bottle of champagne, put on some sexy music, slowly undress her, fondle her breasts, stroke her thighs ..."
"Yes, then what?"
"Call for me."

★ ★ ★

DID you hear about the girl who advertised for a husband in the personal column of the local paper?
She had over 200 replies saying, "You can have mine."

★ ★ ★

THE eldest son was still masturbating at the age of 35 so his dad strongly advised him that it was time he got married.

A year later, having found a girl, the son got married but it was only six weeks later that his father caught him once again masturbating in the garden shed.

"What's going on, I thought this would be a thing of the past once you'd got married," said his father.

"Have a heart, Dad, Doreen's only small and her arms get tired very quickly."

★ ★ ★

A COUPLE have been apart for nearly six months and when they eventually embrace again at the railway station he says, "FF," but she says "No, EF."

He replies, "FF" and at that point the ticket inspector taps him on he shoulder and says, "I couldn't help but overhear, what's going on?"

The man replies, "She wants to eat first."

★ ★ ★

A NEWLY married man comes home from work to find his wife crying in the kitchen.

"What's wrong?" he asks, looking alarmed.

"I'm trying so hard to be a good wife," she sobs "and I've spent all afternoon in the kitchen cooking your dinner but it's turned out to be a disaster."

"Never mind," he says, "Let's just go to bed."

The following day, he comes home from work to find her crying again because she's burnt the dinner and once more he comforts her and takes her to bed. This happens the next night as well. Then on the fourth night he arrives home to find her sliding stark naked down the bannisters. When he asks what she's doing, she replies, "I'm just keeping your dinner warm."

DID you hear about the man who grew a moustache?
He was fed up with his wife calling him a barefaced liar.

★　★　★

A DISGRUNTLED man broke the flies on his trousers when he was putting them on and turned to his wife, saying he'd still wear them just to show his mates what he had to put up with.
"Oh no," replied his wife. "I'll mend them, I don't want them to know what I have to put up with."

★　★　★

MY mother-in-law and I don't get along.
Take our anniversary for instance. She sent us some mono-grammed bath towels.
"Hers and Its."

★　★　★

AFTER a month of being married, the young rather naive wife turned to her husband and said, fondling his private parts, "I thought you said you were the only man who had one of these, but you were telling lies. The man next door has one as well."
"Oh that," he replied. "That's just a spare one I had so I let him have it. "Oh you goon," she laughed. "You've given him the best one."

★　★　★

A NEWLY married couple had experienced their first real argument and she had spent two nights in the spare bedroom. On the third night her husband brought her some flowers home as a way of apologising and it seemed to work. She smiled at him and disappeared into the bedroom, where he found her lying on the bed with her legs wide apart.

"These are for the flowers," she murmured.

"Oh dear, I didn't know we hadn't got a vase," he replied.

★ ★ ★

ONLY one month into their marriage, a young girl finds her 80-year-old husband cheating on her with a woman of 65.

"Why are you doing this? Can't I satisfy you, what has she got that I haven't?", she complains

"Patience," he replies.

★ ★ ★

"IT'S very simple," said the newly wed husband to his bride. "I don't want to be too demanding, so if you want it tug on this twice, but if you don't want it, tug on it 400 times."

★ ★ ★

A HUSBAND and wife were always arguing. This time it was about sex.

"You're so frigid, I wouldn't be surprised if you put cold cream between your legs!" he yelled.

"Oh yeah!" she sneered. "And I wouldn't be surprised if you put vanishing cream between yours."

★ ★ ★

A MARRIED couple are in bed one night when he turns to her and says, "Darling, I've got a new position for us to try. We must lie back to back."

"But I don't understand," she says, "how can that be?"

"It's OK. We've got another couple joining us."

THE snow was thick on the ground when Jack went into the public toilets for a pee. As he was fumbling around in his flies, his mate Bob walked in.

"Hello Jack, it's hard to find in this weather, isn't it!"

"It is that," replied Jack, "Even at home when two of us are looking for it!"

★ ★ ★

A WOMAN comes back from the doctor's smiling all over her face.

"You're in a good mood," remarks her husband. "What's happened?"

"The doctor has just told me I've got the boobs of a 21-year-old."

"Oh yeah, what did he say about your 50-year-old arse?"

"Nothing, we didn't mention you," she retorted.

★ ★ ★

DID you hear about the totally selfish husband? Every night in bed he would shout, "Coming, ready or not!"

★ ★ ★

OVERHEARD in a bus:

"I'm worried about my wife. It's her appearance, she's let me down."

"Oh, how come?" replied the other.

"Well, I haven't seen her for three days."

★ ★ ★

A REPORTER from the local newspaper was interviewing a couple who were celebrating their 25th anniversary.

"And after all this time, can you still say you're in love" he asked. "Oh yes," said the husband "I'm in love with her sister and she's in love with the man next door."

★ ★ ★

"DO you know I found a great way of getting my husband to increase the housekeeping. Last week I went shopping with him wearing a low-cut blouse with no bra on. When I bent down to get something from the bottom shelf one of my boobs fell out. He was so angry until I told him it was because I didn't have enough money to buy a good bra, so he increased the housekeeping straightaway."

"What a great idea," said her friend, "I'll have to try something like that."

The two women met up the following week but her friend looked very downcast.

"What happened, didn't it work?"

"I remembered what you said and just before we went out on Saturday night I lifted up my dress and said, "Look Alf, I'm wearing no knickers cos I can't afford to buy any, and you'll never guess what the old bugger did. He gave me a couple of quid to buy myself a comb, telling me that at least I could look tidy."

★ ★ ★

THREE women are talking about their husbands and the subject of nicknames comes up.

"My husband's called Big Mac cos he's got the largest, juiciest donger you ever did see," said the first woman happily.

"I call my husband 'Surfing Willy' cos when he gets going I feel like I'm floating on water," said the second.

"Mine's called Cointreau," said the third.

Puzzled, one of the other women asked, "Isn't that a special kind of liquor?"

"That's exactly what I mean," she answered dreamily.

★ ★ ★

A MAN and a woman find themselves sharing the same carriage on an overnight sleeper to Glasgow. After half an hour the woman shouts down to the man, "It's quite cold in here, do you think you could pass me another blanket?"

"I've got a better idea," he says, "Why don't we pretend we're married?"

"Well, OK then."

"Good, then get your own bloody blanket."

★ ★ ★

THE young couple have been married for six months and one day when they are in bed he asks her if she is happy.

"Oh yes," she replies. "Everything is wonderful."

"But is there nothing that bothers you?" he persists.

"Well.... only a couple of things. You're always picking your nose and we always make love with you on top."

"I can explain that," he says. "When I was growing up my father gave me two pieces of advice which I try to follow - 'Keep your nose clean and don't fuck up.'"

★ ★ ★

A MARRIED couple go into the pub and the man (a bodybuilder) goes up to get the drinks while the wife goes to get a seat. When he returns he finds her visibly upset and asks her what's wrong.

"Oh Bert, that horrible little man over there has said some

dreadful things to me."

"Like what?"

"He said he'd like to take me back to his place, strip me and caress every part of my body."

"Why, the bloody swine!"

"And then he said he had a very long tongue and he'd like to lick me all over."

"That's it, he's gone too far," says the husband, rolling up his sleeves.

"And then he said he'd like to turn me upside down, fill my fanny up with best bitter and drink the lot."

The husband sits down quickly. "Well let's not be too hasty about this."

"What the hell are you waiting for? He's only half your size!" she cries.

"Maybe, but you don't fuck with a man who can drink that much bitter."

★ ★ ★

THE woman sobbed quietly into her handkerchief as the engineer came to cut off the gas supply for non-payment of bills.

"We just couldn't afford to pay it," she cried. "We've got ten children and it takes all our money to feed them."

"Perhaps you shouldn't have had so many children," replied the engineer. "It's irresponsible if you can't meet your bills. One of you is to blame, though I would guess it's six of one and half a dozen of the other."

★ ★ ★

TWO men talking in the bookies:

"What's wrong Charlie? You don't look so good this morning."

"It's the bloody wife; she's keeping me awake at night dreaming of this driving test she's taking next week. Every so often she grabs hold of my willie and moves it around like a gear stick. It's no joke."
"I've got an idea Charlie. Next time she starts, turn her over and stick it up her backside - maybe that will stop her."
The next night, Charlie does as his mate suggests, turns her over and gives her one up the backside.
"£5 of 4-Star, please," she says.

★ ★ ★

"DOCTOR, you've got to help me. My dick isn't big enough to satisfy my wife," said the distraught man.
"Do you drink special brew?" asked the doctor.
"Yes."
"Well, that's your problem, special brew tends to keep it small, you'd better try some brown ale."
A few weeks later, the doctor bumped into the man in the off-licence.
"Was it a success? I see you've got some brown ale there," said the doctor.
"Oh yes, the sex is great now. Thanks, doc. I don't drink the brown ale, though; I give it to my wife."

★ ★ ★

ON their second honeymoon night a couple discovered there had been a mix up with the booking and they would have to sleep in a twin bedded room. They got into bed and the man said, "Sweetie pie, are you going to bring that beautiful big body of yours over here so that I can show you how much I love you?"
As she came across to him, she bumped into the bedside table

and knocked the lamp on the floor.

"Never mind, my darling, accidents will happen."

Some time later, when the 'party' was over, the wife slipped out of bed to return to hers. But again she bumped into the bedside table.

"For goodness sake, watch what you're doing, you stupid, fat bitch!" he said.

★ ★ ★

AFTER watching a steamy video at work, a man goes home to his wife and asks her why she doesn't moan when they make love.

"If that's what you want, I'll do it tonight," she says.

That night, in bed, he gets on top of her and after a couple of minutes she says,

"When are you going to paint the kitchen? Why can't I have a new dress? Next door have got a far better car than we have ...."

★ ★ ★

AFTER a heavy night drinking with his pals, Jack staggers home at one in the morning and falls into bed. Three hours later, he wakes up to find he's wet the bed so being a real prat, he climbs over his wife onto the dry side and rolls her into the wet. It's not long before the wife wakes up and an almighty row erupts over who has actually wet the bed.

"I'll prove it," says the wife, and she takes out the pot from under the bed, squats down and enjoys a nice long pee. "Now it's your turn, you won't be able to, because you've just peed the bed."

Jack takes his turn on the pot and tries with all his might until he's finally rewarded with a long and satisfying pee. Alas! One minute later he wakes up to find he's wet the other side of the bed.

"HELLO, Fred, what have you been up to?"

"I've just got married to an identical twin."

"How can you tell them apart?"

"The other one's got a beard and a very deep voice."

★ ★ ★

"OH John, do you remember, the last time we were up here was 25 years ago and we made love for the very first time near an old disused barn. I wonder if we could find it again."

"I shouldn't think it'd be there after all this time," he said, "but we'll go and have a look."

Surprisingly enough, the barn was still there.

"Look Doreen, I sat you on that fence over there and we made love, let's do it again."

She agreed and he sat her on the fence and began the business. Doreen went completely wild, thrashing her arms in the air and waving her feet around.

"Wow, Doreen, you didn't do that last time."

"I know" she stammered, "but it wasn't electrified then."

★ ★ ★

A STREET busker is trying very unsuccessfully to play his cello and the noise he's making is driving most people away.

"Cor, Flo," said May, as they passed him by, "he reminds me of our Bert's nasty habits. He sits and scratches his instrument too, instead of learning how to use it properly."

★ ★ ★

A MAN living way up in the Highlands of Scotland goes down into the village to post a letter. His wife has not long died after 45 years of marriage.

"How's it going then, Jock?" asks the sympathetic store owner.

"Well, the sex is just the same but the ironing is getting bigger."

"NOW you've just got married, let me tell you about sex," said the man's father.

"You go through three different stages. First of all, when you're newlyweds, you have sex anytime, anywhere - the kitchen, the bedroom, the garage, whenever the urge takes you. But then, when you've been married for a while, you usually keep sex to the bedroom - that's stage 2. Stage 3 comes after many years of marriage, it's when you pass each other in the hall and say, 'Fuck you!' "

★　★　★

WHAT did you have for breakfast this morning?
Oh, the usual argument.

★　★　★

"DOREEN, ring for the vet, I feel terrible."
"But why the vet?"
"Because I lead a bloody dog's life."

★　★　★

MY wife's so ugly she's even got a French pleat under her arms.

★　★　★

A WIFE went to the doctor's complaining that her husband couldn't make love. The doctor gave her some pills to give to him and told her to let him know whether there was any improvement. The following week, he met her in the street.

"How did it go?"

"Oh wonderful doctor, thank you. On the first day we did it in the morning, on the second day in the morning and in the evening and only yesterday he did it five times before he died."

IN YOUR MOMENTS OF DOUBT

"OH Fred, I'm pregnant," said Eileen to her boyfriend. "And if you don't do the decent thing, I'll put my head in the gas oven."
He replied, "Oh Eileen, that's great. Not only are you a good fuck, but you're also a good sport."

★ ★ ★

"I DON'T know what's going on," said worried Bob to his mate. "Last month we moved parishes and I left our church which had a message pinned up outside saying 'Sex is your worst enemy' only to get to the new church and read 'Make your worst enemy your best friend.' "

★ ★ ★

AN angry husband was complaining to his friend about his slovenly wife.
"She never does any housework, I never get a cooked meal, everything's dirty, including her. I'm so fed up I sleep on my own and I wish she was dead."
The friend suggested that he try killing her with sex. It wasn't an offence, after all.
So the man returned home, dragged his wife upstairs and kept her there the whole weekend. By the time Monday morning came he could hardly drag himself to work, but when he came home that night the house was spotless, a steak was cooking and she was standing there with a sexy see-through nightie on.
"You see, darling," she said. "Treat me right and I'll treat you right."

WHAT do you do if a pet bull terrier gets randy and tries to mount your leg?
Fake an orgasm.

★ ★ ★

SHE was so naive the man tricked her into marrying him by telling her she was pregnant.

★ ★ ★

IT was so cold in the park last month that the local flasher was reported to be describing himself to the women he met.

★ ★ ★

A FAMOUS footballer was asked if he would appear nude in a glossy magazine.
"We'd like you to pose holding a ball" explained the editor.
"OK, but what do I do with my other hand?"

★ ★ ★

FOR 20 years, a man has been writing to a woman in Norway but they have never met. At long last, the man decides they ought to do something about it and he suggests that she should fly over and he'll meet her at the airport.
"I think that's a wonderful idea," she replies, "but I think I ought to tell you that I'm completely bald, I suffer from a nervous complaint and don't have any hair on my body."
"No problem," he replies.
Another letter arrives soon after and in this she says, "I think you should also know that I don't have any arms, I write by putting the pen between my toes."

A LITTLE startled to receive this news, he still tells her to come, but by return of post she writes that she meant to tell him she only has one eye in the middle of her forehead.

It's too late for him to back out, so he writes to say he's looking forward to seeing her and could she wear a carnation in her buttonhole so that he will recognise her.

★ ★ ★

OVERHEARD on the top deck of a bus:
"Do you know, Jack, if girls are made of sugar and spice and all that's nice, how come they taste like fish?"

★ ★ ★

THE wife of the Head of State was accompanying a visiting VIP through the streets of the capital in a horse drawn carriage. Suddenly, one of the horses gave a rip roaring fart.
"Oh, I do apologise!" she said to her guest.
 "That's alright," he replied. "In fact, I thought it was the horse."

★ ★ ★

THEY'VE just come up with a novel way to stop you smoking. When you buy a new packet of cigarettes, stick the first one up a mate's backside, filter first, put it back in the packet and mix them up. You'd have to be pretty brave to pick one out and smoke it after that.

★ ★ ★

DID you hear about Santa Claus going to the psychiatrist?
He didn't believe in himself.

IT'S Christmas time and the dustman knocks at the door for his Christmas tip. The door opens and a beautiful shapely blonde invites him in, takes him upstairs, strips off and makes mad passionate love to him for the next two hours. They then go back downstairs have some breakfast and before he leaves she give him £1.

The astonished dustman asks her what the £1 is for and the woman replies.

"When I asked my husband if I should give you a £10 tip for Christmas he replied, "'Fuck the dustman and give him £1.' The breakfast was my idea."

★ ★ ★

THE mystery in life that's never been solved is why, when men get drunk, someone creeps into their bedroom in the dead of night, pees in the wardrobe and pukes in their shoes

★ ★ ★

THE King was due to set off for the crusade and knew he would be away for more than a year. Not trusting his knights who would be left behind, he had a special chastity belt made for the queen containing a little guillotine.

A year passed and when the King returned, he asked the knights to bare all and every single one of them except one had lost their manhood.

The King turned to the Knight who was still intact, saying, "You are the only one who has remained loyal to me. You may pick their punishment. Come on, speak up, or have you lost your tongue?"

IN YOUR MEN TALK

TWO girls talking, one says, "I got picked up by the fuzz last night."

"Did it hurt?" the other asks.

★ ★ ★

IT was pouring down with rain and two girls were late for their date.

"Come on, Jane, put your foot down or we'll never get there."

"Oh no," said the driver. "The ground is too wet for us to buy off any speed cops today."

★ ★ ★

A LADY sitting alone in a bar gets pestered all night long by men trying to proposition her, but she sends them all away with a flea in their ear.

Then, towards the end of the evening, an alien walks in, sits down, orders a drink and completely ignores her. She is intrigued and asks him why he is not interested in her.

"On our planet we have sex in a different way and it's much more powerful. Would you like to try it?"

He then puts his middle finger on her forehead and she immediately begins to feel quite stimulated. This feeling gets more and more powerful until she reaches an orgasm never experienced before by any human being. It was so wonderful, she begs for more, but he says, "Give me half an hour"

as he holds up his bent finger.

THE Sheikh always knows which wife to choose for the night. He goes to the harem, throws a bucket of water over them all and takes the one that fizzes.

★ ★ ★

HAVE you heard the mating call of a blonde?
"Oh I'm soooo drunk."

★ ★ ★

WHAT did the Jewish lady say to the flasher?
"You call that a lining?"

★ ★ ★

TWO girls are walking along the prom when a holiday photographer steps forward.
"Hold on Jean, he's going to focus."
"What! Both at the same time?"

★ ★ ★

A WOMAN said to her friend, "Do you smoke after sex?"
"Gosh, I've never looked," she replied.

★ ★ ★

THREE girls were talking on a bus about safe sex.
The first said she always carried a packet of condoms in her bag; the second said she was on the pill; and the third said she used a tin with a few pebbles inside. The other two looked at her in amazement.
"How does that work?"

"Oh, it's quite simple. I make him stand on it and when it starts to rattle I kick it out from under him."

★ ★ ★

THREE daughters all got married on the same day and all spent the first night of their honeymoon in their parents' house.
As mum locked up, turned out all the lights and went up to bed she passed her daughters' rooms.
In the first room she heard her daughter laughing, in the second her daughter crying, but in the third room not a sound.
Next morning at breakfast she asked her daughters about what she had heard.
The first said, "Well you always told me to laugh when something tickled me."
"And you always told me to cry when something hurt me," said the second.
"And you always told me not to speak when I had my mouth full," said the third.

★ ★ ★

WHAT do "good time" girls have written on their underwear?
Next.

★ ★ ★

THREE women at an antenatal clinic were asked what position they were in when they conceived.
The first said he was on top.
"In that case you'll have a boy," said the doctor.
The second said she was on top.
"In that case you'll have a girl," came the reply.

But before the third woman could reply she burst into tears. "Oh no, please tell me I'm not going to have puppies."

★ ★ ★

TWO women were chatting on a bus:
"I've got a dreadful sore throat," said one.
"Oh you poor thing! When I've got a sore throat I suck on a Life Saver."
"Ah, that's easy for you to do. You live near the seaside."

★ ★ ★

TWO women are talking on a bus and one says to the other. "I was so embarrassed this morning. I met my son's new teacher. What a hulk, he made me go weak at the knees and instead of telling him I had come about our Billy, I said I'd come about his willy."
"Never mind," replies the other. "Sometimes we all say things we didn't mean to say. For instance, this morning I made my husband his breakfast and accidentally told him I hated his guts and that was why I was sleeping with his best friend."

★ ★ ★

TWO ladies talking in the laundrette:
"Has your husband been circumcised?" said one.
"No" replied the other. "He's always been a complete dick."

★ ★ ★

TWO women talking:
"How do you keep your youth?" said the first.
"I lock him in the cupboard," replied the second.

MOTHER was trying to console her daughter who was crying her eyes out because her boyfriend had dumped her.

In case it was sex that had caused the split, mother told her about the birds and the bees but was suddenly interrupted by daughter.

"Oh no mum, I can fuck and suck with the rest of them, but he says I'm a useless cook."

★ ★ ★

TWO girls talking on a bus:
"Last night I had three orgasms in a row."
"That's nothing, I had over 50."
"Golly, he must be good."
"Oh, you mean with just one guy?"

★ ★ ★

TWO women talking on a bus:
"No, Doreen, you've got it wrong. If you think the way to a man's heart is through his stomach, you're aiming too high."

★ ★ ★

TWO girls talking:
"What do you think of the new salesman? He dresses fashionably."
"And quickly too," replied the other.

★ ★ ★

OVERHEARD on the top deck of a bus:
"My husband's away at sea so much, when he comes home he's like a stranger."
"Oh you lucky thing, how exciting."

OVERHEARD on the top deck of a bus:
"I've been out with every player in the rugby team and I haven't bonked one of them" said the girl.
"Oh, I know who that'll be" replied her mate.
"It's that timid scrum half."

★ ★ ★

WHY do married women have so many wrinkles?
From squinting down and saying, "Pull what?"

★ ★ ★

"BUT Joan, if sex is a pain in the arse, you're doing it wrong."

★ ★ ★

WHAT'S the definition of a lazy man?
One who weds a pregnant woman.

★ ★ ★

WHY did God create men?
Because a vibrator can't dig the garden.

★ ★ ★

WHAT are the three most popular female lies?
1. Of course you're the best lover I've ever had.
2. Size doesn't mean everything.
3. Only interested in your money? How can you say that? Of course not.

IN YOUR PARENTHOOD

A MAN rushed into a newspaper office saying "I hope I'm not too late to put an announcement in the paper - my wife has just given birth to a baby girl after 10 years of trying."
"Of course, sir" replied the clerk. "How many insertions?"
"Oh, I can't remember - bloody thousands!"

* * *

A MAN is loading his kids into the car, five squeezed in the back and two in the front. As he gets in himself he's heard to mutter, "Wow, I almost screwed myself out of a seat!"

* * *

DID you know there's no chance of a cock-up if you use artificial insemination?

* * *

**A SIMPLE-MINDED couple go to the doctor's because the wife is pregnant again with the fifth child in as many years. "Why didn't you use the condoms that I instructed you to wear?" asked the doctor.
"I'm sorry doc" they replied "but we don't have an organ so I put it over the flute instead."**

* * *

A VERY ugly couple were walking along the road with two beautiful children when they overheard a passer-by express amazement

at the fact that two such ugly people could have such lovely children. They turned to the passer-by and said, "You imbecile, we
didn't make them with our faces!"

★   ★   ★

**DOREEN was absolutely amazed. She was nearly 50 and her
husband was 75 and the doctor had told her she was pregnant.
She couldn't wait to tell her husband and rang him up immediately.**
**"Henry, wonderful news; I'm pregnant; you're going to be a
father."**
**"Well, that's terrific," said Henry proudly, "and who is that
speaking?"**

★   ★   ★

A MALE and female astronaut landed on an undiscovered planet
and soon met up with some of the inhabitants. These inhabitants
showed them many things, including a baby machine which produced the new offspring. On seeing this, the astronauts were asked
how their little ones were made. Rather than explain, they stripped
off and gave a full and satisfying demonstration. The inhabitants
looked puzzled.
"But where are the new ones?"
"Oh that won't happen for another nine months," they replied.
"Goodness me, if it takes that long, why were you rushing so much
at the end?"

★   ★   ★

**ON seeing her friend pregnant, the woman offered congratu-
lations but added sadly, "We've been trying for years but with
no luck."**

"Well, do as I did," replied the happy woman. "Go to a faith healer," and then lowering her voice she murmured, "but go on your own."

* * *

A HUSBAND and wife and their six children sat down in the restaurant and called over the waiter to order their meal. It was obvious that the six children were three sets of twins and the waiter couldn't help but remark, "I hope you don't mind my asking, but do you always have twins?"
"Oh no," replied the wife without thinking. "Sometimes we don't get anything."

* * *

DID you hear about the woman who had a hard time breast-feeding her baby? She couldn't get her husband out of the way.

* * *

WHAT'S the similarity between toys and women's breasts?
They were both intended for kids but it's the dads who keep playing with them.

* * *

TWO women talking:
"My first pregnancy resulted in triplets and that only happens once every 250,000 times."
"Wow!" said her friend "I'm surprised you ever had time to do any housework."

* * *

IT was decided to add sex education to the school curriculum and the parents were asked how they felt about this. The majority were in agreement with one proviso - no graphic demonstrations, just keep it oral.

★   ★   ★

JUST as the young girl is coming out of the school gates, a car draws up and a man leans over to ask her if she'd like a lift home.

"No, thank you," she replies.

But he asks again. "Come on, it's raining, you'll be soaked by the time you get home."

"No! Go away and leave me alone."

The man follows her up the road. "Look, get in please, I'll get you some sweeties."

"No!" she yells and starts to run.

"I'll get you some sweeties and your favourite comic."

"No, no, no!" shouts the girl. "Just because you bought the Lada doesn't mean I have to ride in it, dad."

★   ★   ★

"GOOD gracious" said Flo's friend, putting down the newspaper. "It says here that there are 19 women in the village all expecting a baby on the same day - June 23. Your baby's not due until July is it?"

"No, it's not, but then I didn't go on the Mothers Union trip to Weymouth."

★   ★   ★

A KINDLY old curate happened upon three young girls crying in the deserted old graveyard. Taking pity on their distress he invited them into the rectory for a cup of tea and a slice of cake. In the warmth of the kitchen and the smell of freshly baked cakes, the three girls cheered up.

"Now," he said, smiling as he brought over the tea tray, "Who's going to be mother?" and they all burst into tears again.

★ ★ ★

"JOHN, your dad's not very good at these things, so I wonder if you'd tell your brother about the birds and the bees," asked Mum. John sought out his brother and said, "Hey Bill, d'you remember what we did last night?"

"Sure, we went down the Palais, picked up a couple of birds, had a dance, then took them round the back of the bus station for a good 'one two'. Why do you ask?"

"Mum just wanted you to know that what you did last night is the same for the birds and the bees."

★ ★ ★

POOR old Sammy. He was a Caesarean baby and even now, 20 years later, he still goes out of the house through the skylight.

★ ★ ★

TWO husbands are in hospital anxiously awaiting for their wives to give birth. One of them is so nervous, the other tries to comfort him. It'll be alright mate, I've been through this before."

The nervous man asks a lot of questions, finally saying, "Can you tell me how long it will be before I can have sex with my wife again?"

"Are you private or NHS?"

"NHS."

"In that case, you'll have to wait until you get home."

"DOCTOR, I've only got three weeks to go before my baby is born, can you advise me on the best position for delivering it?" she asked. "Well, the most common way is exactly the same position as when you conceived."
"Oh goodness, you mean in the dark under the stairs, standing on an orange box!"

★ ★ ★

BOB and Sheila had a small flat in the city and decided the only way they could have a Sunday afternoon 'quickie' was to send their 10 year old son out on the balcony and ask him to report on the neighbourhood activities. It was sure to distract him for an hour. The boy began his commentary as the parents got down to business.
"An ambulance has just stopped at old Mrs Jenkin's place, Mr Wales is walking his dog, Mat and Jenny are on their bikes and the Davidsons are having sex."
Mum and Dad sat up in bed astonished.
"What do you mean?" said dad. "How do you know?" he spluttered.
"Their kid is standing out on the balcony with binoculars too," replied the son.

★ ★ ★

MOTHER receives a telephone call from school telling her they are sending home her son for weeing in the swimming pool.
"But everyone does that," she says.
"Not from the top diving board."

★ ★ ★

A YOUNG boy at school called Tommy is always in trouble.

Stealing, pinching, bullying, his misdemeanours are endless. Then one day, the head teacher calls his mother in to tell her that they have no choice but to expel the boy. This time he's been found wanking in the classroom.

"You know it's a big problem," says the head teacher. "You've got to stop him from doing it."

"How?" she asks.

"Well, tell him he'll go blind if he carries on like that."

When they get home, mum insists that dad goes upstairs and has a word with him."

"Go and explain what will happen" she says.

So dad goes up to his son's bedroom and starts to talk to him.

"Hold on a minute, dad," says the little boy. "I'm over here."

★ ★ ★

GRANDPA takes his grandson to Blackpool for the day and they go on every ride in the fair except for the big dipper. But the boy's not satisfied, he wants more.

"Oh please, Grandpa, please, please let's go on the big dipper."

After ten minutes of constant pestering, Grandpa relents and they go on three times.

"Can I have an ice cream now, Grandpa, please, please can I have an ice cream?"

Grandpa knows his mother has said 'No' but it's anything for a quiet life, so he buys the boy a cornet. In the afternoon, they go down onto the beach and the boy has a donkey ride. He loves it. In fact, he loves it so much, he wants Grandpa to buy the donkey.

"No, no, no," says Grandpa, but the boy screams and yells and pesters him that he eventually buys the donkey for £50.

"What are you going to call it?" he asks.

"Tosser," said the boy, "cos he kicks a lot and is always tossing people off his back."

Later on, at 3am in the morning, Grandpa is woken up by the little boy because the donkey has broken his leash and disappeared.

"Grandpa, grandpa!" cried the boy. "Tosser's off."

"Now look here boy, I've taken you to Blackpool, you've had a good time at the fair, filled yourself with ice creams, bought a donkey. Don't you think I've done enough for one day?"

IN YOUR PINK

HOW many gays does it take to screw in a light bulb?
One, if he takes it slowly and uses special lubricating jelly.

★ ★ ★

HAVE you heard? There are now special pool tables in lesbian bars - no balls.

★ ★ ★

POLICE were called today to break up a fight at the drag races.
Two gays arrived wearing the same dress.

★ ★ ★

**IN the gay shop down the road they're selling a strong kind of condom.
It's called seal-a-meal.**

★ ★ ★

A YOUNG man was introduced to the Queen as the new royal photographer.
"How amazing!" she said, "My uncle is a photographer."
"Well that is a coincidence," he replied. "My uncle's an old Queen."

★ ★ ★

**THE social climber confided to her friend over a cup of coffee.
"It's awful, my son's just told me he's gay...
Oh well, at least his boyfriend's a judge."**

PERCY and Alan had a little tiff at the funfair, so Alan went off on his own on the Tunnel of Love. Suddenly there was a huge explosion and the tunnel collapsed.

Percy rushed over, beside himself with worry, and scrambled through the debris until he found Alan.

"Alan, Alan, are you alright?"

"No, I'm not," said Alan, "I went round three times and you didn't wave once."

★ ★ ★

DO you know the difference between a general rodeo and a gay rodeo?

At a general rodeo they all shout, "Ride that sucker!"

★ ★ ★

IN a smoky old night-club the pianist leant over to a man on the front table and said, "You see, I told you I could make you forget about that girl."

"You sure did" he replied. "Play with it again, Sam."

★ ★ ★

REMEMBER, if you are a bisexual, it doubles your chance of a date on a Saturday night.

★ ★ ★

DID you hear about the woman who married a bisexual?
She didn't know which way to turn.

★ ★ ★

APOLOGY from the latecomer:

"Sorry. I'm late. I met a man on a narrow path and didn't know whether to toss him off or let him block my passage."

★ ★ ★

A VERY small guy walks into a bar and finds himself standing next to a huge man. The man turns to him and says,
"Hi, I'm 6'6", 345lbs, 22" penis, 3.5lb left testicle, 3.5lb right testicle, Turner Brown.
The small guy immediately faints. When he comes around he is being helped to a chair by the big man, who asks, "What's wrong with you, man?"
"I'm sorry, can you repeat what you said before?"
"Sure, 6'6", 345lbs, 22" penis, 3.5lb left testicle, 3.5lb right testicle, Turner Brown."
The small guy sighs with relief.
"Oh, wow, I thought you said turn around."

★ ★ ★

FOUR gay guys walked into a pub but there was only one barstool.
It was no problem, though, they turned it upside down.

★ ★ ★

TWO men talking over a pint of beer.
"How's your son getting on?", one asked.
"Very well, thank you. He's just been given a seat on the board, and because it means he's going to be so busy all the time, he's given his deluxe cruiser away. Such a kind hearted boy."
"Mmm, that sounds a bit like my boy," replied the second man. "He's just successfully floated his company on the stockmarket and as a gesture of goodwill gave away his BMW sports car."

Just then a third man joined them.

"We were just talking about our sons. How's yours doing?"

"Funny you should ask," he said. "We've just found out he's a homosexual, but he's made some good friends. One's given him a car and the other's given him a beautiful boat."

★　★　★

A GAY walks into a club holding a very small paper bag.

"If anyone can guess what is in this bag, they can come home with me tonight."

A wisecracking hell's angel replies, "Yeh, you've got an old Triumph 500 in there."

Everyone starts to laugh as the gay man takes a peek in the bag and he replies, "Yep, we have a winner."

★　★　★

"DOCTOR, doctor, I've got a pain up my backside."

"Bend over, let's have a look. Oh yes, I can see what the trouble is, you've got a dozen red roses stuck up it."

"Oh really," said the man happily. "Is there a message on them? Does it say who they're from?"

★　★　★

SUPERMAN'S cruising around, looking for some fun when he suddenly sees Superwoman lying flat out on her back, absolutely naked, in her garden.

Now he's a bit of a cheeky bugger and he thinks to himself, at my speed I could go down, have my way with her and then fly off before she realises what went on.

So he dives down, does the business and is away at the speed of light.

"Bloody hell, what was that?" says Superwoman.

"I don't know," says the Invisible Man, "but it bloody hurt."

★ ★ ★

ADVICE to prison inmates - never volunteer to play the female role in the Christmas panto.

★ ★ ★

AFTER a disastrous love affair, the young man decided to get away from it all and took a cabin up in the woods, miles from civilisation. All went well for a few weeks but then he started to get bored, so he was delighted to see a man coming up the road one day towards his cabin.

"Hi," said the newcomer. "My name's Bob. Just heard you've moved here, so there's a party in your honour tomorrow night."

"That's great" said the young man, thinking how friendly people were.

Bob continued, "Yep, there'll be singing, dancing, lots of beer and plenty of sex."

"I'll be there," said the young man. "What shall I wear?"

"Oh come as you are, there'll only be you and me."

★ ★ ★

A MAN goes into the local deli and asks for a pound of German sausage. The shopkeeper is just about to place it in the slicing machine when the man shouts, "Don't do that... my arse isn't a money box, you know!"

★ ★ ★

AFTER travelling for some hours, the motorist realised he was completely lost, so it was with a sigh of relief that he saw a little village nestling in the valley. Arriving on the main street, he knocked at the door of the first house.

"Excuse me, sir, can you tell me the name of this village?"

"Of course, you're in Little Poofsville."

"That's a strange name. Why's it called that?"

"I don't know, I'll just call the wife. Hey, Bob, why's it....?"

★ ★ ★

IT was very late at night when the man pulled up at the only hotel in town and asked for a room.

"I'm sorry, sir, all the rooms are taken, there's a county fair here tomorrow."

Horrified at the thought of having to travel further, he pleaded with the man for somewhere to stay.

"Well...," said the owner, "we do have a spare bed but it means you'll have to share a twin room with one of our local residents and he snores so badly you'll never get any sleep."

"Don't worry, I'll sort it," said the man and off to the room he went.

Next morning, the man came down to pay his bill, looking well rested.

"Everything alright, sir, you weren't disturbed too much?"

"Oh no, not at all. Before I went to sleep, I went over to the other man who was still awake, gave him a kiss on the forehead and wished him, 'Pleasant dreams darling.' He stayed awake all night watching me."

★ ★ ★

"DOCTOR, doctor, I think I might be gay," said the young man.

"What makes you think that?"

"My father was gay, my grandfather was gay, my two uncles and my older brother."
"Good gracious," said the doctor. "Is there no one in your family who likes women?"
"Yes, my sister does."

★ ★ ★

WHAT did one Lesbian say to the other?
Your face or mine.

★ ★ ★

WHAT do you call a lesbian dinosaur?
A lickalotapus.

★ ★ ★

A LESBIAN goes to the gynaecologist and after being examined, he says, "Well, this is meticulously well kept."
"Oh yes," she replies, "I have a woman in three times a week."

★ ★ ★

"DAD, now that I'm 15, can I wear a bra and suspender belt?"
"No, you can't, John."

★ ★ ★

IS a Lesbian a pansy without a stalk?

IN YOUR PROTECTION

A MAN goes into a chemist's and asks the lady assistant for a packet of condoms, but he's not sure what size he needs.

"That's no problem," replies the lady. "Just pop into the back where we have a board with a number of different holes and that way we'll know your size."

The man does as he's told and sticks his willy in the different holes, not knowing that each time he does so the lady assistant, hidden on the other side, is fondling him.

Eventually he discovers his size and returns to the shop.

"Did you find your size?" she asks.

"Oh, yes, but bugger the condoms, how much do you want for that board?" he replies.

★ ★ ★

THE local doctor was asked to give a talk on sex education to the girls at the local high school but, knowing his wife was a bit of a prude, told her he was speaking on hot-air ballooning.

Some days later the headmistress met the doctor's wife in the street.

"Please tell the doctor again how much we enjoyed his talk. I think the girls learnt a lot from him."

"Well, I am surprised," exclaimed the wife.

"As far as I know he's only done it twice and the second time he couldn't get it to rise properly."

★ ★ ★

HAVE you heard about the man who put a condom on inside out ... and went?

MY girlfriend is fanatical about practising safe sex. She even makes me use dental floss after it.

★ ★ ★

A YOUNG man out for a good time pops into the local chemist's to stock up. The shop is empty.
"Anyone there?" he shouts and from the back room comes the chemist's wife, a bitter and unhappy woman.
"Four French letters, please, Miss."
"Don't you Miss me," she replies.
"Oh, sorry, make that five then, please."

★ ★ ★

WHAT'S the difference between 365 days in a year and 365 condoms?
One's a good year and the other's a fucking good year.

★ ★ ★

WHAT does a man and a packet of condoms have in common?
They both come in three sizes; small, medium and liars.

TWO friends meet in casualty:
"Hello, John, how did you break your ankle?"
"I pulled out to avoid a child," he said angrily, "and fell off of the bloody bed."

★ ★ ★

A LOCAL nymphomaniac is out walking in the country when she spies two brothers harvesting the wheat. Now the two boys are ideal specimens of manhood but not very worldly.

"Hi boys, why don't you take a break from work and we can all have a good time. But you'll have to wear these condoms because I don't want to get pregnant."

The boys are entranced by her and immediately agree to anything she suggests.

A year goes by and one day one of the brothers says, "Our Jack, do you remember the time we met that girl in the cornfield?"

"I do that," he replied dreamily.

"Well, do you care if she gets pregnant?"

"No, not anymore."

"Nor me. Let's take these things off now."

⋆ ⋆ ⋆

CHEMIST to young man:
"Sir, I would recommend these condoms; they're guaranteed by the makers."
"Ah, but what if they break."
"Then sir, the guarantee runs out."

⋆ ⋆ ⋆

A MAN walked into a chemist's shop complaining angrily.

"I bought a gross of condoms here on Friday but it turned out to be only 130."

"I'm so very sorry, sir," apologised the chemist, and he immediately wrapped up another 14, saying sarcastically, "I hope it didn't spoil your weekend."

⋆ ⋆ ⋆

THE C.O. walks into a chemist's and enquires the price of a condom.

"Well, we don't usually sell them singly but it would be 30p," says the assistant.
"And how much would it cost for one to be repaired?"
"Oh sir, it wouldn't be worthwhile, there's so much work involved - it would cost at least £20."
The man leaves and returns the next day.
"I've had a word with the men, we'll buy a new one."

★ ★ ★

A MAN rang the vet in some distress.
"It's an emergency! My dog has swallowed a condom! What shall I do?"
"No need to get too alarmed, just keep him in and I'll get back to you at the end of surgery."
Half an hour later, the vet rang back. "How's it going?"
"Oh, it's alright now, we found another condom in my wife's handbag."

★ ★ ★

"WHAT'S wrong, Jack, you look a bit down in the dumps this morning. Is the wife giving you a lot of lip?"
"Dead right she is. She's just had a coil fitted - it picks up the local CB radio, so now I'm getting hassle at both ends!"

★ ★ ★

A NEW film is being premiered in London next week, about the dangers of having casual sex. It's called Germs of Endearment.

IN YOUR PURCHASING

I BOUGHT my girlfriend a fur coat. I said to her, "Your knickers are coming down." "No they're not" she said.
"Then that coat's going back!"

★ ★ ★

"IS it in?" he asked.
"Yes, it's lovely," she replied.
"Does it hurt?"
"Oh no."
"Good. These shoes are all the rage this year," replied the salesman.

★ ★ ★

A WOMAN tries on a low cut evening dress and asks the shop assistant for her opinion.
"Do you think it's a little too daring?"
The girl replies, "Have you got hair on your chest?"
"No."
"Then it's too much."

★ ★ ★

A MAN goes to the most exclusive shop in Mayfair to buy his wife some exquisite lingerie for their wedding anniversary.
The sales assistant shows him some outfits around £100 but he shakes his head saying, "No, it's got to be more sheer than that."

She then shows him an outfit at £150 but he insists on having something even more sheer. So eventually she brings out some lingerie at £400, extra, extra, sheer.

He takes the lingerie home and asks his wife to go and put it on so that he can see what it looks like. The wife, however, decides to play a trick on him. She is convinced that because it is so sheer he wouldn't be able to tell whether she was wearing it or not, and then she would go back to the shops and pocket the refund.

So she appears before him with nothing on.

"Well what do you think?" she says.

"Crikey!" he replies. "You'd think at that price they'd iron out the creases first."

★ ★ ★

A MAN went into the menswear department to return a pair of underpants and was served by a young girl.

"Why do you want to return the underpants sir?" she asked.

"Because, er.... they're not satisfactory," he mumbled in embarrassment.

"In what way?"

The young man was clearly at a loss as to what to say but suddenly a smile appeared on his face and he answered, "Miss, you know the Grand Hotel on Dalton Street?"

"Yes", she replied.

"And you know the ballroom underneath?"

"But there is no ballroom underneath."

"Exactly," said the man triumphantly, "and that's just what's wrong with these underpants."

★ ★ ★

A MAN went into a furniture shop to buy a dressing table. He saw one he liked and asked the price.

"That'll be £900," said the assistant.

"What!" gasped the man. "It's only small, why, it's only got two drawers."

"That may be so," said the assistant, "but it costs so much because it has special powers. Watch this."

The assistant went up to the dressing table and asked it how much money the man had in his pocket. The table started to move and knocked against the wall ten times.

"That's amazing," said the man, "I do have £10 in my pocket. I must have that dressing table."

The next day, the table is delivered just as the man's friend arrives. "That's a nice dressing table. Did it cost much?"

"Indeed it did, but that's because it has special powers. Here, let me show you." He thought for a moment and then said, "How much money has my wife got in her account?"

Suddenly, the dressing table went completely berserk, knocking into the wall time and time again. Open mouthed with shock, he croaked, "But how did she get all that money?"

Suddenly, the dressing table stopped moving, its legs fell apart and its drawers dropped out.

★ ★ ★

"OH no, not another hat? Where will I get the money to pay for it?"

"But sweetheart, you know I'm not nosey."

★ ★ ★

A WOMAN walks into a pet shop and asks the owner for some wasps.

"I'm sorry, Madam, we don't sell wasps in here."

"But you do," she insists.

"No, I think you're mistaken," replies the owner.

"Well, in that case, why have you got two in the window?"

★ ★ ★

A MAN walks into a shop and asks for a kipper tie.
"This is a clothes shop, not a café," comes the reply.

IN YOUR QUICK REPARTEE

"HOW do you say 'screw you' in agent talk?"
"Trust me."

★ ★ ★

WHAT is the first thing elephants do before they make love?
They remove their trunks.

★ ★ ★

"DRINK makes you look beautiful and very sexy."
"But I haven't been drinking."
"No, but I have."

★ ★ ★

AN ornithological meteorologist is a man who looks at birds
and can tell whether....

★ ★ ★

WHY doesn't Father Christmas have any children?
He only comes once a year and then it's down the chimney.

★ ★ ★

HAVE you ever had Chinese beer?
It doesn't get you drunk, but after a few pints you get the urge
to take your clothes off and iron them.

I WENT to this discussion group on premature ejaculation. In fact, I was five minutes early, but it was all over.

★ ★ ★

"YOU'VE got to hand it to Bob when it comes to petting."
"Why, is he that lazy?"

★ ★ ★

SHE was only an architect's daughter but she let the borough surveyor.

★ ★ ★

WHAT happens when you eat onions and beans?
Tear gas.

★ ★ ★

YOU know John, as soon as I get home I'm going to tear the wife's bra off - the elastic's killing me.

★ ★ ★

WHAT did the art critic say to the flasher?
"Well hung, sir, good show."

★ ★ ★

WHAT is the greatest test of courage?
Two cannibals having oral sex.

★ ★ ★

WHAT'S the difference between a virgin and a light bulb?
You can unscrew a light bulb.

★ ★ ★

THE man was so fat he used to rock himself to sleep trying to get up.

★ ★ ★

AND maybe the unluckiest person alive would be the man who
fell into a pool of tits and came up sucking his own thumb.

★ ★ ★

DO you know the definition of a hen-pecked man?
One who is sterile but daren't tell his pregnant wife.

★ ★ ★

WHAT'S pink and moist and split in the middle?
A grapefruit.

★ ★ ★

HE'S not only unlucky, he's also very short.
Yesterday he walked under a black cat.

★ ★ ★

I WISH I hadn't bought that cheap suit.
Yesterday I went out. It was only cloudy but it shrank three
inches.

★ ★ ★

WHY do bald men have holes in their pockets?
They like to run their hands through their hair.

★ ★ ★

DO you know why pubic hair is curly?
If it wasn't it would blind you.

★ ★ ★

HOW do you get rid of unwanted pubic hair?
Spit it out.

★ ★ ★

"HEY, Jack, what do you grow in your garden?"
"Tired."

★ ★ ★

WHAT do you call a man with a one inch willy?
Justin.

★ ★ ★

WHY is the Irish pound called the punt?
Because it rhymes with bank manager.

★ ★ ★

WHAT is a woman's belly button for?
It's somewhere to put your chewing gum on the way down.

★ ★ ★

IS it true that a man who goes to sleep with a sex problem on his mind will wake up in the morning with the answer in his hand?

★ ★ ★

I KNOW a man who has submarine hands.
You never know where they'll turn up next.

★ ★ ★

WHICH one is the odd one out?
Luncheon meat, soya bean or a vibrator?
Luncheon meat, because the other two are meat substitutes.

★ ★ ★

THERE'S one thing wrong with oral sex - the view.

★ ★ ★

A BRASSIERE is a device for making mountains out of mole-hills.

★ ★ ★

A LADY is a woman who doesn't smoke or drink and only swears when it slips out.

★ ★ ★

HE was so lazy he preferred masturbation to regular sex because he didn't have to get up in the middle of the night to drive his hand home.

WHAT do video games and Men Only have in common?
They both improve hand-to-eye co-ordination.

★ ★ ★

WHY do men prefer big tits and tight pussies?
Because they have big mouths and little willies.

★ ★ ★

WHAT does an ugly girl put behind her ears to make her more attractive?
Her legs.

★ ★ ★

WHAT'S the definition of indefinitely?
When your balls are bouncing off her arse, that's when you're in - definitely.

★ ★ ★

HAVE you noticed the difference between men and women when they fill the car up with petrol?
The men always give the hose a few shakes when they're finished.

★ ★ ★

WHAT do you get when you turn three blondes upside down?
Two brunettes.

★ ★ ★

WHAT do you say to a girl who can suck a marble through a hose pipe?
Will you marry me?

WHY is a nymphomaniac like a door knob?
Everyone gets a turn.

★ ★ ★

WHAT have ugly girls and mopeds got in common?
They're both fun to ride as long as no one sees you.

★ ★ ★

WHY is virginity like a balloon?
One prick and it's gone.

★ ★ ★

WHAT did the fat woman say to the fat man?
Thanks for the tip.

★ ★ ★

DISAPPOINTED party agent to friend a week before the General Election.
"I'm having trouble getting my member in."
"Oh dear," replied friend. "Have you tried Vaseline?"

★ ★ ★

WHAT are the two words men don't like to hear?
'Stop' and 'don't.'

★ ★ ★

DID you hear about the girl who went out with the undertaker?
He only wanted her for her body.

ADAM came first.
But then men always do.

★ ★ ★

**HAVE you heard about the man who's so lazy, instead of tak-
ing his teeth out at night he sleeps in a six inches glass of
water?**

★ ★ ★

WHAT do you do if a bird shits on your car?
Never take her out again.

★ ★ ★

HOW do you know if a man's a bachelor?
He comes to work every morning from a different direction.

★ ★ ★

WHAT is the difference between men and Opal Fruits?
Men don't come in four refreshing fruit flavours.

★ ★ ★

DID you hear about the girl who came second in a beauty contest?
She was the only entrant.

★ ★ ★

OFFICE boy to new secretary:
"You may use my dictaphone."
"No thanks, I'll use my finger, just like everyone else."

WHAT'S the similarity between nymphomaniacs and turtles?
When they're on their backs, they're screwed.

★ ★ ★

WHAT lives in a hole and only comes out for food and sex?
Your tongue.

★ ★ ★

WHAT'S the difference between a skunk and an estate agent
both lying dead in the middle of the road?
There are skid marks in front of the skunk.

★ ★ ★

WHY are men like snowfalls?
You don't know when they're coming, how many inches you'll get
or how long they'll stay.

★ ★ ★

OLD proverb:
A regularly serviced relationship is like a car.
It'll give you trouble-free rides for many years.

★ ★ ★

AND don't forget - if you shake it more than three times, you're
playing with it.

★ ★ ★

HAVE you noticed how cars only break down on the way home
and never when you're going to work?

WHAT'S the difference between a nymphomaniac and butter?
Butter is difficult to spread.

★ ★ ★

WHAT'S the similarity between cabbage and pubic hair?
You push them both to one side and continue eating.

★ ★ ★

DO you know why it's called sex?
Because it's easier to spell than Ahhhhm ooohmm, uggghh, eeeeee....

★ ★ ★

DID you hear about the unhappy atheist?
He had no one to talk to during orgasm.

★ ★ ★

WHAT'S pink and hard first thing in the morning?
The Financial Times crossword.

★ ★ ★

WHAT do you get if you cross a rooster with a disobedient dog?
A cock that doesn't come!

★ ★ ★

DID you hear about the nymphomaniac who when asked how many husbands she'd had, replied, "Shall I count my own?"

DID you hear about the poor old spinster who dreamt she'd got married but when she woke up there was nothing in it?

★　★　★

HAVE you heard about the 'good time' girl in the newsagent's? When asked by the man if she kept stationery she replied, "I do up to the last ten seconds and then I go absolutely mad."

★　★　★

DID you hear about the miserly man who enjoyed being constipated?
He hated to part with anything.

★　★　★

THE man was so unlucky - one day when he approached a prostitute she said she had a headache.

★　★　★

DO you know there are only two kinds of people who know how to govern this country?
Hairdressers and taxi drivers.

★　★　★

WHY can't you be an estate agent if you've been circumcised? You have to be a complete prick to be an estate agent.

★　★　★

WHAT'S the definition of natural dental floss?
Pubic hair.

WHY is sex with an SAS man so unsatisfactory?
He slips in and out unnoticed.

★ ★ ★

WHAT'S the difference between a bumpy road and Marilyn Monroe?
One knackers your tyres....

★ ★ ★

WHAT do you get if you cross a nymphomaniac with a dictionary?
A fucking know-it-all.

★ ★ ★

DID you hear about the man who had five dicks?
His trousers fitted like a glove.

★ ★ ★

HOW many fish do you get in a pair of tights?
Two soles, two eels and a wet plaice.

★ ★ ★

DID you hear about the drug addict?
He started on heroin, went onto curry, progressed to madras, then vindaloo, and now he's in a Korma!

★ ★ ★

WHY do MP's wives always get on top?
Because MP's always fuck up.

WHY does a poor butcher remind you of a poor example of manhood?
Neither of them have any meat worth bothering about.

★ ★ ★

WHAT'S the similarity between Guy Fawkes and a 'poor excuse for a man'?
They both have a limp fuse when it comes to a blow job.

★ ★ ★

WHAT'S the similarity between a man and a stamp?
One lick and they stick to you.

★ ★ ★

WHAT'S the similarity between a Hepatitis B injection and sex with a useless man?
A quick, short prick in the bum and it's all over.

★ ★ ★

WHAT'S seven inches long and buzzes?
A mobile telephone.

★ ★ ★

DID you know? The last person to catch AIDS is a wanker.

★ ★ ★

WHAT'S the difference between Ohh.. and Agh?
Four inches.

DID you hear about the lady who had trouble getting up in the mornings?
She had a velcro nightdress.

★ ★ ★

WHAT is the similarity between your dick and a Rubik's cube?
The longer you play with it, the harder it gets.

★ ★ ★

WHAT do you get if you merge Xerox with Wurlitzer?
A company that makes reproductive organs.

★ ★ ★

WHAT'S the similarity between a bank account and sex?
After a withdrawal you lose interest.

★ ★ ★

DID you hear about Bob?
He lost his Christmas list, so he has no idea who his friends are.

★ ★ ★

A MAN goes up to a girl he fancies and says, "Excuse me, but I don't think your hand and my leg have been introduced."

★ ★ ★

WHY do women rub their eyes when they get out of bed in the morning?
They don't have balls to scratch.

WHAT'S better than roses on your piano?
Tulips on your organ.

★　★　★

AND don't forget - Vaseline makes the coming easy, and the going back.

★　★　★

WHAT'S the similarity between a soldier and a carthorse?
One darts into the fray and the other ....

★　★　★

WHAT'S got four legs and an arm?
A rotweiler.

IN YOUR RIP

IT was Bob's funeral. His wife and three children were sitting in the front row listening to the vicar as he spoke enthusiastically about the man's life.

"He was a wonderful father, a hard-working man and a great asset to the community ...."

At this point, the widow suddenly jumped up flustered and shooed her children out of the door.

"Oh dear, I think I must have got the wrong time, this can't be Bob's funeral."

★ ★ ★

THE devil tells a man who's just arrived in hell that he must choose one of three doors to enter and in the room beyond he will spend eternity.

The man is very worried that he will choose the wrong door so eventually persuades the devil to let him have a quick look behind the doors before making his choice.

Behind the first door he sees everyone standing on their head on a wooden floor. He doesn't fancy doing that for eternity but the second door is even worse. Everyone is standing on their head on a stone floor. However in the third room everyone is standing around drinking tea, ankle deep in manure. Oh well, thought the man, at least I'm not standing on my head, so he tells the devil his choice is room 3.

He goes into room 3 and just as the door slams shut behind him he hears the devil shout out, "OK everyone, break's over! Get back on your heads."

TWO neighbours, one upright and a pillar of the church, the other a drinker and fornicator. Eventually the wicked one dies from his excesses, a few years later the other one dies goes up to heaven and is astonished to see the wicked one with a large barrel of beer and a naked angel on his lap. The upright man is outraged and complains to St. Peter.

"I denied myself all the good things in life so that I could come to heaven and when I get here I see him enjoying himself when he should be in hell."

"Don't worry, he is in hell. The barrel's got a hole in it and the angel hasn't."

★ ★ ★

A WOMAN returns from her husband's cremation and tips his ashes onto the kitchen table. She then says to them, "You see this beautiful fur coat which I always asked for and never got. Well, I've bought it myself. And you see this pearl necklace I always longed for. Well, I've bought that too. And you see these exclusive leather boots, the one's I always wanted - I've also bought these."

Then she stands up, leans over the table and blows all her husband's ashes on the floor saying, "And this is the blow job you always wanted and never got."

★ ★ ★

DID you hear about the suicide club that held a special meeting? It was the only one.

★ ★ ★

A MAN was up before the judge accused of making love to his wife after she died. In his defence the husband said he didn't know she was dead, she had been like that for years.

DID you hear about the wife who couldn't afford a headstone for her husband ? She left his head out.

★ ★ ★

TWO men are walking through a graveyard when they stop to read the writing on one of the headstones which says, "Not dead, just sleeping."
One man turns to the other and says, "He ain't fooling nobody, only himself."

★ ★ ★

"I'M sorry to hear you buried Jack yesterday," said the neighbour. "Had to," replied Joan. "He was dead, you know."

★ ★ ★

A MAN goes to a fortune teller because he fears he's going to die.
"Don't be silly," replies Gypsy Rose. "You'll live till the ripe old age of 95."
"But I am 95," he replies.
"There, you see, I'm always right."

★ ★ ★

DID you hear about 'good time Sal'?
When she died they had to bury her in a Y-shaped coffin.

★ ★ ★

THREE nuns at the pearly gates were being questioned by St. Peter before being allowed to enter.

He said to the first nun, "Who was the first man?"
"Adam" she replied, the gates opened and in she went.
To the second nun he asked, "What was the name of the first woman?"
"Eve," came the reply and in she went.
Then to the third he said, "What were the first words spoken by Eve to Adam?"
"Wow, that's a hard one!" replied the nun and at that the gates opened and she disappeared inside.

★ ★ ★

DID you hear about the woman who wore black garters?
To commemorate those who passed beyond.

★ ★ ★

A WOMAN died, went to heaven and asked if she could be reunited with her husband.
"What's his name?" asked the angel.
"Smith."
"Oh dear, we have thousands of Smiths. Is there anything you can tell me about him that would make him easier to find?"
"Well, not really," she replied, "except that he did say just before he died that if I was unfaithful to him, he'd turn in his grave."
"Ah yes, said the angel. "You'll be wanting revolving Smith."

★ ★ ★

A MAN died with a full erection and no matter how hard the undertakers tried to put the coffin lid down, it would not close. Eventually they rang up the wife and told her their problem.
"I'll tell you what to do" she said. "Cut it off and stick it up his backside."

The day of the funeral came and as the wife passed the open coffin she looked down at the pained expression on his face and hissed, "There you are you bugger, you wouldn't believe me when I said it hurts."

★ ★ ★

A NEW group of men had arrived in heaven and were told to get into two lines. One was for henpecked men, the other for independent, liberated men. However, only one man stood in this second line and when asked why, he replied, "Because my wife told me I had to."

★ ★ ★

A MAN arrived in heaven and had to answer a few questions before he was allowed to stay.
"Have you ever done anything good in your life?" asked the angel.
"Well, um... I once gave a blind beggar 5p."
"Anything else?"
"I put 15p in the charity box when they were collecting for the local hospital."
At this the angel turned to the gatekeeper and said, "Give him his 20p back and tell him to go to hell."

★ ★ ★

AN estate agent named Bill Strange was making out his will and one of the instructions he put in was to have his gravestone inscribed with the words"Here lies a truthful man."
"But they won't know who it is," replied the lawyer.
"Oh yes, they will," he smiled, "When people pass by and read the headstone they'll say, 'That's strange!'

THE husband was dying and called his wife, three strapping sons and one small son to his bedside. He beckoned his wife to come closer and said, "I've not got long to go. Please tell me, is that small lad really my son?"

"Yes John, with my hand on my heart, he really is."

At that the husband passed away and the wife sighed with relief, "Thank goodness he didn't ask about the other three."

★　★　★

A LAWYER and the Pope die on the same day and arrive in heaven together. St. Peter takes the Pope to his room which is quite small, poorly furnished and only has a skylight. He then takes the lawyer to his quarters, which are 5-star in comfort and outside is his own swimming pool set in landscaped gardens.

"Wow, I can't believe it!" he gasps. "Why have I got this when the Pope has so little?"

"It's like this; we have many popes up here and it gets a little boring, but we've never had a lawyer before."

★　★　★

AT the funeral of his wife, Bob was absolutely distraught, his hands over his eyes, moaning and crying. The vicar thought he'd better go and comfort the poor man, so went over, put his arms around his shoulders and said, "Come on Bobby, time will help heal the loss and who knows, maybe one day you'll meet someone new."

"So what?" cried Bob. "But where will I get a fuck tonight?"

★　★　★

TWO men arrive at the gates of heaven together and get asked

some questions by the gatekeeper.

"Right, Mr White. I see from your records that you've lived an exemplary life. You've done a lot for your community, you've been a good husband and a loving father. Just one question, have you ever been unfaithful?"

"Never," replied the man.

"In that case, I grant you a BMW and free petrol to get you around heaven."

The gatekeeper then turned to the second man.

"Well, Mr Black. I see you've not had a bad life, you've been good to your parents, you've worked hard and lived fairly modestly, but just one question, have you ever been unfaithful?"

Mr Black had to admit that he'd been unfaithful on four occasions.

"In that case, I grant you a mini for your transport around heaven."

Some days went by and the two men happened to meet up. Mr White was sitting dejectedly at the wheel of his car.

"What's wrong?" asked Mr Black. "You've got a lovely car, free petrol, why are you looking so down in the mouth?"

He replied, sadly, "I've just seen my wife riding around on a bicycle."

★ ★ ★

AN old couple in their eighties die and both go to heaven on the same day where they are met by one of the angels.

After signing in, the couple are shown to their new house. It is magnificent - wonderful views, plush interior, all mod cons and push button controls, plus a limousine in the garage outside. The old man turns to his wife and says, "Bloody hell, Flo, if you hadn't made us stop smoking, we'd have been here enjoying this years ago."

ONE of the world's best wicket keepers had just taken his place on the field when he was struck by a bolt of lightning and died instantly. When he got to heaven he was met by St Peter, who showed him to his new quarters saying,
"If you look out of your back window, you'll see our cricket pitch being prepared for a very important game tomorrow against Hell. It would make us winners of the ashes."
"That's amazing," said the wicket keeper. "I didn't know there was cricket up here."
"Of course, why do you think we sent for you!"

⋆ ⋆ ⋆

A WOMAN asked her friend at work if she would look after her budgie while she was away on holiday. Unfortunately, the bird was quite old and died within a couple of days. Arriving back at work, the woman asked how her budgie was and her friend replied bluntly, "It's dead, dropped off its perch and that was that."
The poor woman collapsed in floods of tears. "You could have broken it more gently to me, you could have said one minute he was singing his heart out and then all of a sudden he lay quietly down and went to sleep with a smile on his face. At least I could have imagined he died happy. Anyway, I bet my mum next door was sad to hear the news as well."
"Yes, the day after it happened she was singing merrily in the garden when all of a sudden...."

⋆ ⋆ ⋆

FLO goes along to the local seance to try and get in touch with her late husband.
She's in luck and it's not long before she's asking him how he spends his time in heaven.
"Well, I get up in the morning, have something to eat, do a bit

of bonking, take a nap, have something to eat, do a bit more
bonking, go for a walk, eat, bonk, eat again and then go to
bed," he said.

"But, Alf, you were never like that down here," said Flo, quite
amazed.

"No, but I wasn't a rabbit then."

⋆ ⋆ ⋆

"DOCTOR, doctor, was the operation successful?"

"Sorry, I'm not the doctor, I'm the Angel Gabriel."

⋆ ⋆ ⋆

THE funeral was halfway through when the vicar got up to
talk.

"Come on, someone must have something nice to say about our
departed brother" he said.

Silence.

"He must have done something good during his life, can't anyone remember?"

Still there was silence.

"Perhaps he once helped an old lady across the street.... or put
some money in a collecting box. Come on, someone say something," he pleaded.

All of a sudden, a man stood up at the back and said, "His
brother was worse!"

⋆ ⋆ ⋆

AN old fellow in Yorkshire died of a bad chest and on the day of
the funeral, they got him into the coffin and took him up to the
cemetery at the top of the hill. Unfortunately, just as they got there
the hearse doors opened and the coffin slipped out back down the

hill, across the main road and smashed through the door of the chemist's shop. It hit the counter and the top burst open.

"What's going on?" asked the lady in the shop.

The old man in the coffin sat up and said, "Can you give something to stop me coughing?"

★ ★ ★

THE Chairman of a leading travel agency dies and finds himself sitting alone on a cloud. Along comes an angel and says, "Hello, we're having trouble deciding where you should go, whether it should be heaven or hell. So we've decided you can choose for yourself from these brochures."

The angel gives the man some brochures containing pictures and descriptions of both places. Heaven looks very nice and peaceful with lots of lovely scenery and people sitting around reading or listening to music. Hell looks a lot more lively. Scantily clad girls are frolicking in pools, there are pictures of tables sagging under the weight of sumptuous food, there's dancing, drinking and generally 'a good time' feel. It doesn't take long for the Chairman to decide he'd like to go to hell and with that he's whisked away. A month goes by and the angel happens to be passing Hell's gateway when he sees the Chairman chained to a rock with a pair of bellows in his hand, frantically keeping the flames of Hell burning. He spots the angel and says bitterly, "This is nothing like I thought it was going to be."

"Ah well," said the angel. "You of all people should know better than to believe all it says in the brochures."

IN YOUR SIMPLICITY

"HA, ha," laughed the simpleton. "I've just found out that Jack pays my wife £50 to sleep with him I get it for free."

★ ★ ★

DID you hear about the simpleton who thought oral sex was just talking about it?

★ ★ ★

THIS Irishman's car broke down and the garage mechanic said, "Yeah, shit in the carburettor."
"How often do I have to do that?", replied the Irishman.

★ ★ ★

TWO Irishmen on a train. One turns to the other and says, "I'm sure that fella over there is the Pope."
"Holy Mary," said his mate, "It can't be, go and find out."

★ ★ ★

THE first Irishman goes over to the man and says, "Are you the Pope?"
"Fuck off!" came the reply.
The man went back to his mate.
"He won't say."

★ ★ ★

AN Englishman, a Scotsman and an Irishman were all sentenced to be guillotined. The Englishman was asked if he would like to face upwards to the blade or down to the earth. He said he would prefer to look down. The knife descended but stuck an inch from his neck, so under the law of the country, he was reprieved.

Next came the Scotsman. He said he wasn't afraid to see what was coming and would look upwards. Again the knife stuck and he was reprieved.

Lastly came the Irishman who said he too was not afraid to see what was coming and he would look upwards.

Just as the knife was to be released he shouted, "Stop, bejeezers - I think I can see what the trouble is here."

★ ★ ★

WHEN a peasant is caught stealing onions he is given a choice between paying 100 rupees, receiving 100 lashes, or eating 100 onions.

He chooses the onions but after eating 20, his eyes streaming, he asks for the lashes. But after 20 lashes he finds it too painful and pays the fine.

When he gets home, he tells his wife, "I really cheated them this time. I only ate a few onions, received only a few lashes and delayed the fine as long as I could."

★ ★ ★

HAVE you heard about the Irish jellyfish?
It set.

★ ★ ★

AN Englishman, an Irishman and a Scotsman were walking down

the street when they got stopped by a mugger.

"Hand over your money and valuables or I'll inject you with AIDS."

Immediately, the Englishman and Scotsman did as he asked but the Irishman said, "Bloody hell, no, inject away."

The mugger injected him and then ran away.

The other two looked aghast at the Irishman.

"Don't you realise what you've done?"

The Irishman smiled, "It's alright, I'm wearing a condom."

★　★　★

TWO simple brothers talking on the village green. One says to the other, "Eh John, have you heard about the new pub in Dunscombe Bottom? You buy one drink and then all your drinks are bought for you for the rest of the night. Then when the pub closes you go out the back and they give you sex all night long."

The other looks at him with eyes popping.

"Are you sure you've got it right our John?"

"Oh ay," he says "The whole thing happened to our sister the other night."

★　★　★

DID you hear about the simple-minded tennis player who negotiated a £12 million contract? £12 a year for a million years.

★　★　★

"EXCUSE me, are you game?" asked the simple minded man on his first hunt in Africa.

"Sure am," said the naked woman lying on the ground.

So he shot her.

A NAIVE young girl went to work in a broom factory but after a couple of months handed her notice in.

"What's the matter?" asked the foreman. "I thought you were happy here."

"Oh I am, but it must be something to do with handling all the bristles because I've now got hair growing between my legs."

The foreman told her it was just a natural development which happened to everyone but she didn't seem too convinced so he took her aside, dropped his trousers and said, "See, it happened to me just like it happens to everyone."

"Oh no!" she gasped. "It's even worse than I thought, you've started to grow the broom handle."

★ ★ ★

ANOTHER man had a thin, grumpy old wife who made his life hell. So he took advice from his friend who said he should get into training and have sex with her for three hours every night.

"She'll never be able to take it and within a month she'll be dead."

Two weeks later, the two men met up again and the husband was in an awful state. He'd aged dramatically, trembled and walked like an old man.

"How's your wife?" asked the friend. "Well, she may have put on weight and she may look happier, but the last laugh's on me. She doesn't know, but I do that she's only another two weeks to live."

★ ★ ★

A SIMPLE man was pacing up and down in the maternity ward waiting for his wife to deliver their baby when out came the nurse to give him the good news.

"Congratulations, you are now the father of beautiful twins."

"Oh no", he replied. "She's been unfaithful, how could she!"

"What do you mean?" asked the nurse.

"Well, I only had my way with her once, so one of them's not mine."

★ ★ ★

A COUPLE got married but had no knowledge of sex, so they went along to the doctor to ask him to show them how.

The doctor agreed, asked the woman to strip off, got on top of her and made love. When it was over he turned to the man and said, "That's what sex is. Do you understand now?"

"Yes, thank you," replied the man, "and how often do I have to bring her in to see you?"

★ ★ ★

THREE men, two friends and a naive hillbilly, were on top of the World Trade Centre in New York. They were bemoaning the fact that it was so cloudy there wasn't much of a view. One of the friends turned to the hillbilly and said, "I bet you didn't know that when you're up this high these very thick clouds are so solid that if you jump on one you bounce right back up."

"You're having me on?" said the hillbilly. "No, I'm not. Watch this," and the man jumped off the building, landed on the cloud and bounced back again.

The Hillbilly was amazed.

"Look, I'll show you again." And he repeated the action.

Now convinced, the hillbilly decided to have a go himself. He jumped off the building went straight through the clouds and landed on the pavement below. Never to rise again.

The other friend turned to his mate and said, "You know Superman, sometimes you can be a real wanker."

A SIMPLE man was walking down the street when he got pushed into an alley and mugged by two masked men. The man put up a terrific fight but was eventually pinned to the ground.

All the muggers got was some small change.

"Why did you put up such a fight if this is all you've got?" they asked, amazed.

"Oh no," said the man, "I thought you were after the £200 I've got hidden in my sock."

★ ★ ★

A COUPLE are sitting on the pier in the midday sun when a sea-gull flies over and splatters the top of the man's head.

"Just a moment, I've got some tissue paper here," says the wife.

"Don't be silly Marge, it'll be miles away by now."

★ ★ ★

A RATHER simple man was stopped by the traffic police when they saw him driving a brand new, top-of-the-range BMW.

"Pull over, get out!" shouted the policeman. I don't believe this is your car, so until you tell me whose it is, you won't move." And he drew a chalk circle around the man saying, "Don't step out of that circle."

The man remained still but didn't say a word.

"Right, if you're not going to speak I will damage this car."

With that he kicked in the indicator lights, but the man did not speak.

"OK, if you won't tell me the owner of this car, I'll do even more damage."

The policeman slashed the tyres, but still nothing was said, the man just grinned.

Seeing this, the policeman got more and more enraged and

went completely berserk. He ripped out the seats, smashed the dashboard and pulled off the mirrors. Instead of making the man talk, it made him laugh. Beside himself with fury, the policeman shunted the car until it ran off the road into a tree. It was a complete write-off. By this time the man was in hysterics.

"If you're laughing like that, I know it can't be your car, now tell me whose it is." demanded the policeman.

The man spoke.

"I'm not laughing because of the car. I'm laughing because every time you turn round, I jump out of the circle."

★ ★ ★

A RATHER naive girl and a cocky young man find themselves waiting at the same bus stop. After some time, they strike up a conversation and he tells her that he works on the local community radio - he does the request show.

"Oh how wonderful!" said the young girl, very impressed. "I would do anything to wish my parents a happy anniversary on the radio."

"Anything?" asks the young man with a gleam in his eye.

"Oh yes," she replies.

So with that he takes her behind the bus stop and whips out his ever increasing member. As soon as she sees it she grabs it with both hands saying "Hi Mum, Hi Dad, Happy anniversary from...."

★ ★ ★

MILES out in the middle of nowhere, a motorist suddenly finds himself faced with a fast flowing stream across the road. Uncertain of what to do he notices an old simpleton sitting on a gate watching him.

"Will it be alright if I take my car through the water?" he shouts.

"Ay, no problem" comes the reply.

However, halfway across, the water comes seeping in through the windows and the car stalls.

"I thought you said it would be alright!" yells the angry man.

"Ay" replies the old simpleton, scratching his head. "'Twas all right yesterday when we took the ducks across, it only came up halfway on them."

★ ★ ★

TWO couples go on their honeymoon together and on the first night the men have a last drink in the bar before going upstairs.

"Let's have a small bet," suggests Bill. "Let's see who can make love to their wife more, and we'll tell each other in the morning."

Jack agrees and next morning at breakfast he tells Bob he made love four times.

"That's nothing!" replies Bob. "I made love 22 times."

Jack is flabbergasted, but determined to do better.

"OK," he says, "double or nothing."

The next morning, they meet up and Jack is looking knackered.

"It's no good. After six times we couldn't do anymore, the wife's had to stay in bed this morning."

Bob laughs and replies. "Well, I did it 35 times last night."

"I can't believe it," says Jack, "how do you manage it?"

"Easy, I'll show you. I put my hips back, like this, and then quickly forward - that's one - then I put my hips back and push forward again - that's two.... ....."

★ ★ ★

A YOUNG girl, naive to the ways of the world, became a nun but after a year she confessed to the Mother Superior that she was pregnant.

"Why, you foolish girl! Who is this man?"

"Oh Reverend Mother, it's not a man; it's an angel."

"Then you're even more stupid than I gave you credit for."

"Oh, but it's true. When I asked him what his name was he said St Michael and showed me the name tag on his underwear."

★ ★ ★

THE hostess was making a last minute inspection of the dining table before her guests arrived.

"Dodds," she called to her waitress. "For goodness sake, don't forget the sugar tongs. You know what men are like. They go to the toilet, fiddle with their 'you know what', forget to wash their hands and then, alas, handle the sugar lumps."

Halfway through the evening, the hostess called over Dodds again.

"I thought I told you to put out the sugar tongs?"

"But I did Madam."

"Well, I can't see them here."

"Of course not, I put them in the loo."

★ ★ ★

A BLOKE goes into the local DIY store and orders 20,000 bricks.

"May I ask what you're building?" says the storekeeper.

"Yes, it's a barbecue."

"Gosh, that seems a lot of bricks for one barbecue."

"Not really; we live on the 18th floor."

★ ★ ★

DID you hear about the simpleton who stood before the mirror with his eyes closed?

He wanted to see what he looked like when he was asleep.

★ ★ ★

"HEY Jack, I've just been reading in the paper about this bisexuality. What do you think?"
"Yeah, why not, if you can afford it?"

★ ★ ★

TWO drunks came staggering out of London Zoo, their clothes in tatters and their hands and faces covered in blood.
"That's the last time I try lion dancing," said one to the other.

★ ★ ★

THE Antiques Roadshow was coming to the Welsh borders and all the local people were busy looking out any family heir-looms. Simple Sam had lived in one of the outlying villages all his life, and so had his father and grandfather before him.
"I bet you'll have something in the attic that's been there for years. Why don't you go and see?" said Sam's next door neigh-bour.
"Ay, I'll do that," said Sam.
On the day of the show, many people queued up, carrying all sorts of items and amongst them was Sam dragging a very heavy item wrapped up in brown paper. When it got to his turn, a lot of people took an interest in this mysterious package so it was with bated breath that they waited for it to be unwrapped. Gasps of astonishment went up from the gather-ing crowd as the expert turned to Sam and said, "You say you found this in the attic?"
"Ay, I did that. It must be very old, I knows it was there when my grandpapa was alive."

"Well, yes, it would have been," said the expert, "it's the water tank."

⋆ ⋆ ⋆

DID you hear about the yachtsman who took a naive young girl aboard his boat and asked her to toss him off?
They're still searching the waters for any sign of him.

⋆ ⋆ ⋆

A YOUNG couple were picnicking in the woods and as they ate they also fed the birds, squirrels and any other inquisitive animals that came to see what was going on. When they'd finished they lay out on the grass and soon fell asleep. What a surprise they got on waking, to see a man sitting on the ground nearby. He told them he had been one of the squirrels they had thrown some crumbs to and that showing such kindness to him had broken a wicked spell and he had been restored to human form. He continued to explain that as a thank you for setting him free, he had three wishes, one for each of them. What two wishes would the couple like?
The husband and wife thought about it for a few moments and then told him that their first wish would be to win the jackpot and the second to become famous Hollywood stars.
"OK," said the man, "your wishes have been granted. Now it's my turn."
He turned to the husband and said, "My wish is to have sex with your wife."
The couple had to agree and after an hour of continuous bonking they lay back exhausted. Then the man turned to the woman and said, "How old is your husband?"
"Thirty five" she replied.
"My goodness, he's a bit old to still believe in magic wishes."

"How dare you ask me if I've been to bed with anyone, that's my business."

"Oh sorry" said the young man. "I didn't know that's what you did for a living."

★ ★ ★

A TOUGH-LOOKING cowboy walked into the saloon, had three shots of whisky and then left. A moment later he returned and shouted.

"Whichever bastard has taken my horse, better return it in five minutes or I'll do the same thing here as I did in Tucson."

Five minutes passed and when he went back outside the horse had been returned.

"Hold on a moment," said the barman, following him out. "What did happen in Tucson?"

"I had to travel on foot."

★ ★ ★

A MAN who had lived all his life up in the hills was finally re-housed in a small cottage closer to civilisation. A couple of days after he had moved in a council worker stopped him in the street and asked how it was going.

"Not bad," he admitted, "but I can't get the hang of this strange contraption in the bathroom - a tank thing with a chain."

"Oh it's quite simple, you just pull the chain and the water flows."

A few days later, they met up again.

"Everything alright?" he was asked.

"Not really; as soon as I tried to wash most of the water had disappeared."

★ ★ ★

OUT walking one day, a young but 'experienced' girl came upon a youth masturbating by putting his willy between two pieces of best frying steak.

"Hey, my lovely, come home with me and I'll show you what it's all about," she murmured.

So the youth went back to her house and up to the bedroom, where she stripped off, parted her legs and said, "Now you put it in here."

"What, both pieces!" he said.

★ ★ ★

A ROUGH, slovenly looking woman had fallen on such bad times it looked as if she would have to abandon her six children. But fortunately, a woman who lived nearby and who was renowned for her kindly deeds saved the family by finding a place for them to live and alerting the welfare services so they could help her get back on her feet. It wasn't much but they survived. And then 18 months later the slovenly old hag turned up on the woman's doorstep three months pregnant.

"My goodness," said the woman. "What on earth were you thinking of - you can barely feed and clothe the children you've already got. Whose is it?"

"It's the next door neighbours," she said sadly. "I was just so flattered that he asked me."

★ ★ ★

A MAN in a Rolls Royce stops to buy petrol. Putting his hand in his pocket for the money to pay, he brings out a couple of golf tees.

"What are those for?" asks the garage attendant.

"These are to put your balls on when you're driving off."

"Cor blimey, these Rolls Royce people think of everything."

★ ★ ★

A MAN went to the doctors to have a medical for joining the services.

"Just go behind the screen and strip off" said the doctor. "I'll be with you in a moment."

After he had examined the man he told him that he was in excellent condition.

"There's just one thing that's quite remarkable. Your penis is like a corkscrew."

"Oh yes" said the man "I've only just recently realised why that is so, it's my mother's fault."

"Really, that's an odd thing to say."

"When I was small there was only the two of us. I didn't have a dad, and my mum didn't like to talk about certain things so I never knew that when you went to the toilet you shook it dry, not wringed it out."

IN YOUR SPORT

THE steward at the local cross-country race asked one of the competitors what time he pulled out.

"I didn't," replied the runner," and now I'm really worried."

★   ★   ★

A WORLD class gymnast, away from home at an athletics meeting, spends a night of passion with one of her fellow athletes. On returning home she's overcome with guilt and goes off to confession. When the priest gives her absolution she's so relieved she comes out of church doing handstands and double somersaults just as Mrs O'Neil is going in.

"Oh no," murmurs the woman.

"What a day to do that as the penance and me with no knickers on."

★   ★   ★

MY girlfriend is a real athlete.

Always ready to play ball with me.

★   ★   ★

JACK had just played a gruelling game of tennis down at his local club when he looked at his watch and realised he was going to be late for his mother's cocktail party.

"Damn," he muttered to himself as he hastily changed and rushed off home forgetting about the two tennis balls that he'd put in his pocket.

In fact he didn't realise anything was wrong until he started getting very odd looks from a lovely young girl.

Blushing madly, he stammered, "Oh er... they're just my tennis balls."

"Golly," she replied. "I bet that's even more painful than tennis elbow."

⋆ ⋆ ⋆

A DEVOUT church woman happened to see a scruffy looking man sitting on a park bench and as she went past him she pressed £5 into the palm of his hand, saying, "Have faith, young man, have faith."

Two days later, she walked through the park again and sitting on the bench was the same scruffy man. When he saw her his eyes lit up and he ran to meet her.

"Here you are, Ma'am, Have Faith came in at 10-1", and with that he stuck a wad of notes in her hand.

⋆ ⋆ ⋆

TWO blokes meet up on the river bank to do a day's fishing. One turns to the other and says, "Haven't seen you around for a while; have you been away?"

"Yes," says the man looking glum, "I've been on my honeymoon."

"Congratulations. Is she pretty, your wife?"

"No, she's plug ugly, she can't cook and she's bad in bed."

"Then why on earth did you marry her?"

"She's got worms."

⋆ ⋆ ⋆

DID you hear about the world's worst boxer?

He had advertising on the bottom of his boots. He eventually gave up when he saw a face in the third row that he recognised and after two minutes realised it was his own!

CRICKET

THREE cricket managers meet up to talk over the previous cricket season and as they are strolling back to their hotel they notice a sign saying 'Come and find out what the future has in store for you - Speak now to Mystical May.' They've had a bit to drink, so decide to go in and have some fun.

"We'd like to know if God's a cricket fan, and if so, can he tell us how our teams will do in the future?" says one of them, winking at the other two.

But Mystical May takes them very seriously and asks them which teams they manage and what they want to ask.

The first says, "When will Somerset win a major trophy?"

After a moment's silence, a loud voice is heard: "2040."

"Damn, I'll have gone by then."

The second man asks the same question for Lancashire and the voice says, "2038."

"Oh no, I won't be here either."

Then the third man, one of the England Selectors, asks, "When will England win the Ashes"

This time, there is an even longer silence before the voice booms out. "Bloody hell, I won't be around either."

★ ★ ★

A MAN found himself hurtling to earth after his parachute failed to open. Thinking this was the end, he was suddenly amazed to see a group of men standing in a circle shouting to him, "Don't worry, you'll be alright, we'll catch you!"

Unable to believe his luck, he was just about to relax when looking down again he realised they were the English cricket team.

★ ★ ★

HE was the laziest boy in the class. Only yesterday, the children were asked to produce an account of a cricket match. All the others spent an hour writing while he took 30 seconds. When the teacher saw it later she read, "Rain stopped play."

★ ★ ★

A VERY famous cricketer who could play right-handed or left-handed was asked how he decided which way to play that day. The man explained.
"If my wife is lying on her left side, I play left-handed and if she's lying on her right side, then I play right-handed."
"Ah, but what if she's lying on her back?"
"In that case, I ring up and tell them I'll be late that morning."

★ ★ ★

A PASSER by happened to see a coffin being brought out of the church, with a cricket bat and pads on it's lid. He turned to one of the mourners and said, "Like his cricket did he?"
"He still does, he's straight off to a match after this, once they've burned his wife."

★ ★ ★

DID you hear about the fanatical cricket fan?
On the day his pregnant wife was rushed to hospital he was to be found in the waiting room listening to the test match on a Walkman. Suddenly, his anxious mother in-law arrived and asked

him for the latest news.

"It's going well," he replied enthusiastically. "They've got five out and there's only two to go."

At that she fainted.

FOOTBALL

WHY are football managers like nappies?
They're always on someone's arse and full of crap.

★   ★   ★

THIS Glasgow Celtic fan was such a fanatic even the house was painted green and white.

His wife said, "I'm pissed off, you think more of Rangers than you do me."

"Christ Almighty, woman," he said, "I think more of fucking Rangers than I do you."

★   ★   ★

WHAT do the fans on the football terraces of Borussia Munchengladbach dread to hear?
Someone stand up and shout, "Give us a B."

★   ★   ★

A BLOCK of flats is on fire and a woman with a baby is trapped on the eighth floor. She is leaning out of the window, screaming for help.

Below her on the pavement, the crowd are urging her to throw down the baby, saying they will catch it, but she is afraid it might be dropped. Then along comes a world-famous goalkeeper who persuades her that the baby will be safe in his hands. So at last convinced all will be well she throws down the baby and to much cheering and clapping he catches the baby .... bounces it twice and boots it up the street.

★ ★ ★

ON holiday, Bob was amazed when he went to see the local football team and halfway through the match they all suddenly stood stock-still except one, who put the ball behind his back.
"What's going on?" he asked the supporter next to him.
"They're just posing for this week's 'Spot The Ball' competition."

★ ★ ★

DID you hear about the disappointed nymphomaniac?
She volunteered to put up some of the men from the visiting football club. Six of them should have arrived after the match but one called Dix injured himself during the game and had to go to hospital.
On hearing the doorbell, she opened the door and greeted them enthusiastically.
"So how many do I get?" she said. "There are five of us here without Dix," they replied.
And she slammed the door in their faces.

★ ★ ★

A PROFESSIONAL footballer was out on a first date and after the pubs closed he invited her back to his place. Removing his jacket, she noticed UMBRO tattooed on both arms and he explained it was part of an advertising campaign

and he received £1,000 for each arm. When he saw how impressed she was he removed his shirt and there across his chest was the word PUMA.

"I got £1,500 for this," he said. "And £800 each for these" and he dropped his trousers to show the word KAPPA tattooed on both ankles.

"But this is the best," he laughed and with that he showed her his penis.

"Oh" she exclaimed. "Why SLAG?"

"No, no" he replied, "I got £8,000 for this and if you stay around a while you'll see it says SLAZENGER."

★ ★ ★

WHO says girls can't make the football team?
Suzie did! She's so athletic, she'll play ball with anyone.

★ ★ ★

"I'M transferring you to North Nogoland," said the boss to his salesman.

"But, sir, all you ever get there are whores and footballers."

"My wife comes from there!"

"Really, what position did she play?"

★ ★ ★

"FOOTBALL, football, football! I'm sick of it. If you took me out on Saturday afternoon instead of going to the match I think I'd die of shock."

"Now, now, dear" said her husband. "It's no good trying to bribe me."

★ ★ ★

DID you hear about the two football managers of a local derby? They promised their players a pint of beer for every goal scored. The result was 50-49.

★ ★ ★

IT was the women's football league final and a large crowd had turned out to watch. But 10 minutes into the game, the goalkeeper was thrown against the post and knocked to the ground. Immediately, all the linesmen and officials rushed over to give her help but after five minutes and no sign of recovery, the referee walked over to find out what was going on.

"We're trying to give her the kiss of life," explained one of the officials, "but she keeps trying to get up and walk away."

★ ★ ★

"HEY ref, are you blind or what?" shouted a very angry man in the crowd as he saw another player on the opposing team get away with a foul. The ref walked over to the heckler and shouted, "What did you say?"

"Bloody hell," replied the man, "he's deaf as well."

★ ★ ★

DID you hear what happened when two men went to watch the worst football team in the league? When they handed over £10 and asked for "Two, please", the ticket seller replied, "What will that be, defence, midfielders or strikers?"

★ ★ ★

A MAN walks into the local pub with a parrot on his shoulder to watch England playing Brazil on Sky Sports. The match soon starts to go Brazil's way and after 10 minutes they score from a free kick. All of a sudden, the parrot starts to make awful moaning noises.

"Sorry," says the man, "he's a fanatical England supporter, so he's obviously quite upset."

The score remains the same until half-time but Brazil score a second goal only 5 minutes into the second half. This time the parrot is besides himself with anguish - moaning, stomping up and down and burying his head in his feathers. When a third Brazilian goal is scored, there's absolute chaos. The bird starts pulling out all his feathers until there is a pile of them on the floor.

"Heavens" says the barman, "if he reacts so frantically when they lose, what's he like when they win?"

"I don't know, I've only had him a year."

★ ★ ★

"NOW, listen son, we can't afford for you to get injured before the Cup match next week, so I'll put you on for the first 45 minutes and pull you off at half-time."

"Wow, thanks Boss, all I got at my old club was a slice of orange at half time."

GOLF

"WHAT happened to you?" exclaimed his mates, as Jack walked into the bar with a black eye.

"I got it playing golf," he said rather sheepishly, "and before you ask, it wasn't a golf ball it was a club."

Laughing into their beer, his mates insisted on hearing the full story.

"Well, I hit a bad shot and my golf ball landed in a field of

cows. When I went to retrieve it, one of the women golfers was in there also looking for a lost ball. Luckily I found mine quite quickly and was about to leave when I noticed one of the cows frantically flipping its tail. I walked over, lifted the cow's tail and saw a golf ball wedged in its crack. So I called the lady over, raised the tail and said, "'This looks like yours'.
That's when she hit me with the club."

★ ★ ★

ANGRY wife to husband:
"You were twice as long on the golf course today. Why's that?"
"A slight problem," replied the husband.
"Old Jack died on the ninth hole and from then on in it was play the hole, drag Jack, play the hole, drag Jack, play the ....."

★ ★ ★

AN Englishman, Scotsman and Arab were talking about their families.
"I have 10 children" said the Englishman. "One more, and I'll have my own football team."
"I have 14 children. One more, and I'll have my own rugby team." replied the Scotsman.
"Well, I have 17 wives," said the Arab. "One more and I'll have my own golf course."

★ ★ ★

TWO men were playing golf on the eighth hole when a funeral procession went by. One of the men stopped playing, put down his club and bowed his head.
The other said, "That was very decent of you."
"Well she was a good wife to me you know," replied the first.

FOR more than six months a woman had been having golf lessons but still couldn't hit the ball more than a few yards down the fairway.

Unable to take it any longer, her coach shouted, "You're not holding the club properly. Hold it like you hold your husband's willy."

So the woman did and the ball flew through the air landing on the green.

"That's terrific," said the stunned coach. "You can take the club out of your mouth now."

★ ★ ★

DID you hear about the world's worst golfer?

He stood on a rake and yelled, "That was the best two balls I've hit today."

★ ★ ★

A YOUNG couple meet on holiday and after a whirlwind romance decide to get married.

"I must warn you," says the man, "that I'm golf crazy. I like to play everyday, you'll hardly ever see me."

"Don't worry," she says. "I have something to confess as well. I'm a hooker."

"That's OK," he says. "You're probably not keeping your wrists straight."

★ ★ ★

IT was competition day at the local golf club and the retired colonel found himself paired up with the bishop.

They set off and it wasn't long before the colonel forgot who he was playing with and on missing a short putt exclaimed, "Bugger, I missed!"

The bishop shook his head reproachfully.

A little later, the same happened again, and the colonel missed an easy putt.

"Bugger, I missed!" he shouted loudly, at which point the bishop was forced to tell him that the Almighty would not be pleased with his language and that something dreadful might happen to him.

But almost immediately on the next hole the Colonel missed his drive and was so incensed he shouted and swore for a good half minute.

All of a sudden the skies opened, there was a terrible clap of thunder, and lightning struck the Bishop dead.

After a short pause a voice was heard from above,

"Bugger, I missed!"

★ ★ ★

EACH week the vicar and retired colonel played a round of golf and no matter how well he did, the vicar was never able to beat him. After one very close defeat the colonel turned to him and said, "Don't worry Vicar, you win in the end. You'll be burying me in the not too distant future."

"That's true," said the vicar dispiritedly. "But even then it's your hole."

★ ★ ★

A GROUP of men, who were very competitive when it came to golf, were arguing on the ninth tee. When the Captain arrived and asked what was wrong they replied.

"See my partner Bob over there lying in the bunker? He's just died of a stroke and these buggers want to add it to my score."

★ ★ ★

COLIN Moanalot was drinking in the club bar and complaining about his morning's golf.

"I only hit four balls properly this morning," he moaned.
"Ay," came a voice from the other end of the bar, **"and two of those were when you stepped on the garden rake."**

★ ★ ★

IT was the honeymoon night and the happy couple strip off as quickly as possible and jump into bed. But just before they start, she whispers to him,

"Before we start, I feel I must tell you that one of my previous lovers was the Captain of our local golf club."

"Listen love," he replies "Whatever went on before doesn't matter; we're married now so let's get down to it."

And for the next 30 minutes they vigorously do the business. Afterwards the husband lights a cigarette and picks up the phone.

"What are you doing?" she asks.

"I'm going to get us some smoked salmon and pink champagne - we deserve it," he says smiling.

"Oh no," she says, "the Captain of the golf club would have made love to me again."

So once again they have 30 minutes of unbridled passion and then once again he calls for room service.

"No, no," she cries, "he would have done it a third time."

Again, they do it but by this time the husband is feeling knackered. He reaches for the phone and before she can say anything, he says wearily, "I'm just ringing the golf Captain to find out what the par for the hole is."

★ ★ ★

"MOLLY, would you get married again if I died?" asked her **husband.**

"Probably," she replied.

"And would you share with him all the little things we did together?"

"I expect so," she said.

"And would you let him have my prize golf clubs?"

"Oh no," she replied, "he's left handed."

★ ★ ★

A LOCAL golf club was being built for the less well off in the district and it was agreed that the women's team would practise once the men had finished and they would share the same equipment. That night, once the men had gone, the ladies walked out to the first hole when they suddenly heard an anguished voice behind them.

"Hold on," shouted Doreen. "I've got the clubs but the men have gone home and taken their balls with them!"

★ ★ ★

AN old man knocked at the door of the solicitors' offices and asked one of the partners if his grandson, an articled clerk, could have the afternoon off to accompany him to the last day of the Open at Wentworth.

"I'm afraid you're out of luck. He's taken the afternoon off to go to your funeral" came the reply.

★ ★ ★

EVERY Sunday afternoon when her husband was away on the local golf course, the wife would entertain her lover on the sofa. The two were humping away so passionately one afternoon that they didn't notice how bad the weather had got until they heard her husband walking up the garden path. In blind panic, the man jumped off and hid behind the sofa as he walked in.

"Couldn't play in that weather," he complained. "Can't see a yard in front of you" And with that he settled down to read the newspaper. An hour passed and the man behind the sofa had such bad cramp he couldn't take it any more. He stood up, picked up the husband's clubs and strode confidently to the door remarking, "Bloody weather, you didn't happen to see a ball coming this way?" And with that, he was gone.

★ ★ ★

THE local golf club was having an 'Open Day' to attract new members and one man from the wrong side of town asked the official, "Is this where the changing rooms are at?"
"My dear, sir, you do not finish a sentence with a proposition, I'll have you know."
"OK, by me" replied the man. "Is this where the changing rooms are at, fuck face?"

★ ★ ★

A MAN joined the local golf club and before taking a walk round the greens, he decided to have a couple of drinks in the bar. When he tried to pay he was told,
"That's alright Sir, it's on the house for new members."
He then decided to have lunch and again they refused his money.
Feeling well pleased with himself, the new member decided he'd have a go at a few practice shots so he went too the club shop for some golf balls.
"That'll be £5 each - £30 please Sir."
"Goodness" commented the man, "they've got you by the balls round here."

★ ★ ★

"MY doctor has told me I must give up golf."
"Oh, I see he's played with you too!"

FOR a whole week, the golfing instructor has been giving lessons to a new female member of the club and at the end of the session he invites her out for a drink. She accepts and they go off into town. After a couple of drinks, he invites her to dinner, then to a club and finally back to his place.

"Look, Ron," she says as they sit close together on his sofa, "I think I ought to tell you that I'm not really a woman, I'm a transvestite."

"Why you awful, you dreadful, you... you... immoral..."

"Come on, Ron, we are living in a more tolerant society."

"But it's unforgivable. You've been playing off the women's tee all week!"

★ ★ ★

ON his tour of the world's best golf courses, a man ends up on a course in Africa. As he sets off for the first hole, he is accompanied by a caddie who carries a shotgun.

"Surely we don't need that," he says.

"Believe me, we do," replies the caddie.

All goes well until they get to the 7th hole and the man's tee shot lands in the bunker. As he steps into the sand a huge cobra suddenly looms up and as quick as a flash, the caddie aims his gun and shoots the snake dead.

"Bloody hell, I see what you mean," says the golfer, sweating profusely.

Then at the 12th hole, the ball lands in the rough and as the golfer goes over to hit it, a lion appears unexpectedly. Again, the caddie immediately takes aim and frightens the lion off with a gun blast. The rest of the holes are played without interruption but on the 18th the golfer finds he's hit the ball close to the water. As he steps up to take the shot a crocodile rears up out of the lake and grabs hold of him.

"Quick man, do something!" he yells at the caddie.

"Sorry, sir, I can't give you a shot at this hole."

IN YOUR STATE OF HEALTH

DID you hear about the woman who went to the doctor for exhaustion and was told to stay out of bed for a few days?

★ ★ ★

WHEN they buried Jack the hypochondriac, the words on his headstone read, "There, you see - I told you I was ill."

★ ★ ★

OLD Jack hadn't been feeling too well but had to go out to collect his pension. All went well until he set off for home when suddenly he felt an eruption in his stomach and knew he had to get to the toilet as soon as possible. He wasn't too far from the public toilets, which was lucky really because all hell was about to break loose. He raced into the cubicle backwards to save time, pulling his trousers down as he did, sat down and relaxed .... But as he looked down, he saw two pairs of shoes.

"Bugger me!" he cursed, jumping up quickly. "Sorry mate, I didn't see you there, I didn't mean to shit all over you, it was an emergency."

"Oh that's quite alright," replied the man. "It's a good thing I saw you coming and pulled your trousers up before you sat down."

★ ★ ★

"ALCOHOL is a dreadful thing," said Bob. "It's bad for the health. Do you know, it killed my first wife?"
"No, how dreadful!" said Fred. "Alcoholic was she?"

"Oh no, I came home pissed and shot her."

★ ★ ★

A FITNESS fanatic was doing his regular 100 press-ups in the park when along came a drunk. After watching him for a few moments the drunk doubled over in hysterics.
"What are you laughing at?" demanded the man.
"See here, mister, I don't want to upset you but somebody's stolen your gal."

★ ★ ★

WITH a few hours to kill before the pubs open a man limps into a faith healing meeting and finds a seat on the front row. After the 30-minute service, the faith healer comes down from the platform and starts to touch some of the people. To the first one he puts his hands over the woman's eyes and she jumps up shouting, "I can see, I can see!"
He then lays his hands on a man who cannot walk and to everyone's delight he gets up out of his wheelchair and begins to dance. And so it goes on, people are being healed left, right and centre. Suddenly, the healer is standing in front of the newcomer and is just about to put out his hands when he shouts, "No, no, don't touch me! I've waited weeks for the orange disability stickers for my car, and they only came this morning."

★ ★ ★

A MAN went into the chemist's shop to see if they had anything for a permanent erection. He felt highly embarrassed when he realised the shop was owned by two women but it was too late to walk out, so he said, "I've got this permanent erection, it won't go down and I wondered what you could give me for it."

"Just one moment, sir" and the two women went to the back of the shop to confer.

They came back smiling.

"We can offer you the shop and £100 in cash."

★ ★ ★

A WOMAN was so dreadfully upset about being flat-chested that she travelled to deepest Africa to see a witch doctor. When she told him of her plight he gave her a simple spell to make and told her that when she returned home her boobs would grow every time a man said 'Pardon' to her.

A few days later, she was shopping in the High Street when a man came up to her and said, "Pardon me, Miss, could you tell me the way to the Post Office?"

After she had directed him she noticed with delight that her boobs had grown an inch. The following week she was coming out of the bank when a man bumped into her.

"Pardon me, Miss," he said.

Again her boobs grew an inch and she was very pleased with the way things were turning out.

The next night, she and her mates went for an Indian and as the waiter was serving up their meal, he tripped and dropped some madras curry on her clothes.

"Oh Miss, I am so sorry, a thousand pardons to you."

Sadly the restaurant was cleared due to an obstruction.

★ ★ ★

AN old spinster, ill in bed and not wearing her glasses, was visited by what she thought was the vicar. After he had gone she said to her next-door neighbour,

"Wasn't it nice of the vicar to come visiting?"

"That wasn't the vicar, it was the doctor."

"Oh dear," replied the spinster downheartedly. I thought he was rather familiar."

★ ★ ★

DID you hear about the alcoholic who was staggering home with a bottle of whisky in his pocket?
He slipped over and feeling something wet running down his leg, prayed to God it was blood.

★ ★ ★

DID you hear about the hypochondriac who received a Valentine's Card and thought it must be from his cardiologist?

★ ★ ★

HOW do patients in a burns unit pick their noses?
From a catalogue.

★ ★ ★

DID you hear about the unlucky man who had a wet dream and had to go to the VD clinic?

★ ★ ★

DO you know how Alcoholics Anonymous practises Russian Roulette?
They pass round six glasses of tonic water - but one of them is a gin and tonic.

★ ★ ★

THERE'S one definite way of giving a person amnesia.
Lend them money.

A LONDON man had an awful time last week when he didn't realise the difference between fixative and laxative.
His teeth have been stuck on the lavatory for three days.

★ ★ ★

DID you hear about the gynaecologist who papered his hall through the front door letter box?

IN YOUR HOSPITAL WARD

"HEY, haven't we met somewhere before?"
"Yes, I'm the nurse at the VD clinic."

★ ★ ★

YOUNG nurse in nurses' home knocks on matron's door while she's having a bath.
"Yes, who is it?" asks the matron.
 "I have Mr Thompson to see you."
"Come, come nurse", responds matron. "I'm naked in the bath."
The nurse continues, "Mr Thompson, the blind man."
"OK, bring him in" says matron.
The door opens and the nurse and Mr Thompson enter the bathroom. Looking at the matron, Mr Thompson says, "Fair pair of tits matron. Now where do you want these blinds?"

★ ★ ★

SAID the plain nurse to the pretty nurse, "When I gave the man in bed five a bed-bath yesterday, I noticed he had LUDO tattooed on his er.. thing."
"That's not LUDO" replied the pretty nurse. "That's Llandudno."

A YOUNG nurse is walking along the corridor with one of her boobs hanging out of her uniform. Matron appears and on seeing this is outraged. She asks for an immediate explanation. The nurse, with a resigned air, replies, "Sorry, Matron, it's these young house doctors. They never put anything back where they found it."

★ ★ ★

TALK about the cutbacks in the NHS!
One hospital has just installed coin operated bed pans.

★ ★ ★

TWO nurses locked out of the nurses home late at night, shinned up the drainpipe and in through an open window. The first nurse turned to her friend and said, "Doing this makes me feel like a burglar."
"And me" said the second, "but where will we find two burglars at this time of night!"

★ ★ ★

A WOMAN is visiting her sick aunt in hospital and as she's leaving, she notices a ward completely enclosed by glass.
"Excuse me, nurse, what's that for?" she asks.
"That's the Isolation Ward. The man in there has got distemper, the plague, hepatitis and AIDS."
As they look, they see a man going towards the glass pushing a trolley.
"Is that his lunch?"
"Yes, he has Ryvita, After-eight chocolates and dried sheets of lasagna."
"Goodness, will that make him better?"
"No," replied the nurse, "but it's the only thing that we can slide under the door."

AN unscrupulous young man decided to embarrass the new student nurse so when she came round to make his bed, he asked, "Excuse me nurse, where does a woman's hair grow blackest and thickest and curliest?"

The poor nurse turned scarlet and went off to find the Sister.

A little later, Sister came over to the young man's bed and said, "Mr Jenkins, I hear you've been upsetting one of our nurses. Just exactly what did you say to her?"

"All I asked was where does a woman's hair grow blackest, thickest and curliest, Sister?"

"Indeed, and where might that be?" she said, glaring at him.

"Why, in Africa of course."

★ ★ ★

"DOCTOR, we have had to buy three new operating tables this month alone. Will you please try not to cut so deeply?"

IN YOUR ORGAN EXCHANGE

SHE must be the unluckiest person in the world.

She's just had a kidney transplant from a bed wetter.

★ ★ ★

A VERY rich young man, hearing about the amazing advances in body part transplants, decided he would like a new brain. He went to the specialist to find out what was on offer.

"Well, at the moment we have a computer analyst for £10,000; a university professor for £15,000 and a high court judge for £20,000."

"Money is no object" said the young man.

"Tell me, what is the best and most expensive brain you have?"

"Well,"said the specialist, "We do have an MP's on offer at £50,000."

"I don't understand, why is that so much more expensive?"

"That's simple," said the specialist. "It's hardly ever used."

★ ★ ★

A MAN went into hospital to have a penis transplant, having lost his own in an industrial accident. After the operation, he immediately asked the surgeon how it went.

"Well," hesitated the surgeon, "mixed results really. The transplant was a success. I think you'll agree it's an impressive member, but unfortunately your hand has rejected it."

IN YOUR PSYCOTHERAPY

A WORRIED wife sent her rugby-mad husband to see a psychiatrist. What she didn't know was that the psychiatrist was also a fanatical supporter of the game.

"Now Mr Owen, let's try some word association. What do you think of if I describe something as smooth, curvy and sometimes difficult to handle?"

"A rugby ball," came the reply.

"Good. Now what about the act of coming up behind someone who is bending down and putting your arms round their waist?"

"A scrum."

"Excellent. And lastly - firm, athletic thighs?"

"A top class rugby player."

"Well, Mr Owen, I can see no problem there. Your reactions are absolutely normal considering some of the silly answers I get in here."

"HELLO, is this the right number for the Downside Psychiatric Hospital?"

"That's right."

"May I speak to the man in Room Four?"

"I'm sorry, sir, there is no man in Room Four."

"Hooray, I've escaped, I'm free."

★　★　★

A MAN walks into a bar, orders a pint, drinks it and then wets himself, leaving a puddle all over the floor. The landlord is livid but the man is so embarrassed and so apologetic, he allows him to stay. But after another pint the man does it again - pisses all down his leg. That's it, the landlord throws him out of the pub, telling him never to come back.

A month later, however, he sees the man walk through the door.

"You're banned" he bellows across the room and the poor man is so embarrassed he rushes out sobbing. Six months go by and one lunchtime the same man appears again.

"Hold on landlord, everything's sorted out now, it was a nervous affliction."

"Well, OK" says the landlord who could see that the man had changed, and he serves him a pint of beer. No sooner had he drunk it than he weed all down his leg onto the carpet.

"You bloody twat' roars the landlord. You told me you had it sorted."

"I do" smiles the man. "I went to a psychiatrist and he has taught me not to be embarrassed and upset about it. I'm quite confident now, in fact I feel proud."

★　★　★

"I THINK I know what's wrong with you," said the psychiatrist to his patient.

"You're feeling all screwed up."
"Yes, that's right, how did you know?" replied the patient. "Well, ever since you walked in, you've been trying to get into the waste paper basket."

★ ★ ★

DID you hear about the psychiatrist who was so busy, instead of a couch he used bunk beds?

★ ★ ★

A MAN goes to the psychiatrist. The psychiatrist says, "You're mad".
The man says, "I want a second opinion."
"OK," answers the psychiatrist. "You're ugly too."

★ ★ ★

A THERAPIST is trying to find out if there is any link between the number of times people have sex and the way they live their lives. He gathers together a group of people and asks, "How many have sex four times a week?"
Half the class put their hands up.
"How many have sex four times a month?"
Ten hands go up.
"Four times a year?"
Two hands go up.
"And once a year?"
Up pops a hand at the back of the group, belonging to a man who is jumping up and down and smiling all over his face."
"Well," says the therapist, "You're very happy considering you only have sex once a year."
"I am, I am," he cries, "and it's tonight."

A MAN goes to see a sex psychologist because he has a fetish about eggs.

"Just look at this, doc," he says, pulling an egg out of his jacket pocket.

"Look at these beautiful curves, the smoothness of the shell, the beautiful colour..."

The psychologist is amazed.

"Do you really believe all this?"

The man whispers quietly to him, "No, not really, but you've got to say these things if you want it to go to bed with you!"

IN YOUR SKIN GRAFTS

A PLASTIC surgeon was complaining to his colleague about one of his regular patients.

"I'm being sued by Cynthia Prighorse. I told her she was unwise to have so many facelifts."

"Why, what happened?" asked the colleague.

"She's got a beard."

★ ★ ★

A YOUNG man goes to a plastic surgeon because he's got a very small dick. The surgeon tells him he could be helped but it would mean implanting part of a baby elephant's trunk. The man agrees and the operation is a great success.

A few days later, he decides to celebrate and takes out an old girl-friend for a romantic meal to tell her how everything could be different between them now.

Suddenly, his new appendage flies out of his trousers, grabs a bread roll and disappears.

"Wow, that's quite a trick!" says the girl. "Do it again."

But the young man, with a pained look on his face, replies, "I'm not sure if my arse could stand another bread roll."

★ ★ ★

A WIFE'S face was so badly injured in an accident it required plastic surgery.

"We can do it," the surgeon said, "but it will cost you £2,000 and we will need to take skin off your backside."

The man agreed and the operation was a great success. His wife was even more beautiful. A few days later the plastic surgeon rang the husband to tell him he had paid £500 too much.

"Oh no," said the husband, "the extra is for the extra pleasure I get everytime I see my mother in law kiss my arse."

★ ★ ★

A FLAT chested woman tells her husband that she wants to go and see a plastic surgeon.

The husband replies, "Well, before you go, try this first. Rub some toilet paper on your nipples four or five times a day."

"Will that make my breasts get bigger?"

"Well, look what it did for your rear end."

★ ★ ★

A MAN went back to the plastic surgeon to complain about a new hand he had grafted on after his own hand had been smashed up in an accident.

"Well, it looks alright to me," said the plastic surgeon.

"It is most of the time. Trouble is you gave me a female hand and every time I go for a slash, it won't let go."

IN YOUR SPECIALIST'S CHAIR

A MAN went into the chiropodist's and, taking his dick out, laid it on the table.

"But that's not a foot," said the chiropodist.

"I know," the man said proudly, "but it's a great ten inches."

★ ★ ★

A MAN went to the optician's to replace his glasses, because the others were broken.

"But you only had a new pair last week," said the optician. "We can't just replace them like that, without a good explanation. What were you doing?"

"I was kissing my girlfriend," he said.

"Well, that shouldn't have broken them."

"She crossed her legs" he replied.

★ ★ ★

"YOU don't have to open your mouth that far, madam," said the dentist." I expect to stay outside while extracting your teeth."

★ ★ ★

A VERY nervous woman walked into the dental surgery, saying, "I'd rather have a baby than a tooth out."

The dentist replied, "I hope you're sure about that because I'll have to adjust the chair."

IN YOUR SPERM BANKS

A WOMAN goes to the doctor to tell him she wants a baby but she doesn't want a relationship with a man.

The doctor tells her it's no problem. Just take her clothes off, lie on the couch with legs wide apart and he'll go and get a bottle of semen.

However, coming back from the storeroom he catches sight of her on the table and is overcome by her beauty and stunning body. He leaves the bottle behind, drops his trousers around his ankles and comes back into the room saying, "Sorry, but we're out of bottles. You'll have to have draught."

★ ★ ★

THREE of the top scientists in the country decide for posterity to make a donation to the national sperm bank. The first goes in, the nurse does her business and out he comes. The second scientist goes in, again the nurse sees to him and out he comes. The third then goes in and the other two decide to take a peek, but when they pull the curtain aside they see the nurse on her knees giving him a blow job.

"Hey!" they cry out in dismay, "Why are you using your mouth when you only used your hands on us?"

"Ah," the nurse replies "but he's got private health insurance."

★ ★ ★

A MAN went to a sperm bank but found the whole atmosphere of the place made it impossible for him to perform. So he asked one of the young nurses who was new to the clinic if she would help him.

Some time later, he emerged with a very small sample and was asked by the doctor why he had been so long.

"Sorry, doc," he replied. "I would have been out sooner but it took ages to get your nurse to cough it back up."

★ ★ ★

OF all the sperm that lived in Jack's body, one was fitter and more active than the rest. It was determined that when the time came, it would fertilise the egg and make the woman pregnant.

Some time later, all the signs showed that the moment was coming and off they raced, the fittest one out front. But suddenly, it stopped dead, turned round and tried desperately to swim back the other way.

"What's wrong?" they shouted.

"Quick, get back! It's a blow job."

IN YOUR SURGERY

A WOMAN went to the doctor's because she was feeling tired and listless. He asked her to strip off and noticing she was somewhat overweight said, "Why don't you diet?"

She looked down and replied, "Do you think so? What colour do you suggest?"

★ ★ ★

MUM was so worried about the small size of her son's penis, she took him to the doctor. Knowing she would only be satisfied if he gave her son something for it, the doctor told her that marmite on toast would soon cure the problem. Next morning at breakfast there was a huge pile of marmite toast on the table.

"But mum, I can't eat all that," protested the son.

"Don't be daft," replied Mum. "Three are for you, the rest is for your father."

★ ★ ★

SHE told the doctor that every time she sneezed she experienced an orgasm.

"Are you taking anything for it?" he asked.
"Yes, pepper," she replied.

★ ★ ★

"MR Jones, you're health is very poor," said the doctor. "Try going on a healthier diet: eat more fruit".
"But, doctor, I have three cherries in every martini."

★ ★ ★

A GIRL goes to the doctor's because she's found two green marks on the inside of her thighs. After examining her, the doctor asks a few questions.
"You're not a prostitute, are you?"
"How dare you? No I am not," she says.
"Do you have a boyfriend?"
"I am engaged."
"Ah, would he happen to be a gypsy?"
"Yes, he is."
"Then just tell him that his earrings aren't real gold."

★ ★ ★

"DOCTOR, doctor, there's something wrong with me. I can't stop farting, but they don't smell."
"Really?" said the doctor, waving his hand in the air and opening a window. "I think you may need an operation."
"Oh no, on my insides?"
"No, on your nose."

★ ★ ★

"DOCTOR, doctor, I've got a penis growing on my forehead, what can I do?" said the distraught young man.

"I'm afraid there's not much that can be done, it would be too risky to surgically remove it."

"Does that mean that everytime I look in the mirror I'm going to see a penis staring back at me?"

"Well, er... no" said the doctor hesitatingly, as he didn't like giving bad news to his patients. "You won't see the penis because you'll have a pair of bollocks hanging over your eyes."

★ ★ ★

A MAN goes into the doctor's, takes his dick out and lays it on the table. After looking at it for a few minutes, the doctor says, "Well, it looks alright to me."
The man smiles, "Yes, it's good isn't it?"

★ ★ ★

THE doctor pointed to a jar on the shelf in his surgery and said, "I want you to fill that."

"What!" gasped the patient. "From here?"

★ ★ ★

"JUST go over to the window and stick your tongue out," said the doctor to his patient.
"Why?"
"Because I don't like the person who lives opposite."

★ ★ ★

A WOMAN goes into the doctor's surgery.

"Say aah" said the doctor. "Good, that seems alright, but what's with the postage stamp on your tongue?"

"So that's where I left it!"

THE doctor's trainee assistant was always getting things round the wrong way and it was hard to find jobs for her to do that she wouldn't cock up. One day a man arrived for a blood test. It seemed a straight-forward job, so he asked his assistant to do it for him. However after 30 minutes, she hadn't returned, so he went looking for her and on opening the door stopped dead in his tracks.
"You silly bitch!" he cried. "I said prick his finger."

★ ★ ★

A VERY small woman went to the doctor's complaining that her fanny was painful. After a complete examination, the puzzled doctor could find nothing wrong.
"Do you have this pain all the time?" he asked.
"No, only when it's wet outside."
"OK, well next time it's wet come and see me" he suggested.
The following week it had rained heavily and the woman appeared once more at the surgery. Again the doctor examined her and immediately discovered the problem.
"Just lie there a moment," he said, "while I find some scissors."
A moment later she sighed with relief.
"Oh doctor, the pain's gone. It's wonderful, what did you do?"
"Oh, quite simple really. I just trimmed an inch off the top of your wellingtons."

★ ★ ★

A MAN takes a girl back to his flat but after some heavy petting, he suddenly stops and says, "It's no good, I'm so frightened of getting AIDS, would you mind if I used my toe?"
She doesn't mind, so he sticks his toe up and she sits astride him.
A few days later, he notices something wrong with his toe, so he goes to the doctor.

"My goodness, I'm getting some odd cases at the moment," says the doctor. "You've got thrush on your toe and only yesterday I had a woman in who had athlete's foot in a most unusual place."

★ ★ ★

A MAN went to the doctor because he could not get an erection. Some weeks passed but none of the treatments worked so finally the doctor gave him an ancient remedy which involved injecting him in his member.
It was such a success that the man had a permanent erection, so he went back to the doctor to ask if it could be reduced.
"I'm sorry, it's impossible," said the doctor.
"But surely you can do something. All drugs have antidotes."
"I agree," said the doctor, "but this injection was not a drug. Just three of sand to one of cement!"

★ ★ ★

"IT'S incredible" said the doctor to the man.
"You're pregnant! This will make medical history."
"Oh no," said the man, "I'm not married. What will the neighbours say!"

★ ★ ★

A MAN went to the doctor's covered in blood and bruises.
"What happened?" asked the doctor.
"It's my wife; she had another nightmare."
"But surely she couldn't have done this."
"Listen doctor, when she shouted out, 'Get out quick, my husband's coming home!' Being only half awake, I jumped out of the window."

A WOMAN goes to the doctor feeling very unwell. He takes some tests and tells her to come back in a week for the results. The following week her husband comes to collect the results because she is too ill to leave the house.

"Her name is Jane Smith," he says.

Unfortunately, the doctor has two Jane Smiths on his books and tests for both of them have just come back.

"Oh dear," says the doctor, having read both results.

"Your wife either has VD or Alzheimer's disease."

"Oh no, what shall I do?" says the distraught husband.

The doctor replies, "Take her on a long journey changing trains and buses at least four times then leave her there and see if she finds her way home. If she does get back on her own, then don't fuck her!"

★ ★ ★

A MAN goes to his doctor because he has not been able to have an erection for five years. The doctor tells him that after such a long time the condition has become very serious and there's only one pill that can help. But beware, the pill is so powerful that once taken the man will have three huge erections and that will be it for the rest of his life. He also tells him that the pill is voice-activated and will only work when the man says, "Ding dong." Once the man has had his erection it will return to normal by saying, "Ding dong" again.

It's a hard decision to make, knowing that these three erections will be the last he ever has, but he reasons it's better than not at all, so he takes the pill.

On the way home, he starts to have doubts as to whether it works, so he decides to try it out.

"Ding dong" he says, and this huge todger comes hurtling out of his trousers.

"Blimey!" says the man and quickly says "Ding dong" to return back to normal.

Now full of anticipation, the man races home and crosses the road without looking properly.

"Ding dong" goes the ice cream van and once again this huge appendage appears, frightening the passers by.

"Ding dong" and it goes back to normal.

Thankfully he gets home without any mishap, knowing he's only got one left. He rushes into the house, pushes his beautiful, but frustrated wife to the floor, tears her clothes off and says, "Darling, darling, I love you so much, ding dong."

"What's the ding dong for?" asks his wife.

★ ★ ★

A MAN goes to the doctor and tells him he swallowed three 10p pieces four weeks ago.

"Can you get them out?" he asks.

The doctor looks at him puzzled.

"You swallowed the money four weeks ago and it's only now you're coming to see me?"

"That's right," replies the man. "I didn't need the money then."

★ ★ ★

THE man was so boring, when he masturbated, his hand fell asleep.

★ ★ ★

A MAN goes to the doctor with a most unusual complaint. His penis is so big it drags his vocal chords down and causes him to stutter. The doctor tells him he can be cured but it will mean an operation to take away eight inches from his very large member. The man agrees and the operation is a complete success. However some weeks go by and the man misses his extra long penis - after all, it made him quite a celebrity. So he goes back to the doctor to ask if it can be put back on.

"I'mmm sorrrry thaaat's nooot posssiible."

★ ★ ★

A WOMAN went to the doctor to tell him that every time she went to the toilet, pennies, Ten pence pieces and 50p pieces came out. "Don't worry," said the doctor. "You're just going through your change."

★ ★ ★

A MAN had over 100 dogs in his house. The doctor told him to stop whistling in his sleep.

★ ★ ★

A BUXOM young lady goes to the doctor and he asks her to undress. When she's completely naked, he starts to feel her thighs. "Do you know what I'm doing?" he asks.

"Yes, you're checking to see if there are any abnormalities."

Then he starts to fondle her breasts.

"Do you know what I'm doing now?"

"Yes, you're checking to see if there are any strange lumps."

Then the doctor lays her down on the table, jumps on top of her and starts making love.

"Now do you know what I'm doing?" he asks.

"Yes" she replies. "You're getting VD."

★ ★ ★

A WOMAN goes to the doctor to get her husband's test results, only to learn that he has a very serious illness and will be dead by the following morning. In a most terrible state of shock and crying uncontrollably, she returns home determined to make his last night on earth the best he's ever had. That night, she wears her sexiest black lacy underwear and makes love to him passionately for five hours without a break. The husband is over the moon at his wife's incredible performance and after an hour's rest asks her if they can do it again .. and again .. and again. Another two hours of lovemaking take place until the wife lies back completely exhausted.

"Just once more, please," begs the husband, and at that, the wife turns to him with a spark of anger.

"OK, OK, it's alright for you, you don't have to get up in the morning."

★ ★ ★

A MAN went to the doctor complaining of a severe migraine-type headache and constant ringing noises in his ears. After a very thorough examination, the doctor told him that his symptoms were caused by an infection in his testicles and the only cure was to have them removed.

The man was aghast at the news and insisted on a second, third and even fourth opinion, but all the doctors agreed that having his testicles removed was the only cure.

At first, the man thought he would try to live with his afflictions, but it became unbearable, so he agreed to the operation. A little later, on leaving hospital and feeling very low, he decided to pop into the local gentlemen's outfitters and cheer himself up by buying a new suit. The tailor took one look at him and said, "Yes, you'll need a 36" waist, a 35" inside leg and a 15" collar. Chest size is 44".

"That's amazing," said the man. "How do you know all that?"

"After 40 years in the trade I'm an expert at all men's size. For instance, I also know you take a size 11 shoe, an 8" hat and medium sized underpants."

"Absolutely spot on," replied the man, "except that I take a small size in underpants."

"Oh no, sir, no sir," said the tailor. "If you wear a small size in underpants it could make you sterile, you'd certainly suffer from severe headaches and ringing noises in your ears."

★ ★ ★

THE doctor told the old deaf man he needed a sample of his urine, a stool specimen and a sperm specimen.

"What's he saying?" said the old man to his wife.

"He wants you to leave your underpants here."

★ ★ ★

"YOU'VE got to cut down on your smoking, drinking and sex life, otherwise your heart is going to give out on you," said the doctor to his 70 year old patient.

"Only two cigarettes a day and one pint of beer."

"What about sex?" asked the man.

"Only with your wife," replied the doctor. "You mustn't get excited."

★ ★ ★

"DOCTOR, doctor, my balls have turned green."

"Well, you've heard of cauliflower ears.

Those are brothel sprouts."

★ ★ ★

"DOCTOR, every bone in my body hurts."

"Then be thankful you're not a kipper."

A DOCTOR is the only man who can tell a woman to take all her clothes off and then send her husband the bill.

★ ★ ★

I HAVE a great doctor. If you can't afford the operation, he touches up the x-rays.

★ ★ ★

A MAN goes to the doctor, upset because every night he has the same dream where two gorgeous women are trying to get into bed with him but he keeps pushing them away.
The doctor asks what the man would like him to do and the patient replies, "Break my arms."

★ ★ ★

THE old woman says to her next-door neighbour who she knows is suffering from piles, "Put some tea leaves up there. It's a good remedy."
So she does, but it's no better. In fact, it gets worse so she goes to the doctor. As she's bending over, she says to him, "Can you see anything?"
The doctor replies, "No, but you're going to meet a tall dark handsome man on Monday."

★ ★ ★

A MAN was asked to send a sample of his urine to the surgery before the doctor could complete his examination. Unfortunately, the man had to go to work, so asked the young boy next door to drop it in for him. On the way, however, the boy spilled most of it and fearing trouble, topped it up with a cow's in a nearby field. It wasn't long before the doctor called

for him to come to the surgery as soon as possible, and when he returned home later he was in a raging anger.

"So much for trying all your fancy positions," he said to his wife. "You would have to try on top, now I'm going to have a baby."

★ ★ ★

THE man said, "Every time I sneeze, I get a hard on."
His doctor said, "What do you take for it?"
"Pepper."

★ ★ ★

"I AM very sorry to say that I have two bad pieces of news for you," said the doctor to his patient.
"Oh dear, what is it?" asked the patient.
"You have only 24 hours to live," came the reply.
"Oh no, what other piece of bad news could there be?"
"I tried to get you on the phone all day yesterday."

★ ★ ★

A MAN went to the doctor complaining of a sharp pain in his willy.
"And what about sex?" asked the doctor, "How often do you perform?"
"About twice a week," he replied. "Does it burn after intercourse?"
"I don't know, doctor, I've never put a match to it."

★ ★ ★

A MAN went to the doctor and said he couldn't stop farting. It was dreadful. He just couldn't stop.

The doctor went away and came back with a huge long pole.
"Oh no," said the man.
"It's alright" replied the doctor, "I'm only going to open the window."

⋆ ⋆ ⋆

A YOUNG wife went to the doctor's complaining that her husband never made love to her. She wanted to know if it was her fault. After a complete examination, the doctor concluded it was not her - it must be her husband.
"Give him two of these pills every morning and by evening you should be happily satisfied. But let me know how it goes because these pills are still experimental."
Only one day had passed before she stormed back into the surgery.
"I am so angry," she said. "One minute we were sipping tea, the next moment he lunged at me, lifted my dress, pulled down my knickers and took me on the table there and then."
"But isn't that what you wanted?" puzzled the doctor.
"Yes, but not in the middle of the coffee shop; I'll never be able to show my face in there again."

⋆ ⋆ ⋆

"DOCTOR, I'm so overweight, I've tried hundreds of different diets but nothing seems to work. Can you help me?" asked the fat man.
The doctor gave him some pills and told him to come back in a month. This he did, having lost over a stone in weight.
"It's wonderful," said the man. "Every night I'd take a pill and then all night I dream of being stranded on this desert island with 20 beautiful girls, each one of them demanding sexual satisfaction. No wonder I've lost weight."
"That'll be £40 then," said the doctor and the man went away very happy.

Now this man had a friend, a miserly sort of fellow who was also having trouble losing weight so he was recommended to go along and see the same doctor and get similar treatment. However, after a month had gone by he returned in a very disgruntled mood even though he had lost a stone in weight as well.

"What's wrong, the pills have worked, haven't they" asked the doctor.

"Oh sure, every night when I went to sleep I dreamt I was in the jungle being chased by wild savages brandishing machetes. Every morning I was knackered. But how come I get this nightmare and my mate is surrounded by beautiful women?"

"Well what did you expect? You insisted you have it on the NHS." said the doctor.

★ ★ ★

"DOCTOR I want to get married but I think my cock's too small. What shall I do?"

He replied, "Go and stay down on the local farm, dip your cock in fresh milk every day and have it sucked by a calf."

Some weeks later, they met in the street and the doctor asked him how his marriage was going?

"Oh, I didn't bother in the end, I bought the calf."

★ ★ ★

DOCTOR to woman patient.

"You have acute appendicitis."

"Thank you, and you have a real neat bum," she replied.

★ ★ ★

A MIDDLE-AGED couple go to the doctor's and ask him if he

would mind watching them have sexual intercourse. It's an odd request, but the doctor agrees and charges them £40. They come back a second week and request the same thing even though the doctor tells them they're doing nothing wrong. However, they insist and he charges them another £40. After the third visit, the doctor asks them why they are doing this and the man replies,

"Well, she's married, so we can't go to her house. I live with my mother, so we can't go there, and the hotels are so expensive. But here I can get half the cost back on my private health insurance."

★ ★ ★

A MAN took his wife to the doctor's complaining about her sex drive. It was non-stop, whatever time of the day, whatever place, she was always hankering after sex.

"I'll see what I can do," said the doctor and he asked her to go into the consulting room and strip off. As soon as he started to examine her, she began to make little groaning noises, and tempt him forward with her open legs. It was too much for him and in no time at all he was astride her.

But all the noise attracted the attention of the husband waiting outside, so he opened the door to find out what was happening.

"What the hell's going on here?" he shouted.

"Oh er... nothing to worry about, I'm taking your wife's temperature" said the sweating doctor.

"Really?" said the man taking a flick knife out of his pocket. "When that thing comes out it better have numbers on it."

★ ★ ★

"DOCTOR, it's my husband, he thinks he's a chicken."

"Good gracious," replied the doctor. "Why didn't you tell me sooner?"

"Well, we needed the eggs."

IN YOUR STATE OF WEALTH

AN old spinster was walking home one night when she was accosted by a burglar.

"Hand over your money," he demanded.

She said she hadn't got any money, but he didn't believe her and started to search her. He frisked her up and down, put his hands inside her bra and also inside her pants. Satisfied there was no money he was just about to go when she said, "Hold on a minute. Keep trying. I can always write you a cheque."

★ ★ ★

A WOMAN rings her husband up at work to tell him she's won the jackpot on the lottery and that he'd better start packing.

"Darling that's wonderful" he shouts with glee.

"Where are we going?"

"I'm not bothered," she replied. "Just make sure you're gone by the time I get home."

★ ★ ★

A SMART talking man who thought he could charm the birds off the trees met his match one night. The man had just learned that his father only had days to live and then he would inherit over half a million pounds. Overjoyed at the promised wealth, he celebrated at the local wine bar, where he saw a ravishing long legged blonde. He couldn't wait to brag to her and indeed she was so interested in him, they went back to his house together. The next day she became his stepmother.

A GIRL went into the local police station to report a theft. "He stole £50 I had pinned inside my knickers," she said. "Did you put up a fight?" asked the policeman. "No," she replied. "I didn't know he was after my money."

★　★　★

BOB suggested to his wife that a good way to save money would be to put £1 in the money box every time they made love. A year went by and Bob decided to empty the money box and see how much money had been saved. He couldn't believe his eyes when he found not only £1 coins but lots of £5, £10 and £20 notes as well.

"How come we've got all these notes?" he asked amazed.

"Well, not everyone's as stingy as you," she retorted.

★　★　★

AS it was very windy outside, the lady held onto her hat and took no notice of the fact that her skirt was flying up around her thighs. Realising she was getting funny looks from some of the passing men, she said, "Look lads, this hat cost a fortune and is brand new. What you're looking at is 40 years old."

★　★　★

DOWN at his local social club, Jack was amazed to see a girl lean over the table exposing her bare bum. Not only that, but on each buttock was tattooed the number 6. Jack immediately felt it was a sign he was going to be lucky, so he went over to the Treasurer and bought ticket 66 for the prize draw the next night. It was a bonus prize of £1,000. The following night Jack arrived after the draw had taken place and he turned to his mate at the bar, saying, "Was the winning ticket 66?"

"No, sorry mate, you were almost right."
"What was it, then?" asked the disappointed Jack.
"It was 606."

★ ★ ★

A MAN went round to his mate's, and the wife answered the door.
"Is he in?"
"No," she said.
"I fancy you."
"Go away."
"How about a quick one?"
"Piss off."
"I'll give you £300."
"Alright, come in."
Later her husband comes home.
"Did Jack come round?"
"Yes."
"Did he drop my wage packet off?"

★ ★ ★

LEGEND has it that when a person is born they are kissed on the part of their anatomy that will bring them fame and fortune.
There are a lot of men who make excellent Chairmen - I wonder where the angel kissed them.

★ ★ ★

A MAN receives a letter ordering him to attend the local tax office for an interview about his last year's earnings. Unsure of what to wear, he asks his mate, who tells him to look very smart, wear a suit and a good pair of shoes to show him that

he's an honest man. Later on in the pub he meets another mate, tells him about his impending interview and that he's off to buy a good pair of shoes. But his mate disagrees, telling him he should wear old clothes, look very poor, so the tax man will feel sorry for him. By this time the man is very confused, so on the way home calls in at his cousin's house for advice. His cousin is a wealthy businessman.

"Well, my advice to you is the same as I gave my daughter, Marlene, when she asked me what she should wear on her wedding night - a long bri-nylon nightie or a short skimpy baby-doll nightie. My answer to you both is whatever you wear, it doesn't matter because either way you're going to get fucked."

★ ★ ★

A MAN and woman walked into a bank with a large sack of coins. "Did you hoard all this yourself?" asks the bankteller.

"No," came the reply. "My wife whored, I pimped."

★ ★ ★

"IT'S no good, sir," said the DSS man to his interviewee. "It's no good saying you feel like 65 - you have to be 65."

★ ★ ★

A RICH couple lost all their money, so the husband turned to his wife and said, "If you learn to cook we can get rid of the house-keeper."

And she retorted, "If you were better in bed we could get rid of the gardener."

★ ★ ★

TWO friends on a walking tour of Dartmoor get lost in the mist and after many hours of wandering about finally come across a cottage. A widow lives in the cottage and after hearing their sorry story she welcomes them in and gives them some supper and a glass of beer. She tells them she only has two bedrooms so one can sleep in the spare room and one with her. The two men toss a coin and Jack ends up sleeping with the widow. He has a wonderful night and in the morning after breakfast they depart. After a few minutes Bob asks Jack how it went.

"What a night, mate. It was great, but this morning she asked for my name and address so I gave her yours - you know what my wife's like."

Bob was so incensed by this; it broke up their friendship and they didn't see each other again for nine months. When the widow died, Bob said, "Hello Jack, you remember that widow? Well, I've had a letter from her solicitor and she's ..."

Jack hastily interrupted, "Look, I'm sorry Bob, my wife would have strung me up by the balls."

"Let me finish," said Bob. "The solicitor's letter said she'd died and left me £1million."

⋆ ⋆ ⋆

DID you hear about the debutante who wrote home from the States to say she had a beautiful fur coat and it only cost her 200 bucks? She never could spell!

⋆ ⋆ ⋆

ON the way home to her flat, a young couple passed a jeweller's store. The man stopped and said, "If you're very nice to me tonight I'll buy you that diamond ring."

The girl, who loved material possessions, agreed immediately. The next day, after a night of passion, the couple passed the shop and went in. But instead of buying her a beautiful dia-

mond ring, he bought her a cheap brooch instead.
Later that day she visited her mother and, between the sobs, told her what had happened.
"My darling," replied her mother. "One thing you must learn - when they're hard they're soft and when they're soft, they're hard."

★ ★ ★

TWO men sitting on a park bench reading newspapers. Suddenly one of them puts down his paper and bursts uncontrollably into tears.
"Excuse me," says the other, "I can't help but notice you're very upset about something. Can I help?"
"I've just read that the richest man in the whole world has died."
"I'm sorry. Were you related to him?"
"No," sobbed the man, "that's why I'm crying."

★ ★ ★

A RANDY old financier was bonking his secretary up against his desk when there was a knock at the door. The timing couldn't have been worse. She rushed back to her room and in haste he stuck his dick in the desk drawer. As the door opened the newcomer commented, "Why Mr Large, you're looking pleased with yourself."
Yes" he replied "I've just come into some stocks and shares."

★ ★ ★

WHAT is green and takes an hour to drink?
The family allowance cheque.

★ ★ ★

A JACKPOT winner on the lottery was asked what he was

going to do with his new-found wealth.

"I'm going to travel round the world, visit all the racecourses, spend time in Las Vegas, enjoy myself with the girls, drink lots and buy a super, top of the range sports car."

"And what will you do with any money left over?"

"I don't know, probably just squander it."

★ ★ ★

"HE'LL be alright soon," said the doctor, "he's just suffering from shock after seeing his numbers come up on this weeks jackpot."

"Oh thank you doctor" replied the wife. "Just one thing, how long should I leave it before I tell him I didn't put a lottery ticket on this week?"

★ ★ ★

FLO'S husband dies and because he was such a popular fella, she decides to put an announcement in the paper. But not having a lot of money, she tells the local newspaper she wants to keep it as short as possible. "Just put 'Ben Potts dead'."

"Actually Madam, you can have up to six words for the same price. Is there anything you would like to add?"

Flo thinks for awhile and then says, "Yes, OK, can you add 'Ferret for sale'?"

★ ★ ★

A MAN was always thinking up ways of making easy money and one day he thought he was on to a certainty. He taught his parrot to say the 23rd psalm and then took it down the local pub.

"I bet anyone £5 my parrot can recite the 23rd psalm, from beginning to end" he said.

Quite a lot of interest was shown and the money laid on the bar.

"Go on then, parrot, recite the psalm."

But the parrot remained completely dumb and eventually the man took it home, having lost quite a lot of money.

"Why the bloody hell didn't you do as I taught you, you scrawny old bird?"

"Now hold on," said the parrot. "Think what the odds will be tomorrow when we go back."

★ ★ ★

WHAT'S the difference between a Lloyds investor and a seagull? A seagull can still put down a deposit on a BMW.

★ ★ ★

A GROUP of students were being taught good business practice by a visiting guest speaker from a thriving international company.

"Now here's a tricky problem you may come across. One of your best customers comes in to settle his bill. He pays by cash with £50 notes but two of the notes have stuck together, so he's paid too much. Now the question is - should you tell your partner?"

★ ★ ★

WAS it love at first sight?
No, second. The first time I didn't know he had so much money.

★ ★ ★

AT a party to celebrate her 21st birthday, the daughter put all her presents on display including a cheque from her father to buy a new car. During the evening the guests would wander over to take a look at the presents and on one occasion a man was standing at the table looking at the cheque, doubled up with laughter.

"Mum," whispered the birthday girl, "Who is that man?"

"Oh him, he's your dad's bank manager."

IN YOUR TRAVELS

A MINI-CAB driver had an attractive fare in the back when suddenly the engine failed. He got out and lifted the bonnet to see what was wrong. The attractive girl got out too and came over to see what he was doing.

"Do you want a screwdriver?" she asked.

"In a moment, Miss. I'll just finish up here first."

★ ★ ★

"FASTEN your seat belts, ladies and gentlemen, we'll be landing in New York in less than 10 minutes," said the pilot of Concorde over the intercom. Unfortunately, he forgot to turn the intercom off and the passengers overheard him telling his co-pilot what he would do when they landed.

"First, I'm going to have a bloody good crap ... I'm in agony ... and then I'm going to give that gorgeous new air stewardess a right good rogering."

The new air stewardess, on hearing what the pilot said, blushed deeply and ran up the aisle to warn him, but halfway up she tripped and fell.

An old lady sitting on the aisle seat near her leant over and said. "Don't worry dear, there's no need to rush. He said he was going to have a crap first."

★ ★ ★

WHEN in Madrid, a man is recommended to go to a special local restaurant that serves the testicles of the slain bull from the local bull fight. When he gets there, he sees written up outside the restaurant, "After the killing in the ring, the testicles are on your plate within 30 minutes."

Sitting at table, the man orders the hot testicles, but on arrival, the chap is slightly disgruntled, it looks like two pickled walnuts covered with tomato sauce.

"This is very disappointing," he says to the waiter. "I have seen bulls' knackers and they are huge."

The waiter smiles and says, "Ah yes, sir, but sometimes the bull wins."

★ ★ ★

A PRETTY American girl on holiday in Scotland asked a man wearing a kilt, "I've often wondered what you have under your kilt,"

He replied, "I'm a man of few words. Give me your hand."

★ ★ ★

A JUMBO jet full to capacity is flying across the Atlantic when the pilot suddenly makes an announcement.

"I must apologise, ladies and gentlemen, one of our engines has packed up but we've got three others, so we'll reach our destination, but it will be a little later than scheduled."

Some time passes and then he makes another announcement:

"I'm sorry for the inconvenience; we've lost another engine, so we'll be an hour late getting to our destination."

Then some minutes later he announces the loss of another engine and tells his passengers the delay in landing will be two hours.

At this point, one of the passengers turns to the person next to him and says, "Bloody hell, if we lose another engine, we'll be up here all night."

★ ★ ★

THREE men are sitting in the same railway carriage when suddenly the phone rings. The first man puts his thumb to his mouth and forefinger up to his ear and carries on a conversation, explaining afterwards that he's got microchips implanted in both digits, so he doesn't need to carry around a phone. Some weeks go by and the three men find themselves in the same carriage again. A phone rings and this time the second man starts to talk seemingly to nothing but afterwards he explains he has two microchips, one in his ear and the other in his mouth. Even better than using the finger and thumb technique. Suddenly, the third man gets up, groans slightly and bends over with his legs apart.

"Excuse me," he says "I think a fax is just coming through."

★ ★ ★

A JEW and a black are sitting opposite one another in the New York subway. The Jew is astonished to see the black man is reading a newspaper in Yiddish.

He leans over and asks "Are you Jewish?"

"Hey, man," replies the black man "Give me a break."

★ ★ ★

TWO strangers in a train compartment, a biologist and a young girl. As they are travelling through the countryside they pass field after field of animals, many of them doing what comes naturally.

The young girl starts to get hot under the collar and turning to the man, asks him if he could tell her what attracts the animals to each other.

"It would be a pleasure," he says. "At certain times in the year the female gives off an odour attracting the male to her and heightening his sexual awareness".

At last they reach their destination and on parting the man says he hopes they'll meet again one day.

"Only if the cold in your head is better," she replies.

★ ★ ★

A BUSINESSMAN visited a very up-market restaurant in Paris and ordered moules marinieres, duck a l'orange and a sorbet ice cream. When the first two courses were served, he noticed the man had his thumb stuck in the dishes, but not when he brought out the sweet.

"Garçon, tell me please, why did you have your thumb in the first two courses of my meal, but not when you brought out the ice cream?"

"Certainly, sir, I have bad rheumatism in my thumb and something warm helps relieve the pain."

At this, the businessman was outraged. "It is appalling that in such a restaurant as this, customers have to put up with these disgusting habits. Go shove it up your bum."

Unperturbed, the waiter replied, "I only do that in the kitchen."

★ ★ ★

AN American seaman working on a trawler around the Far East takes shore leave and spends the whole week fucking everything in sight. Alas, he picks up a very serious strain of VD and is forced to go along to an American doctor.

"I'm afraid there is not much we can do for you," says the doctor. "We'll have to cut your penis off or you may die."

The man is dumbfounded but determined to get a second opinion, he visits a European doctor. The diagnosis is exactly the same.

Dismayed beyond belief, he goes to see a local doctor tucked away in the backstreets of the city. The doctor tells him there is no need for the operation, it is just a way for these foreign doctors to make more money. The man is overjoyed.

"You mean I don't have to have it cut off."

"No," replied the doctor,"Just wait a few days and your cock will fall off by itself."

★ ★ ★

THREE men were captured by savage Indians in the depths of the jungle. They were told to go out and collect one type of fruit and bring it back to the camp. Two returned quickly. The first had gathered cherries, and as a torture, he had to put them up his backside. Watching this, the second man looked on aghast as he had gathered oranges, but just then, the third man arrived back and the second man started to smile. "What is it?" said the first. "Aren't you worried? Look at the size of those oranges."

"No", replied the man. "I've just seen Bob return and he's got melons."

★ ★ ★

"I'M a little stiff from rugby."

"That's OK, it doesn't matter where you come from."

★ ★ ★

STRANDED miles from home after an all-night party, 'Good Time Lil' flags down a passing taxi and says to the driver, "Look mate, I'm out of money but if you'll take me back to Brighton, we can do the business on the back seat."

The unscrupulous driver agrees, takes her home and then gets into the back seat with her. He takes down his trousers, she takes off her knickers and sits astride him, when he suddenly complains.

"You haven't got anything smaller by any chance!"

THREE men, one of whom is a bit simple, are captured by savages in the deepest part of the jungle and are told they have one last wish before being killed. The first man asks for a crate of bourbon which he drinks until he collapses unconscious on the ground. The savages then kill him, eat him but keep his skin to make a canoe.

The second man asks for a dozen women, all of whom he screws in turn until he collapses exhausted on the ground. The savages then do the same to this man.

Finally, it's the turn of the 'simple' man to pick a wish and he asks for a knife, which he then starts stabbing himself with all over his body. Puzzled, the savages ask him what he is doing and he replies,

"No bugger is going to make a canoe out of me."

★ ★ ★

NO matter what you do, you can't please everyone. Take the old couple who went away on a weekend break and couldn't find anywhere to stay. As a kindly gesture the manager of a 4-Star hotel offered to let them stay in the bridal suite.

"What the heck do we want that for, I'm 75 years old."

"Excuse me Sir, I've allowed people to stay in the snooker room before now but I haven't expected them to play snooker all night."

★ ★ ★

"I'VE just had the most fabulous holiday in St Tropez," said the office girl to her friends. "I met this dishy masseur."

"You mean monsieur, don't you?" said Doreen. "A masseur is someone who gets you to strip and rubs you all over..."

"So this dishy masseur...."

★ ★ ★

A COUPLE were staying overnight at a country hotel but were unable to get to sleep because of the loud noise coming from downstairs. Eventually, the man could stand it no longer and rang down to reception.
"What the hell's going on? The noise is deafening."
"My apologies, sir, they're holding the Policeman's Ball."
"Well for fucks sake, tell them to leave it alone."

★ ★ ★

A WOMAN from the city stops overnight at a B&B in the heart of the country. The toilet is at the bottom of the garden and after using it she comes back in and complains to the owner. "There's no lock on that toilet."
"No need," he says, "Who'd want to steal a pail of shit?"

★ ★ ★

THE leader of the Western world and a monkey were sent up to space to look for life on another planet. They eventually landed many light years away on an unfamiliar world and each had an envelope with a set of instructions. The monkey opened his envelope which told him to study the terrain, take readings of the air pressure, rocks and minerals and finally, make contact with any alien inhabitants. The leader of the Western world opened his envelope and it just said, "Feed the monkey."

★ ★ ★

BOB was so excited. He'd never been up in a plane before but today he was having a special trip in a two seater. At 3 o'clock, they took off and were soon travelling high up in the sky when all of a sudden, the pilot collapsed and died of a heart attack.

Bob was petrified. After some minutes of total panic he found the radio.

"Mayday, mayday, somebody help me, the pilot's dead and I'm up here on my own."

"Receiving you, loud and clear," came a voice from the control room. "Try and keep calm, can you tell me where you are?"

"I don't know!" he yelled. "But we're flying upside down."

"And how do you know that?"

"Because crap's running out of my collar."

★ ★ ★

FLYING for the first time, an old man was having trouble with his ears, so the stewardess brought him some chewing gum. As he was leaving, he turned to her and said, "Thanks for the chewing gum, but how do I get it out of my ears?"

★ ★ ★

THE man was angry.

"Look, I booked a room with en suite facilities."

"But this isn't your room, sir, this is the lift."

★ ★ ★

A VAN driver picks up a young female hitchhiker and after they've travelled some distance he propositions her. She agrees and suggests they get into the back of the van but he tells her it's full of plumbing equipment.

"I know," he says. "Let's do it on the bonnet." So throwing all caution to the wind, they climb aboard and start bonking away. The passion is getting stronger and stronger, the van is swaying from side to side and at the crucial moment he flings himself away and hits his back on the aerial. The next day, it's still very painful so he goes along to the doctor's.

"Mmm... that's the worse case of Van Aerial disease I've ever seen."

★ ★ ★

A MAN stops overnight at an hotel and rings down to reception asking for one of their local girls.

"How disgusting," says the owner's wife. "Go and tell him we don't allow that sort of thing here."

But the husband thought she was making a lot of fuss about nothing.

"OK, I'll go and tell him," she said and off she stormed upstairs.

Half an hour passed and the man appeared downstairs. He said, to the owner, "The girls round here are a bit feisty aren't they? The one you sent me was a real tough one but I got her in the end."

★ ★ ★

A GROUP of ladies are travelling in a railway carriage that only has a door onto the platform. As it pulls into one of the stations, a drunk climbs aboard, sits himself in the corner and immediately falls asleep. Some time later he wakes up dying for a pee.

"Excuse me, ladies, this is a bit of an emergency. Would you mind if I peed out of the window?"

The women are broadminded enough and tell him to go ahead. However a little further on he needs another one, so he asks the ladies again.

"Go ahead," said the spokeslady, but I think we would all prefer it if this time you peed in the carriage and got rid of your fart out of the window."

IN YOUR UNFAITHFULNESS

AFTER a partying most of the night a young couple woke up the next day with awful hangovers.

"I'm sorry, luv," said the husband, "but was it you I made love to last night in the spare bedroom?"

"I don't know," she replied. "About what time would that be?"

★ ★ ★

WHAT the bloody hell do you think you're doing?" said the angry husband when he caught his wife in bed with another male.

The wife turned to her partner and said, "You see, I told you he was stupid."

★ ★ ★

A DUKE and duchess were not getting on very well; in fact, the duchess believed her husband to be having an affair with the housemaid, so she decided to test her theory.

The duchess sent the housemaid away for the night and when her husband made an excuse to leave his bed, she rushed down the back stairs and got into her housemaid's bed. Lo and behold, in he came and had his wicked way before she turned the lights on.

"You didn't expect to find me here, did you?" said the Duchess.

"Indeed not, madam," replied the Butler.

★ ★ ★

A MAN turns to his friend and asks him why he's looking so puzzled. He replies, "I've received this letter today and it's

from a man who says he'll beat me if I don't stay away from his wife."
"So what's puzzling you?"
"Well, he hasn't signed it."

★ ★ ★

WHEN a man arrives home from work one evening he's greeted by his wife, who's got a bottle of hair conditioner in her hand.
"What's that for?" he asks "My hair's OK."
"Yours maybe, but this is for your girlfriend whose hair keeps coming out all over your shoulders!"

★ ★ ★

AFTER a night of unbridled passion with his beautiful young secretary, the unfaithful husband was afraid to face up to his wife.
"Don't worry," said the secretary "Just put this piece of chalk behind your ear and tell her the truth."
When the man gets home he crept quietly upstairs but she was sitting up in bed waiting for him.
"Where have you been till this time?" she yelled.
"I've been enjoying a night of passion with a beautiful young girl," he replied.
"You bloody liar, you've been playing billiards with your mates all night, I can see the chalk behind your ear."

★ ★ ★

A MAN came home early from work to find his wife in bed with a strange man.
"Let me explain," she said "He came to the door looking for something to eat, so I gave him the breakfast you didn't want this morn-

ing. Then he asked if there were any clothes I didn't want, so I gave him your old blue suit that was going to the jumble sale. At that point he asked if there was anything else you didn't use."

★ ★ ★

"YOU never make a sound when you have an orgasm" said the disappointed husband to his wife.
"How would you know?" she retorted. "You're never there."

★ ★ ★

A GOOD looking young man goes into the chiropodist's and enquires how many customers are before him.
"Well I've got one corn, two bunions and one with toenails to clip."
The young man leaves and doesn't return. On the following three days the same man comes in and asks the same question. Each time there are about four or five customers before him and each time the man leaves again. The chiropodist is so intrigued he sends his receptionist out to follow him.
"I don't know what's going on," replies the receptionist on her return "He just goes straight round to your house."

★ ★ ★

"DID you sleep with my husband last night?"
"No, not a wink."

★ ★ ★

THE inevitable happened. A man came home from work early, and as his wife heard the key in the door, the lover jumped out of bed, grabbed his jacket and leapt into the wardrobe.

The husband, on seeing his wife in bed shouted "I know there's a man here somewhere. Come on, where is he?" He looked under the bed, "No, he's not here." He looked out of the window. "No, he's not here." And he looked in the wardrobe. But seeing a man holding a gun he shouted "And he's not here either."

★ ★ ★

"DO you talk to your wife when you're making love?"
"Only if she rings up."

★ ★ ★

"HOW many wives have you had?" asks Jack to Rob.
"Mmmm, about 50, but only one was my own."

★ ★ ★

"DO you like my new Italian suit?" said Jack to his mate Rob.
"I do. Where did you get it from?" said Rob.
"I didn't get it, my wife did. It was a surprise, I came home early from work and it was hanging on the end of the bed!"

★ ★ ★

A JEALOUS wife suspected her husband of being unfaithful, so when they were both invited to a fancy-dress party she feigned a headache and told him to go on his own. So off he went in his spacesuit costume and an hour later she followed in her own masked outfit. When she got there she spied her husband chatting up every female at the party, so after a while propositioned him herself to see what the response would be. Lo and behold, he had her outside quicker than you could say Jack Robinson and screwed her against the tree. Not long after she left and the next morning at breakfast was ready to confront him with his supposed unfaithfulness.

"How was the party?" she asked.

"Not really my scene" he replied. "I went up to the den to play poker with the boys and lent my spacesuit costume to Freddie Parker."

★   ★   ★

A MAN comes home to find his wife in bed with his best friend. The husband goes to the bed and says to his friend, "I have to .... but you?"

★   ★   ★

TWO men are getting dressed in the changing room. One puts on a girdle. "Since when have you been wearing a girdle?" the other asks.

"Since my wife found it in the glove compartment," he replies.

★   ★   ★

"WHEN I came home from work last night, I found my wife in bed with another man. How can I stop this happening again?" "Work more overtime."

★   ★   ★

MY best friend ran away with my wife, and do you know - I miss him.

★   ★   ★

A BUSINESSMAN away for the week at a conference sends a telegram to his wife saying he'll be home Friday night and is

bringing a colleague with him. Friday night comes and he arrives home only to find his wife in bed with a stranger. The businessman goes completely berserk, threatening to kill them both, but his colleague eventually manages to calm him down by saying there's probably some explanation and they'll sort it out in the morning. Sure enough, the next morning the colleague says to his friend, "You see, there was a good explanation. She's just told me there was a postal strike on Friday, so she didn't get the message."

★ ★ ★

A MAN comes home early from work to find his wife in bed. He's immediately suspicious and opens the wardrobe to find her lover hiding amongst the clothes, stark naked.

"What are you doing in there?" demands the angry husband.

"I'm the local pest controller," stumbles the man, "and we've heard there's a plague of moths about.."

"So how come you're bollock naked?" shouts the husband. "Well bugger me!" replies the man in amazement as he looks down at his body. "The bastards!"

★ ★ ★

WHAT is a vindictive pregnancy?
Someone who's had it in for you while you've been away.

★ ★ ★

"I WANT to divorce my husband," said the shapely brunette to her solicitor.

"On what grounds?"

"Infidelity, he's not the father of my child."

★ ★ ★

FOR many years, the miner had returned home after work and was washed gently by his loving wife. However, one day, he got into the bath and she scrubbed him till he bled.

"What's up?" he moaned.

"I'll tell you what's up!" she shouted. "You've always come home 100% black, today you're later than usual and you're 1% white.

★ ★ ★

TWO men in the barber's, a colonel and a sergeant.

"Shall I put some aftershave on, sir?" asked the barber of the colonel.

"Good gracious man, no. My wife would think I smelled like a brothel."

The barber turned to the sergeant "What about you, sir?"

"Certainly, my wife doesn't know what a brothel smells like."

★ ★ ★

COMING back from work one day, a husband sees his wife wearing a stunning diamond ring. When he asks her where she got it, she tells him she's won it in a raffle. In the following two weeks his wife is also seen wearing a beautiful fur coat and carrying a crocodile handbag. Again, she tells him she won them in a raffle. The following Thursday she informs her husband that she's going out again and would he be kind enough to turn the shower on for her.

"Oh, I don't think so," he said. "You don't want to get your raffle ticket wet."

★ ★ ★

IN the back seat of a car, a couple are having it away time and time again. Every time he finishes she asks for more. Eventually he tells her he's just got to go outside for a breather. While he's standing there he sees a man looking in a shop window at some car stereos. "Listen, mate," he says. "I've got a spare radio which you can have for free if you'll do me a favour. I've got a girl in the backseat of my car who's sex mad. She wants it time and time again and you'd be doing me a favour if you took over for a while."

The man agrees and gets into the car. A little while later a traffic cop comes along, shines his torch through the car window and asks what's going on.

"I'm making love to my wife," he replies.

"Well, can't you do it at home?" asks the policeman.

"Until you shone the light through the window, I didn't realise it was my wife!"

★ ★ ★

TWO men talking in a bar. "Listen, Jack, we've been mates a long time. I'd like you to do something for me. I've got to go out of town for a few days and I'd like you to keep a close eye on my wife. I have suspicions that she's up to something."

A few days pass and they meet up again in the pub.

"I watched your wife carefully, Jack," said Bob. "On the second evening a man knocked on the door and she opened it in a see-through night-dress. They kissed passionately and then went upstairs to the bedroom where I saw him put his hand between her legs - but then they closed the curtains and I saw no more."

"Oh dear," said Jack. "You see, the doubt remains."

★ ★ ★

"YOU'LL never believe this," said the man when he got home that night.

"I saw the paperboy this morning and he boasts he's slept with everyone on the street except one."

"Oh, I bet that's her at Number 8" replied the wife.

★ ★ ★

A MAN walked into a bar and ordered a double Scotch, drank it down in one gulp and immediately ordered another.

"You don't look so good," remarked the bartender. "Is it bad news?"

"Yes," replied the man "I just found my wife in bed with my best friend."

"Oh no," said the bartender "Here, have the next one on me. What did you do?"

"I told her to pack her bags, get out and never come back."

"And what about your best friend?"

"I went right up to him and said 'Bad dog!'"

★ ★ ★

TWO men talking in a bar. One says, "I've got such a clever wife, why she's even found a burglar-proof way of protecting her clothes. Sometimes when I come home from work there's a man in the wardrobe looking after them."

★ ★ ★

JACK lived his life to a strict routine and would go out for a pint every Monday, Wednesday and Friday. However, one Friday night he didn't feel very well, so decided to stay in and watch television with his wife. Half way through the evening the phone rang and his wife heard him say, "Why the hell are you ringing me. Get onto the Met Office!" and he slammed down the phone.

"Who was that?" she asked.

"Some silly bugger asking me if the coast was clear."

SAME man talking in a bar:

"And do you know, she loves me so much. Last week I was off sick. Every morning she was so glad to have me home, she'd run out into the street when the milkman or postman arrived, shrieking, "My husband's here, my husband's at home!""

★ ★ ★

A WIFE who was forever left at home on her own because her husband worked late at the office insisted they go out to the best club in town for her birthday. She was determined he wouldn't get out of it, so that night he was dragged along. At the door the bouncer greeted her husband in a familiar way: "Hello, Bob, nice to see you."

Quickly Bob explained that the bouncer worked in his office during the day and he worked at night for some extra money. In they went and left their coats in the cloakroom at which point the girl in charge also greeted Bob in a familiar way. "Hello, Bob, how are you tonight?"

Again, he remarked that the girl used to work in his office before changing jobs. However, it all went horribly wrong when the stripper also greeted him.

"That's it!" roared the wife as she stormed out and hailed down a taxi. "I could just about accept the explanations about the bouncer and cloakroom attendant but you'll never convince me that the stripper works as a secretary through the day.

No, no, no definitely not!" she screamed.

Hearing this the taxi driver turned round and said, "By Jove, you've got a difficult one tonight, Bob."

★ ★ ★

JACK and Bill are in the urinals, and on seeing Bill's prick, Jack exclaims, "How the heck did you get such a huge prick? It's a real stonker."

"Oh that's easy," replies Bill proudly. "Every night before I get into bed I knock it five times on the bottom of the bed."

That night Jack decides to do the same and before getting into bed knocks his prick on the bottom of the bed five times.

Awakened by the noise, his wife whispers, "Is that you Bill?"

★　★　★

WHY did the unfaithful man buy a dog?

If his wife overhears him saying, "Lie down, roll over, give it to me and I'll give you a bone," she thinks it's the dog he's talking to.

★　★　★

WHAT does the unfaithful man say to his wife after having sex?

"Sweetheart, I'll be home in half an hour."

★　★　★

A WIFE hears the shattering news that she's pregnant and immediately rings her husband.

"I'm pregnant, you bastard, why didn't you wear a condom?" she yells.

"Now, hold on a minute," he replies. "I always wear a condom. Anyway, who is this?"

★　★　★

JACK Carter, chairman of an international company, is outraged one morning when he sees that someone has peed in the snow outside his office window. Not just peed but formed the words, "Fuck the wanker Jack."

He immediately calls in his private secretary and demands that the culprits be discovered.

Later, the secretary returns and rather nervously gives him the news.

"Sir, the urine belongs to the deputy chairman, but ... er..."

"But what, man, come on, but what?"

"Well, sir, the handwriting belongs to your wife."

★ ★ ★

BETTY'S walking down the street when she comes upon her hated neighbour, Doreen.

"Hey bitch, how dare you say my John's got a wart on the end of his dick?"

"I said no such thing," replied Doreen. "I said it just felt like he had a wart on the end of his dick."

★ ★ ★

HUSBAND comes home from the office and sees his wife in the garden.

"Sarah, I have some good news and some bad news to tell you. I'm leaving you for Molly."

"I see," says the wife, "and what's the bad news?"

★ ★ ★

"THAT was a wonderful weekend we spent in Paris," said the Director to his Secretary. "Will you ever be able to forget it?"

"I don't know," she replied. "What's it worth?"

★ ★ ★

DROWSING contentedly after an afternoon of bonking in bed,

suddenly there's the sound of a car pulling up outside. Dreamily, the girl whispers, "Oh, oh, quick get moving, that's my husband." Quick as a flash, the man jumps out of bed, rushes to the window and suddenly stops dead.

"What d'ya mean?" he bellows "I am your husband!"

★　★　★

A COUPLE are having it away on the sofa when the phone rings. After answering it, she replaces the receiver and turns to her lover, saying, "It was only my husband."
"Oh, no" replies the man "I'd better get out of here."
"Don't worry, he won't be home for hours, he's playing pool with you and two other mates."

★　★　★

BOB was off on his usual three day inspection of garden centres when he realised he'd left the house without his new seed catalogue. Returning quietly, he saw his wife in the kitchen, bending over, looking inside the fridge. Unable to resist, he crept up behind her, lifted her flimsy nightdress and was just about to do the business when she said, "Only six eggs this week Jack Bob's away till Friday."

★　★　★

WHEN a husband found his wife in bed with another man he was so angry he knocked the man unconscious, tied him up and took him down to the garden shed. On regaining consciousness, the man realised his offending member was chained to the floor and the husband was standing over him with a machete."
"Bloody hell, you're not going to cut it off, are you?"
"No" said the husband, handing him the knife. "You can do that, while I set fire to the shed."

THE chief executive of an international company pulled up in his Rolls outside a pub where two men were drinking.

"Hey, Jack, you see that man in the Rolls? He was trying to get me for months."

"Really?" said Jack, "Whose company were you with at the time?"

"His wife's."

★ ★ ★

JACK and Bill spent the night drinking heavily in the pub and got so drunk that Jack missed his bus home.

"Never mind," slurped Bill. "Come on home with me."

They staggered back to Bill's house and went inside.

"I'll just show you where everything is," he said. "There's the kitchen and if we go upstairs.... there's the bathroom, you can kip down in here and this is my bedroom."

Bill opened his bedroom door. "And there's my wife and the man next to her is me!"

★ ★ ★

A MAN partners up with a new member of the Golf Club and they've played nine holes when he comments, "I see you've got a club in a special leather case, but you haven't used it yet."

"Oh no, that's not a club" explains the man. "I'm a freelance hit man, so I carry my gun around with me at all times in case someone needs my services."

They continue playing another 2 holes when suddenly the man turns to him urgently.

"I've been thinking of what you've been saying and I'd like to hire your services. Do you see that house across the fifteenth fairway? That's my house, and if I'm not mistaken my wife is having it off with the next door neighbour."

"Let me have a look," says the hit man and he gets out the high-powered rifle, adjusts the telescopic sight and aims at the bedroom window.

"Does the man have red hair and a moustache?"

"Yes, yes, that's him" he says excitedly.

"Shoot them both. Take away my wife's good looks - the cause of all my misery, and get him right in the balls - the bastard."

"Hold on a minute," says the hit man, "I think I'm going to be able to save you a bullet."

★ ★ ★

GUNS don't kill people; it's husbands that come home early.

★ ★ ★

OVERHEARD on the top deck of a bus.

"I hear your old man's in hospital, Flo. I hope it's nothing too serious."

"Just his knee. I found a blonde sitting on it."

★ ★ ★

DID you hear about the unfaithful film star who, when a flash of lightning lit up his bedroom, jumped out of bed shouting, "I'll pay for the negatives!"

★ ★ ★

"MUM, dad, I have something to tell you. I'm getting married to Julie from the post office, she's agreed to be my wife."

"That's wonderful news," says Mum.

"Er... yes ..." says dad, a little hesitantly.

Later, when they are on their own dad confesses to his son that during his marriage he did have one teeny weeny extra marital affair and that in fact Julie is his half sister. The boy is devastated. He breaks off the engagement but it takes over two years before he can ever look at another girl. Then one day, he comes home again.

"Mum, dad, I've asked Tracy to marry me and she's accepted."

Mum's delighted, she's been so worried about her poor boy, but once again dad doesn't say much until later.

"I'm sorry son, I did have one other fling and I'm afraid Tracy is also your half sister."

The boy collapses in despair but then a fierce anger takes over and he decides to tell his mum all the dreadful details.

"Don't you worry about your father," she says. "Go ahead and marry Tracy. What he doesn't know is that he's not really your dad."

★ ★ ★

AN angry wife went round to the house of her husband's lover and confronted her with the evidence of their liaison

"Look at these photographs," she said, "taken by a private detective over the past month. This is you and my husband swimming naked in the pool, here's one of you and my husband canoodling in the woods and here's one of you both stark naked on the bed upstairs. What have you got to say?"

"Mmm..." pondered the lover. "I think I'll take one of those and half a dozen of that last picture."

★ ★ ★

WAKING up half asleep because he needed a pee, a man saw three pairs of feet sticking out of the bottom of the bed. He dug his wife in the ribs saying

"Hey, Winnie, there's three pairs of feet at the bottom of our bed."

"Don't be silly," she said, "you're dreaming. Go and count them."

"Sorry Mai, there are only two and don't my nails need cutting!"

IN YOUR UNIFORM

A FIREMAN comes home from work with a new idea to spice up his sex life. He tells his wife, "Tonight when we go to bed I'll shout First Bell and you take all your clothes off. Then I'll shout Second Bell and you jump into bed and then on the shout of Third Bell we'll make love all night."

So the following day, the fireman comes home from work, shouts First Bell and she strips off, Second Bell into bed, Third Bell and away they go. But five minutes later, the wife calls out, "Fourth Bell."

"What's that mean?" askes her puzzled husband.

She replies, "It means more hose; you haven't got to the fire yet."

★ ★ ★

PASSENGERS are boarding the plane for Los Angeles and sitting in First Class is a blonde girl.

"I'm sorry, Miss" says the air hostess, "but your seat is in the back of the plane, this is for people with first class tickets only."

But the blonde refuses to move.

"I'm young, I'm beautiful, I deserve to be in First Class."

The air hostess goes and gets the co-pilot, who also asks her to move but again she replies, "I'm young, I'm beautiful, I deserve to be in First Class."

The plane is filling up fast and it's crucial the crew get the problem sorted out so they call for the pilot and tell him the situation. He immediately goes up to the girl, whispers something in her ear and she leaves the first class area straightaway.

"What did you say to her?" asks the co-pilot.

"I simply told her the front half of the plane wasn't going as far as Los Angeles."

★ ★ ★

A LADY got stopped for speeding for the umpteenth time and knew that if she was given another ticket she would be banned from driving. Thinking quickly of something to say to the policeman when he came up to the car she joked, "Have you come to ask me to the policemen's ball?"
Without thinking he said "Policeman don't have balls."
There was an embarrassed silence and he walked away.

★ ★ ★

THE traffic police came across a car that had wrapped itself around a tree. Sitting in the front seat was a young man, still in his safety belt, but screaming with agony.
"Now, now, sir, help is on its way. It's a good thing you had your seat belt on otherwise you might have gone straight through the window like your girlfriend."
"Aaagh!" came the reply "Have you seen what's in her hand?"

★ ★ ★

WALKING along the street, a policeman came across a young man kicking an older man and he stepped in to break it up.
"It's OK Officer, I asked him to do it," said the older man. "Many years ago I was in the flat of this beautiful young girl when she suddenly removed her dress saying she was feeling hot. So I turned the fire off. Then she stripped off completely, so I thought I'd better leave. As I walked out of the door she said that one day I'd remember this and then ask the first person I saw to kick me. Well I've just realised what she meant."
"Keep kicking," said the policeman.

AN old army colonel was awaiting news of the imminent arrival of his son at the exclusive Harley Street Clinic.

"How do you know it will be a son?" asked the doctor.

"Of course it will be, family tradition, man" And in fact it was a son. On hearing the news, the colonel asked for him to be circumcised.

"Family tradition," he said.

Later the doctor called to say the baby was ailing.

"Give it some brandy, don't argue, just do it."

Some time later the doctor rang again to say the baby was no better.

"I'm coming over," said the Colonel. "Meanwhile, put him on the breast."

By the time the Colonel arrived the baby was doing well.

"Excellent!" he chortled, "You see this is a real father's son. Mouth full of tit, belly full of brandy and a sore cock."

★ ★ ★

A COLONEL was posted to the Far East and after three months his wife came to join him. On the first morning she decided to stay in bed, still feeling tired from the plane trip, but at 10.00am the colonel's manservant appeared unannounced, and threw back the bedclothes, saying, "Come on, miss, time's up, go get yourself some breakfast and then be on your way."

★ ★ ★

A UNIT of soldiers returned to base after spending four months in the war zone. The base also had a squad of women soldiers and the colonel in charge of the men took the leader of the women aside and warned her to keep her ladies under lock and key as his men hadn't seen a woman for months. The women replied, "It's all right, there'll be no trouble," and tap-

ping her head she continued, "My girls have it up here."
The colonel retorted, "I don't care where they have it. If my
men start looking they'll find it."

★ ★ ★

A NEW sergeant major had just arrived at the foreign legion outpost and decided to tour the base immediately. In one small shed
he found a camel and when asked why it was there the private
replied hesitantly, "It's for the men to use if their carnal desires get
the better of them, sir."
The sergeant major was outraged.
"Get rid of it immediately, from now on, nothing like that goes on
here."
However, six months later and painfully missing the fair sex, the
sergeant major asked his private if the camel had indeed gone.
"Well, no sir, I'm sorry" came the reply.
"Then let me go and have another look" and the sergeant major
went back to the shed, dropped his trousers, stood on a bucket and
gave the camel a right seeing to."
Afterwards he said to the private, panting, "Is that how the men do
it?"
Embarrassed he replied, "Well, no, sir, actually the men ride the
camel to the nearest brothel."

★ ★ ★

AN army unit was crossing the desert when one of the camels
stopped and refused to move, so it and its rider were left
behind. They were stuck there for four hours and nothing the
soldier did would move him. Eventually along came an ATS
driver who listened to the problem, saying, "Don't worry, leave
it to me."
She put her hand beneath the camel's belly and within seconds

he jumped up and disappeared at a rate of knots.

"That's amazing, miss. What did you do?"

"I just tickled its balls."

"Gracious, then you'd better tickle mine, I've got to catch the bugger."

★ ★ ★

TWO old colonels were talking over their port about a third...

"I say, did you know old Smithers has started living in sin with a monkey."

"By Jove!" replied the other. "Is it a male or female monkey?"

"Now steady on, female monkey of course, there's nothing unnatural about Smithers."

★ ★ ★

TWO retired colonels were bemoaning the younger generation over drinks at their gentlemen's club.

"You'll never believe this," said the first colonel.

"When I told my grand daughter that her grandfather was killed at Waterloo, she wanted to know on what platform it happened!"

"Oh, how ridiculous," replied the second colonel, "As if it mattered what platform he was on."

★ ★ ★

A NEW sergeant major arrived at the base and the retiring sergeant major, who had one more week to go, said to him, "If you've any problems just come and see me."

The next morning a man was brought to him on a charge of homosexuality.

The new sergeant major, not sure what to do, popped in to see the old sergeant major and said, "Sir, what do you give for cock suck-ing?"

"Oh £2-£2.50," he replied.

★ ★ ★

THE conductor told a man off for smoking on the tube.
"Can't you see that No Smoking sign on the wall?" he said.
"Yes, I can," he replied. "But it's not easy keeping all your rules. That one over there says WEAR A WONDER BRA!"

★ ★ ★

A YOUNG man sits down next to a nun in the park and they strike up a conversation. Some time passes and the young man confess-es to the nun that her habit really turns him on and that he would dearly like to make love to her.

"Are you a Catholic?" she asks.

"Yes," he replies.

"OK, let's go behind those bushes."

They do as she suggests and the nun satisfies him with a blow job. Afterwards, feeling very guilty the man tells the nun that in fact he isn't a Catholic.

She replies, "Well, I have something to tell you as well. My name is Bob and I'm on my way to a fancy dress party."

★ ★ ★

A VERY drunk man walked into the police station complain-ing that someone had stolen his horse.
Sighing wearily, the officer on duty asked, "And what colour was the horse, sir?"
"Er... don't know," he replied, "but it was female."
The Officer repeated. "It was female. And how do you know that, sir?"

"Well, I was riding along the pavement when I hears this voice say 'Look at that cunt on the horse'."

★ ★ ★

THE plane is about to taxi down the runway when passengers see the pilot and co-pilot walking up towards the cockpit. Both look as if they are virtually blind, carrying white sticks and bumping into everyone.

At first, the full plane of passengers cannot believe what they have just seen, but as the plane taxis to the end of the runway and turns to pick up speed, a slight panic begins. By the time it's hurtling down the runway, there is ever increasing panic and as the plane lifts into the air an earth shattering scream goes up from the cabins. This sudden change in pitch is followed by the plane rising into the sky.

"Aaah, thank goodness," says the pilot to his colleague. "Safe again. You know, one day the passengers aren't going to scream and then we're really done for."

★ ★ ★

THE man staggered along the street and opened the door of his car just as the police were passing.

"One moment, sir" said the traffic cop. "I hope you weren't thinking of driving?"

"I sure am," he slurred "I'm in no condition to walk."

★ ★ ★

IN a distant outpost of the Foreign Legion, one of the more recent recruits confides to his sergeant that lack of female company is driving him round the twist.

"No need to let that worry you, son. Here, let me show you. See that barrel over there, the one with the hole in the side? You'll find that will help relieve the pressure. You're free to use it on Tuesday through to Sunday."

"That's great, thanks. But er.... What's wrong with Monday?"

"Well, you have to be fair; if you're using it six days a week, then on Monday, it's your turn inside the barrel."

★   ★   ★

IN one of the remotest parts of Outer Mongolia, high up in the mountains, is an outpost of an old regiment. The men have been on duty for six months without a break and only themselves for company. A new recruit joins them and he's only been there a few weeks when a sudden roar goes up from the look-out.

"Hurry, they're' coming!" he shouts.

A might roar goes up and all the troops desert their posts and charge out of the gates. The newcomer turns to his mate and says, "What's going on? It's only a herd of goats. What's all the fuss about?"

"If you'd been out here six months without a break, and without female company, you'd know alright," replies his mate.

"But why all the rush, there seems to be plenty to go around?"

"Oh yes, but no one wants to get lumbered with an ugly one!"

★   ★   ★

A MOTORIST is stopped for going through a red light and is asked to take a breathaliser test.

"I can't blow," says the man. "I suffer from asthma," and he shows the policeman his asthmatics card.

"OK, then we'll have to take you down to the station for a blood test."

"I can't. I'm a haemophiliac" and he produces a doctor's card.

"In that case, it'll have to be a urine test."

Once again, the man produces a card from his wallet. This time it's a Manchester City Supporters Club membership card and as he shows it to the policeman he says, "Please don't take the piss."

★ ★ ★

A MAN driving along in a car hits the kerb and the round-about.

"You're drunk," says the policeman.

"Oh thank you very much, I thought the steering had gone" he replies.

★ ★ ★

"EXCUSE me, Sir, where do you think you're going at this time of night?" said the policeman to the staggering drunk.

"I'm going to a lecture."

"Now? Hardly. Who's giving a lecture at this time of night?"

"My wife."

★ ★ ★

THE young leader could hardly believe his eyes when he saw ten of his best fighters running away down the street being chased by a copper wielding a baton.

"What the fuck's going on?" he said. "There's only one of them."

"We know," they yelled, "but we don't know which one of us he's after!"

★ ★ ★

THE situation looked bad. The platoon had suffered many fatalities and the men were very dispirited. The C.O. felt it was time to give them a pep talk.

"Right, chaps, listen to me. You've done a sterling job, couldn't have asked for better but we have been outnumbered. But we'll fight on, for King and country, until the very last bullet has been fired. When that happens, you have my permission to make a run for it. .... oh, by the way, I've got a bad knee, so I'd better set off now."

★ ★ ★

A DRUNK man was walking down the street, one foot on the pavement and one in the gutter when he was stopped by a policeman.
"I'm going to have to take you in for being drunk," he said.
"Are you sure I'm drunk?"
"Oh yes, completely, you've one foot on the pavement and one in the gutter."
"Oh thank goodness for that, I thought I'd lost part of my leg."

★ ★ ★

AN overbearing, pompous Sergeant Major spends the night with a German prostitute and the next morning he turns arrogantly to the girl and says, "My dear, after last night, you'll have a baby in nine months' time and you can call it Toby, after me."
She replies, "In two days time, you'll have a rash and you can call it German measles."

★ ★ ★

A MAN walked into a police station to report that his wife had gone missing.
"She went out about four hours ago and she hasn't been back to cook my dinner so I know there must be something wrong."
"OK sir, let's not panic. I'll just take down some details. Can

you describe your wife, what she was wearing when she left the house?"

"No, but I did see her walking down the road with our next door neighbour and she's not back either."

"I don't suppose you can give us a description of her?"

"Oh yes, she's about 5'6", black shoulder-length curly hair, 36-24-36, wearing a red mini skirt and a red and white jacket."

★ ★ ★

THIS particular evening, the traffic cop was determined to crack down on drunk and disorderly drivers. He parked near one of the toughest, noisiest and rowdiest bars in town, sat back and waited. A little later, a man staggered out of the bar, tripped over and then attempted to open three cars before he eventually found his own. The man got in and immediately fell asleep. Feeling very pleased with himself, the officer waited all evening until everyone left the bar, got into their cars and drove away. Finally, the sleeper woke up, started the engine and began to pull away.

"Got you," said the police officer to himself and he pulled the driver over and administered a breathaliser test. He was astonished to find the man passed with a zero blood alcohol reading.

"But how can that be?" he said.

"Well, you see, officer," said the man, "tonight I'm the designated decoy."

IN YOUR VANITY

A WOMAN has no luck finding a husband, so she decides to put an ad in the local newspaper, under Personal'.

'Wanted a man with view to marriage, must be loyal, rich and a good lover.'

Some days go by and then one morning there's a ring on the doorbell. To her amazement, when she opens the door there's a man in a wheelchair. He has no arms or legs.

"I've come about the ad in the paper," he says.

"Oh, well er..... are you loyal?"

"Sure am. I was in the army, stationed in Northern Ireland when we came under fire. I ran back to rescue one of my men when there was a loud explosion and I ended up like this."

"Well, are you rich?"

"You bet. I took over the family business and have now built it into an international concern."

"But are you a good lover?" she demanded.

"How do you think I rang the doorbell?"

★ ★ ★

AFTER leading him on for a while, the girlfriend suddenly moves away, telling him, "If you want to go all the way with me, you'll have to have a sports car and a ten inch dick."

"OK, but I'll be back," he tells her.

And indeed he arrives on her doorstep the following week in a gleaming white sports car.

She is very impressed.

"And that's not all," he says "As far as my dick's concerned, my doctor says he can cut it down to any size you want."

THE professor of physiology turned to a young student in his class and asked her what part of the body becomes 10 times its normal size when under emotional stress.

The young girl blushed profusely and said she'd rather not answer. At this point the young student next to her volunteered the answer - it was of course the pupil of the eye.

"That's right," said the professor and turning to the young girl he said, "My dear, your refusal to answer tells me three things. First you haven't studied your homework, second you have a one-track mind and third, I'm afraid you're going to be sadly disappointed."

★ ★ ★

"WOW!" said the man looking at his naked body in the mirror. "If I was five centimetres longer I'd be a king."

"Mmm" said his wife, not impressed. "If you were five centimetres shorter you'd be a queen."

★ ★ ★

"DARLING," said the blushing bride on her honeymoon night. "What is a penis?"

Her husband, joyful that she showed such innocence, dropped his trousers to show her.

"Oh that," she said disappointed. "It's just like a prick, only smaller."

★ ★ ★

A MAN and his domineering wife went into the tailor's to order him some new trousers. When asked if he would like a 5" or 10" zip the man replied quickly, "20" please."

After they left the shop she turned to him scornfully and said, "You remind me of our next door neighbour. Every morning he opens the huge double doors of his garage and wheels out his bicycle."

⋆ ⋆ ⋆

AT the Tuesday coffee morning the ladies got into a heated argument about which of their husbands had the biggest member. The Mayor's wife said it was her husband and was so insistent that in the end she was told she had to prove it. On arriving home she told her husband, who looked aghast.

"Dorothy, you know mine is only small. What are we going to do?"

Fortunately they had a friend whose member was enormous and they asked him if he would do them a favour.

"Don't worry, no one will know because you'll be hidden behind a screen and you'll put it through a hole."

The day came and the friend stuck his enormous member through the hole. The Mayor's wife smiled smugly, sure she had won. However, suddenly a woman's voice was heard to say, "Hold on, that's not the Mayor's, that's the vicar's, I recognise the wart on the end."

⋆ ⋆ ⋆

MAN boasting to his mate:
"What has 250 teeth and guards a monster?
My trouser flies."

⋆ ⋆ ⋆

A TACTFUL girl is one who makes a slow man think he's a wolf.

⋆ ⋆ ⋆

A VERY pompous self-made man decided to pay for his son to

go to private school and the whole family went up to visit the headmaster.

"I'm Sir Dunwell Bates, this is my wife Lady Bates, my daughter Miss Bates and my son Master Bates."

"Don't worry" replied the headmaster. "We'll soon put that right."

★ ★ ★

DID you hear about the man who had an audition with the Chippendales?

He was put on their short list.

★ ★ ★

HAVE you heard of John Little, the nudist who stuck a magnifying glass to his fig leaf and reflected great credit on himself?

★ ★ ★

ALWAYS marry a girl with small hands - it makes your dick look bigger.

★ ★ ★

A RATHER arrogant social climber liked to impress her friends and relations by putting on sumptuous dinner parties. One night, however, as they were all sitting around the table her stomach took a turn for the worse, and she was unable to contain a fart. Without turning a hair, she immediately said, "Jeeves, please stop that!"

But Jeeves replied immediately

"Of course, madam, which way did it go?"

A BODY builder went down to the local antique shop to find a mirror to hang on the back of the bathroom door, so that in the mornings after a shower he could admire his fine physique.

"There are plenty of mirrors to choose from," said the shop owner, "but don't have that one - it's evil."

Well, nothing would satisfy him until he had bought the evil mirror which he took home and hung behind the door. Next morning he looked at himself and realised he wasn't as well endowed as he would like. Knowing the mirror had magic powers, he said, "Mirror, mirror, on the wall, make my tool touch the floor."

And his legs fell off.

★ ★ ★

A GIRL and boy out on only their second date had never done anything more than kiss and cuddle all night because the boy was embarrassed by the size of his penis.

However this night he decided to take the bull by the horns and placed it in her hands.

"No, thanks," she said. "I don't smoke."

★ ★ ★

OUT on their first date, an arrogant man took the girl back to his flat for coffee.

"You don't talk much," she said.

At that he dropped his trousers and proudly said, "This does all my talking for me."

"Well, that doesn't have much to say either," she retorted.

★ ★ ★

A MAN dyes his hair jet black because it had been going grey and is so pleased with the results that when he's buying a paper in the newsagent's, asks the shopkeeper how old he thinks he is.

"Oh, about 32" he says.

"No, I'm 40" laughs the man very pleased.

Then he goes into the chip shop to buy some fish and asks the woman behind the counter how old she thinks he is.

"Oh, about 34."

"No, I'm 40," comes the smug reply.

Later he sees an old woman at the bus stop.

"How old do you think I am?" he says.

"Well," says the old woman, "I'll have to feel your willy before I can tell you."

"What!" gasps the man. "That's the only way I can tell," she says.

"OK then." He unzips his flies and she puts her hand in.

"Ooohooh" she says. "You're 40."

"How can you tell?" he says.

"Ah, I was standing behind you in the chip shop."

★   ★   ★

A VAIN man who thought he had a body "to die for" gave his girl-friend a photograph of himself, posing in the nude.

"What are you going to do with that?", he boasted.

"Mmm", she replied. "I think I'll get it enlarged."

★   ★   ★

DID you hear about the vain man who was trying to impress his new girlfriend? When he stood in front of the mirror admiring himself, he said, "I had to fight hard to get this body."

"Really," she replied.

"I'm sorry you lost."

OR how about the chap who read a sign saying "Wet floor" - so he did.

★ ★ ★

THE vain young man lay back contentedly on the bed after making love to his new girlfriend.
"How was it for you?" he asked.
"Oh, pretty painless," she replied. "I never felt a thing."

★ ★ ★

SOME of the guys out west are so mighty they can run in the three-legged race without a partner.

★ ★ ★

"WHAT are you doing?" he asked excitedly as she put her hand down his trousers.
"Oh nothing," she said. "I thought it might have been the start of something big."

★ ★ ★

TWO young men go on holiday together to Spain and spend all day on the beach and go clubbing at night. By the time they leave the beach each day Bob has usually made a date with one of the many pretty girls round about, but Des never has any luck.
"What am I going to do, why can't I score?" he asks Bob.
His mate looks at him critically - he is rather a poor example of manhood - and says, "Tomorrow, when you come to the beach, stick an orange down your swimming trunks."
The following day, Bob is late joining Des and it's not until lunchtime that they meet up.

"Hi Des, how's it going?"

"Still not pulled anyone," he replies dejectedly.

Bob takes another good look at him and whispers, "Next time Des, put the orange down the front of your trunks."

★ ★ ★

AS he stood at the mirror yet again, admiring his good looks and muscular body, he turned to his long suffering wife and said. "There can't be that many men who are so well endowed."

"One less than you think" came the mumbled reply.

★ ★ ★

IT was the day of the works outing and the boss had arranged for a bus to pick up the employees and their spouses and take them to Blackpool for the day. And what a day they had. The weather was good, the food was great and the booze flowed endlessly. By the time they got back in the bus to go home there was a great deal of merriment. However, an hour into the journey and most of the men needed a pee - they'd swilled down so much beer it was inevitable. "You'll have to stop the bus, we're busting back here!" shouted a voice.

"There aren't any services for miles!" he shouted back. "But if it's a real emergency, I'll stop in the next lay-by."

Soon, twenty desperate and drunk men staggered off the bus and were so relieved to pee they didn't care who was watching. In bed that night, Doreen turned to Bill and said, "Men! You're disgusting, exposing yourself to all us women on the bus .... still," she smiled, hugging him, "ours was grand."

★ ★ ★

THREE 'social climber' women met up at a school reunion

twenty years after they had last seen each other, and the conversation turned to husbands.

"My husband is a regional sales director, responsible for a huge area in the Midlands," said the first.

"Well, mine is a scientist working in the laboratories of a large international company," said the second.

"My husband works on the dustcarts but he has such a big tool. Four pigeons can stand on it at one go."

As the evening progressed and the drinks had a relaxing effect upon the women, they all confessed to having exaggerated a bit.

"My husband's really only a salesman," said the first.

"Well, my husband's not quite a scientist, he's a lab technician," said the second.

"I boasted a little too," admitted the third. "Only three pigeons can stand on my husband's dick at the same time.... mind, a fourth could get on if it stood on one leg."

IN YOUR WORKING DAY

BROWSING around an old second-hand shop, a man spotted a brass rat on one of the shelves and decided to buy it. After haggling over the price, he eventually came away with it and on leaving, the shopkeeper insisted, "Under no circumstances will I take it back," The man walked along the street and suddenly noticed a live rat following him. As the minutes went by, more and more rats joined him until he was surrounded by thousands of them. In blind panic he raced off down the road, came to a river and threw the brass rat into the water. All the other rats followed and were soon drowned. The man went back to the second-hand shop and on seeing him the shopkeeper shouted out, "I told you, no refund! You cannot bring the rat back."

"Oh no, I don't want to," replied the man.

"I just wondered whether you had any brass estate agents?"

★ ★ ★

A SALESMAN was amazed to see a lot of very expensive cars in the hotel car park and commented on it to the hotel owner, a beautiful blonde, as he was signing in.

He asked her who owned all the cars, and she replied, "Actually, they are all mine."

"Gosh, you must have a very successful business to afford all those cars."

"Not necessarily," she said, "I've won them all in bets I've had with the men who've stayed here. You see, I bet them that they can't do what my eight year old nephew can do."

"Well, of course I can," he replied. "Any man could do what an eight year old boy can do."

So the bet was agreed with the car and the hotel as the stake.

First the blonde called the boy over, took out one of her ample breasts and asked him to kiss it. The boy did as she asked and then the amazed man did the same. Then she dropped her panties and asked the boy to kiss her down below. He did and the man followed. At this point the man thought he had won the bet and gleefully asked for the key to the motel.

"Oh no, wait a minute," she said, and she turned to her nephew.

"Just one more thing, bend your willy in half and ask the gentleman for his car keys."

★ ★ ★

A PLUMBER was giving advice to his apprentice.

"Tact is very important in this job, for instance, when I walked into a bathroom to mend a pipe there was a naked woman, so I quickly said, 'Excuse me, sir' and came out. Now that's tact."

Later on the two were called out to a house on an emergency and the plumber asked his apprentice to check the water tank upstairs. A few minutes later he came back down with a black eye.

"What happened?" asked the plumber.

"It's all your fault and your silly tact!" said the boy.

"I walked into one of the bedrooms and saw a couple stark naked on the bed and I said, 'Excuse me, Gentlemen'!"

★ ★ ★

BILL, the local barber, had a secret remedy to restore hair and on the odd occasion he would pass it on to his very special customers.

One such customer came in and asked Bill to give him the remedy for £1,000. After some thought Bill agreed and told him all he needed do to restore hair to his bald patch was apply some female secretions.

"But how do I know it works?" replied the customer. "You've still got a bald patch on your head."

"Maybe," said Bill. "But have you ever seen a better moustache?"

★ ★ ★

THE office boy was obsessed with the secretary's breasts; it was all he could think about at work, so eventually he plucked up his courage to ask her if she would let him fondle them for 10 minutes for £250. The secretary agreed and they disappeared into the backroom where he enjoyed an orgy of fondling her breasts and sucking her tits, all the time murmuring to himself, "I can't, I can't, I just can't fathom it."

At last the girl turned to him and said, "What can't you fathom?"

"I just can't fathom out how I'm going to pay you."

★ ★ ★

HAVE you heard about the local flasher who was going to retire?

He decided to stick it out another year.

★ ★ ★

THREE men were working on a building site when one fell off the scaffolding into the cement mixer. The police were immediately called and the mixer was emptied, revealing bits of bone, flesh and blood.

"Do you know who he was?" asked the police.

"Sure, it was Jack."

"Well it's going to be very difficult to make a formal identification.

Did he have any distinguishing marks?"
One of the men thought for a moment and then said, "Yeah, he did. He had two rectums."
The police looked puzzled at this so the man explained.
"Last time we went down the pub with him I heard the landlord say - Jack's just come in with the two arseholes."

* * *

"CAN you paint me in the nude?" said a beautiful girl to the artist.
"Certainly," he replied, "but I'll have to keep my socks on. I must have somewhere for the brushes."

* * *

A SCIENTIST invented a new piece of confectionery and asked for volunteers to taste it. They were amazed - each side tasted differently: chocolate, liquorice, nuts, spearmint and fruity boiled sweets.
Then the voice of a leering old man at the back shouted out, "You should make one that tastes of pussy."
"Well, try this," replied the scientist.
"Ugh, it tastes of crap."
"Sorry, try the other side."

* * *

I HAVE a boss at work who's really strict on punctuality. One day his assistant came in - broken nose, blood streaming down his face and his arm in a sling. His boss said, "Hey, where do you think you've been? You're an hour late."
"I fell down the stairs," he replied.
"What, and it took you a whole hour!"

AN artist had his wicked way with a beautiful young model in his studio.

He said, "You're the first model I've ever made love to."

"Oh yeah," she replied scornfully.

"Who were your other models?"

"Well," he said, "there was a bowl of fruit, a brace of ducks and the River Thames."

★ ★ ★

DID you hear about the nuclear scientist who was always so preoccupied with formulating yet more amazing experiments that one day he unbuttoned his jacket, took out his tie and pissed himself.

★ ★ ★

AN old woman was handling all the meat on the butcher's slab but not buying anything. Eventually the butcher lost his patience with her and said, "Listen, madam, it's not like your Jack, it doesn't get bigger the longer you handle it."

★ ★ ★

WHAT is professional courtesy?
It's when a shark comes towards a solicitor swimming in the water and then veers away.

★ ★ ★

THIS man was married to the prettiest girl in the office and was the envy of his workmates. One man in particular said to him "I'll give you £250 to smack your wife's pretty bottom."

The husband was furious, but when he told his wife she said, "Come on! We've got lots of bills, what's a few smacks on the bottom?"

Eventually the husband gave in and agreed.

Next day in their bedroom the wife removed her knickers and bent over... the workmate gently stroked her and said, "What curves, what dimples," eventually producing a camera and taking a photo. The husband was besides himself with rage.

"Get on with it or the deals off."

"Oh no," said the workmate, "I could never smack such a beautiful bottom, besides it would cost me £250 if I did."

★ ★ ★

THE local bank was held up by four masked gunmen, and customers and staff were ordered to lie face down on the floor. Everyone did as they were told except one young girl who lay down on her back.

"Don't be silly, lay down the other way, this is a bank robbery not the office party," whispered her friend.

★ ★ ★

THE woman was having her house painted and each night when her husband came home from work she would show him how much had been done that day. On this particular night she was showing him the landing but accidentally he put his hand on the banister and left an ugly mark. So the next morning she said to the decorator.

"Would you mind coming upstairs a minute so that I can show you where my husband put his hand?"

He replied quickly "If it's all the same to you madam, a cup of tea will do."

★ ★ ★

A VERY enterprising young man was determined to be the best salesman for the Higgins Dental Mouthwash Company.

And indeed after one month his sales figures had soared off the top of the graph.

"How did you manage it?" asked one of his colleagues.

"Oh it was quite simple. I set up a stall at the local bus station, selling a new special pate. I ask them to try it and afterwards when they ask me for the ingredients I tell them it's pork, spices and seagull shit. That's when they try to spit it out and that's when I ask them if they'd like some antiseptic mouthwash."

★ ★ ★

THE sleazy young salesman said to his customer - a voluptuous blonde, "If you are keen to have the car we could arrange very easy credit terms with no down payment."

"How do you mean?" she asked.

"Nothing down but your knickers."

★ ★ ★

THE phone rings and it's a man asking to speak to Bob Wankbreak.

"No, I don't think we've got anyone here by that name, just a mo, I'll ask. Is there a Wankbreak here?"

"You gotta be joking," came the reply. "We haven't even got time for a tea break!"

★ ★ ★

DRIVING through the country on a very hot day, an unscrupulous salesman came across a hiker who had collapsed in the heat.

"Water, please, water," he croaked.

"Now, sir, this is your lucky day. Here in my case I have a never-before-seen range of ties and you can have one at a 25% discount."

"Water, please, water," croaked the man again.

"Now, come on sir, you'll never get an offer like this again. For as little as £10 you can have a beautiful silk tie."

"Water, please, water."

After a few more minutes, the salesman realised he wasn't going to get a sale.

"OK, if it's water you want, the local golf club is just round the next bend. They'll be able to help you."

The hiker made one last effort to crawl round the corner and up the drive to the front door where he was met once again by the salesman.

"Water, please, water," begged the hiker.

"Of course, sir, we have all types of water, but you can't come in without a tie on."

★ ★ ★

THE salesman's eyes lit up when he saw the young man walk into the showroom looking for a new car. But after 30 minutes, it was obvious the sale wasn't going to be as easy as he hoped. The young man was insistent on buying a four-door saloon whereas the salesman was trying to persuade him to purchase the more expensive two-door coupe. Suddenly, he had an idea.

"Sir, how many tits does a cow have?"

"Four," answered the puzzled man.

"And how many tits does Madonna have?"

"Two".

"Now, sir, which gives the better ride?"

★ ★ ★

A JAPANESE man went for a job on a building site.

"What are you good at?" he was asked.

"I'm no good at bricklaying, carpentry or painting. I worked in a car factory," he said.

"OK, I'll put you in charge of supplies over there in the shed."

Time went by and two days later there was still no sign of the Japanese man.

"Where the hell's he got to?" asked the boss.

As they started to walk towards the shed, out popped the man shouting, 'Surplies, surplies!"

★ ★ ★

A WINDOW cleaner was doing the upstairs windows of a semi-detached when he noticed a beautiful girl lying seductively on the bed, wearing only a sheer nightie.

"Hello" he said. "You're the second pregnant girl I've met this morning."

"But I'm not pregnant," she said.

"I haven't cleaned all the windows yet."

★ ★ ★

ONE afternoon, a casting director was auditioning an extra for a forthcoming commercial. On meeting, the director looked at him closely and said, "I'm sure we've met before. I never forget a face. You weren't at the last Isle of Wight Festival wearing a long sheepskin coat and dark glasses?"

"No," replied the man.

But the director persisted. "You weren't celebrating New Year's Eve in Trafalgar Square, five years ago, and dived into the fountain?"

"No," replied the man.

"Well, I can't understand it," said the director, "faces are my business. I always remember them."

A moment of silence went by when suddenly the director jumped up shouting, "You weren't playing the fruit machine in the Kings Arms twenty minutes ago?"

"Yes, I was," he replied.

"There, I told you, I never forget a face."

★ ★ ★

THREE surgeons were relaxing in the bar after a conference and the first one said, "I had a pretty easy time last week. I had to operate on a computer analyst and when I opened him up, all the parts were filed and labelled and the retrieval system was very competent."

"Well, my week was even easier," said the second surgeon. "I had to operate on an electronics expert, all the different systems were colour-coded so you could see what was wrong immediately."

"Yes, that sounds good," said the third surgeon. "But I had the easiest of all. I had to operate on an estate agent. They've only got two moving parts - the mouth and the arsehole - and they're both used for the same thing."

★ ★ ★

"EXCUSE me, sir, may I have tomorrow afternoon off. The wife wants me to go shopping with her."

"Certainly not."

"Thank you, sir, I knew you'd understand."

★ ★ ★

TWO men were up a pylon repairing damage caused by recent bad weather. One was at the top and the other, a dimwitted sort of fellow, was halfway down.

"Pass me up the spanner!" shouted the man at the top.

"No thanks, I've had my dinner."

"I said pass me a spanner."

"What did you say, a hammer?"

"No, you prat, I said a spanner."

The fella halfway down finally got the message and threw up a spanner. Unfortunately, it hit the other man on the head, knocked him off his perch and he fell to the ground, dead on impact. A few days later, an inquest was held and the coroner asked for any information that might throw some light on the accident.

His mate got up and said, "I think it had something to do with sex," your honourship.

"Sex? What do you mean?"

"Well as he was passing me I heard him shout 'Cunt'!"

★ ★ ★

"HEY, Jack, quick, come over here mate," shouted a man on the scaffolding of a new building.

Jack put down his trowel, moved the pile of bricks and headed off towards the scaffolding. Unfortunately, on the way he slipped and fell down one of the trenches spraining his ankle, and then in struggling to get out he pulled the cement mixer over on top of him. Feeling quite badly battered and bruised, and hobbling painfully, he eventually got to the scaffolding. Looking up he shouted, "Yes, Reg, what is it?"

"I just wanted to tell you I could see your house from here!"

★ ★ ★

TWO pirates are catching up on all the gossip over a pint or two at the Black Dog. One has a wooden leg, the other, a metal hook and an eye patch.

"How d'ya get that wooden leg then?" asks one of the pirates.

"A big bloody bastard of a shark bit straight through me leg," he says. "What about you, how d'ya get that metal hook?"

"Lost me hand fighting some foreign buggers down past Penzance. One of their swords cut it straight off," he replies.

"Ay.... so what about the patch?"

"Well, I was up in the crow's nest and I looks up to see this big seagull. And this big seagull shits in my eye," he says.

"Do you mean that seagull shit made you blind?" he asks with astonishment.

"No, but it was my first day with the hook."